# Author Reviews of Hippie Cult Leader

True crime documentarian Buddy Day was eating chicken wings in a noisy restaurant when his mobile phone rang. Charles Manson was calling. That quick conversation with the notorious murderer led to a year's worth of phone calls between Manson and Day, an award-winning film, and now Day's book, *Hippie Cult Leader: The Last Words of Charles Manson*. Through hours of conversation with Manson, Manson Family members and their attorneys, friends, and Manson prosecutor Stephen Kay, as well as in-depth study of trial transcripts, police records, and media coverage, Day applies rational thinking to insane acts to create an alternative motive behind the horrific murders of Sharon Tate, Abigail Folger, Jay Sebring, Wojciech Frykowski, Steven Parent, and Leno and Rosemary LaBianca. The result is an intriguing and thought-provoking read. –

—New York Times best-selling author
**Suzy Spencer**


Manson will fascinate true-crimers forever. He was all at once an enigma, carnival barker and clown, but most importantly a bonafide sociopath, whose terrorized victims' stories should never be forgotten. Just when you think you've seen and heard all there is about Charlie Boy, here comes HIPPIE CULT LEADER—an interesting, at times disturbing, addition to the Manson library. Written with passion and detail, James Buddy Day spins a well-told, new take on an old con man.

—New York Times bestselling investigative journalist,

**M. William Phelps**

*"I didn't have anything to do with killing those people. They knew I didn't have anything to do with it. They didn't want to hear it..."*

*Charles Manson, 2017*

For 50 years the legendary Manson Family murders have fascinated and mortified all. Few could phathom that such brutal acts of cold-blooded murder could have taken place in the first place and let alone that women played a key role.

Manson was an enigmatic drifter who drew a group of people into his web of deceit and evil that eventually led to the brutal Tate, and then LaBianca murders. The prosecution would go on to spin what was considered the de-facto theory behind the murder spree. The jury and the world bought into the "Helter Skelter" racial war conspiracy based on the Beatles "White Album." Now for the first time, documentary Film Producer, Director and Author, James Buddy Day takes readers through a more rational and believable set of reasons for the murders.

Day was the last person and author to have interviewed Charles Manson. The reader will be intrigued by Manson's perspective on how the prosecution convicted him for murder when he was forty miles away when the Tate murders took place. For those that are intrigued by the 60's Hippie culture and the most sensational murder spree in history will find the book a compelling and thought provoking read.

The LAPD wasn't even close to finding out who killed Sharon Tate and the others when it ultimately was solved through a conversation in jail between one of the killers and a prostitude. The tale that Vincent Bugliosa then wove was a narrative that he had planned from the beginning and it calls into question his objectivity for the facts of the case. It highlights what ambitions over facts have done for 60 years of American frontier justice, as many have been incarcerated for life or put to death by those that would alter the facts, induce confessions or plant evidence to get a conviction on innocent people.

Today after 50 years, Bobby Beausoleil the convicted murderer of Gary Hinman (the first murder) remains in jail after being granted parole. He had nothing to do with the infamous murders but yet he continues to pay a huge price for his association with the Manson family.   There is no question that Manson and the others were involved with brutal acts of violence and murder and they deserved to be incarcerated for those crimes.  The Governor of the state of California, Gavin Newsom continues the hypocricy of the American justice system based on "Time Served." .

Bobby rightfully should have been granted parole 20 years ago, but today remains one of the longest serving inmates in the American penitentiary system.

Had Bugliosi done his job effectively, rather than grand standing for his own wealth and stature, we might have long forgotten Manson and the murders as highlighted by the assistant DA on the case and brought to light in this book.

Was true justice done for the vicitims and their friends and family by making this the most sensational murder spree of all time?  It begs the question.

Charlie's familiar voice came on the line. "Yeah. Listen, I'm already all around the world. I tricked Vincent Bugliosi in that courtroom. I let him convict me for something I didn't do."
"Why did you do that?" I asked.
"I'd never grown up in that world," Charlie said, beginning a rhythmic freestyle as if he was a beat poet riffing at a coffee house, not someone calling from a communal phone in the hallway of a supermax prison. "I live in rock and roll. I live in the penitentiary. I live in the chain gangs. I live in the south-land. I live in the graveyards. I live in the tomb. Do you realize they're torturing people even today?"

He now lives on in infamy, but let's hope this book provides the perspective for dialogue and debate about the reasons why those innocient lives were taken in the Summer of 69.

Dean Baxendale
Publisher

# THE LAST WORDS
# OF
# CHARLES MANSON

## James Buddy Day

OPTIMUM
PUBLISHING
INTERNATIONAL
MONTRÉAL | TORONTO

Published by Optimum Publishing International a JF Moore
Lithographers Incorporated company.

Canadian Cataloguing in Publication Data

ISBN 978-0-88890-296-2

Digital E-Book version ©Ottawa, 2019 All Rights Reserved

James Buddy Day

Hippie Cult Leader: The Last Words of Charles Manson

Cover and Jacket Design by James Buddy Day
Cover Photo, mugshot of Charles Manson, October 12, 1969, Inyo
County Sheriff's Office, courtesy of Los Angeles Deputy District
Attorney Stephen Kay (retired)
Back Cover photograph,
Printed and bound in Canada by Marquis

For information, address:
Optimum Publishing International
144 Rochester Avenue
Toronto, Ontario M42 1P1
For rights, submissions and media inquiries go to www.opibooks.com

# Contents

prologue
the devil's business

# Prologue - The Devil's Business

*"On the evening of August the 8th, Charles Manson sent his robots out on a mission of murder. There is no evidence that he actually personally killed any of the victims in this case."*
> *- Vincent Bugliosi, final argument to the jury, January 15, 1971.*

*"In all my years I have never seen anything like this before."*
> *- Unknown LAPD Officer, August 9, 1969,*
> *commenting to news reporters outside the scene of the*
> *Sharon Tate murders.*

 

The day that etched Charles Manson into the mind of the world's collective consciousness was Friday, August 8, 1969. That was the fateful weekend when Manson's alleged cult, the Manson Family, slaughtered seven people. It wasn't the first time the group had committed murder, nor would it be the last, but the events of that weekend are why Charles Manson will be remembered as the devil incarnate. A real-life boogeyman capable of untold evil. A maniacal puppet master who carved a swastika into his head with a razor blade. The crimes of that weekend captured the attention of the nation and plunged Los Angeles into a state of panic. Gun sales skyrocketed and parents began walking their kids to school, worried that Manson's satanic family could strike at any moment.

Charles Manson was not physically with the four who came across their initial victim on the night of August 8, but his influence on their actions would be debated for decades to come.

In a tragic twist of fate, the first victim of this infamous crime spree was simply in the wrong place at the wrong time. Steven Parent was an eighteen-year-old California native whose freshman yearbook photo looks remarkably like Buddy Holly. The oldest of five, Steven was raised in El Monte, a city east of Los Angeles. His family was working class and being the eldest, Steven was ambitious. His father had nurtured Steve's love of electronics and by the summer of 1969, Steven was working two jobs with plans to attend community college in the fall. On the evening of August 8, just after 11:00 p.m., Steven had closed up shop at his second job at Jonas Miller Stereo and driven through Los Angeles to visit an acquaintance who lived in a guest house at the far end of a secluded property in Beverly Hills.

The property was located at 10050 Cielo Drive.

The guest house was part of a sprawling lot that sat on a hilltop overlooking a section of Beverly Hills called Benedict Canyon. Cielo Drive itself is a short, winding road that looks like it doesn't belong in the middle of Los Angeles. On the far side of Cielo Drive was a daunting metal gate that guarded the entrance to a driveway leading up to the house. Though driveway is an accurate description, it's not an apt one. The driveway was more like a secondary road that led up a steep incline, so steep that the property was not visible from the gate.

Steven had driven up the winding driveway in the hopes of selling an AM/FM Sony Digimatic radio to Bill Garretson, the property's caretaker. Two weeks earlier, Steven had picked up Bill—who was hitchhiking on Sunset Boulevard—and driven him back home to Cielo Drive. On August 8, Steve stopped by to show Bill a radio he was trying to unload for some quick cash. Bill was listening to The Mamas and the Papas and finishing a TV dinner when Steven arrived just before midnight. Bill admired the radio but decided not to buy it, so Steve called another friend on Santa Monica Boulevard, leaving the guest house just after midnight. With the radio in hand, Steve traversed the property, passing a large swimming pool near the main house and climbing back into a white 1965 Rambler Ambassador, which his father had purchased for him. Steve placed the radio on the passenger seat and began driving down the long, winding driveway.

As Steven pulled away, Bill finished his late-night meal, turned up his stereo, and sat down to write some letters. At the same time, Steven approached the gate at the base of the hill where his headlights lit up the four members of the Manson Family. Three women and one man were hiding in the night—dressed in black, armed with buck knives, and carrying a large rope and a single handgun. The gun, a .22 calibre revolver with a brown wooden grip and long barrel, looked like a comedic prop in a spaghetti western, but the Manson Family knew the gun was capable.

When Steven came upon them, he rolled down his window and was immediately attacked. Using a buck knife, his assailant slashed at him through the driver's side window with quick frenetic motions. Steven raised his left arm trying to deflect the buck knife swinging at him wildly. The knife slashed through the flesh of his palm, scraping bone before catching his wristwatch and severing the band. Steven's reaction sent the watch flying into the back seat, as he screamed for help. With blood gushing down Steven's arm, a second assailant shot him four times with the long-barrelled revolver. The bullets burst through Steven's chest and left arm. The attacker then shot him in the face at point-blank range. The force of the gunshot slumped Steven's head awkwardly to his right, positioning his body with a lifeless gaze into the footwell of the passenger seat, looking past the clock radio. Blood poured down the armrest and saturated Steven's plaid shirt.

With their first victim disposed of, a member of the murder party reached across Steven's corpse and turned off the engine and headlights, leaving the keys in the ignition. They paused, waiting to see if the gunshots had been heard, but to their surprise the night remained silent.

They continued on, going up the steep driveway toward the main house. The group of four were dishevelled, all dressed in a collection of dark clothing picked from a pile at their communal home. The blood from their first victim disappeared into the fabric, further concealed by the night. They were dirty, the women were barefoot, and all were in various stages of an amphetamine high, acid trip, or some combination of the two.

3

When they reached the main house, they looked for a way in. A home invasion is a particularly terrifying crime; the intruders know someone is home and go inside anyway. The occupants are part of the intent.

The de facto leader of the party was named Charles Watson, a six foot two twenty-three-year-old who spoke with a distinct southern drawl, earning him the nickname "Tex." The girls waited by the front door while Tex crawled inside through an unlocked window, opening the front door to let them in. As Tex crept through the living room he moved quietly, aware that the home's occupants could not call for help as he'd cut the phone lines prior to coming up the driveway.

Bill remained in the guest house listening to music and going about his evening, unaware that his friend was lying dead in the driveway and the Manson Family was stalking their prey in the main house. At one point, he attempted to make a call and realized the phone line was dead. He shrugged and didn't think much of it, attributing the interruption to a similar problem they'd had with the phone company the month before.

Inside the main house the Manson Family convened in a dark living room with a cabin-style decor, eyeing a man sleeping on a sofa. The man was dressed in casual clothes, which contrasted with a blanket made to look like the American flag that was strewn across the back of the sofa. Unbeknownst to the home invaders, the sleeping man was Wojciech Frykowski, a house guest who had passed out while the home's other occupants had retired to their rooms. Wojciech stirred, still asleep with his shoes on and his back to the door, as the intruders gathered around him. The girls giggled and crept closer, which pulled Wojciech out of his slumber. "What time is it?" he asked, still in a semiconscious fog, not realizing he was speaking to four people who had broken into the house to kill him.

Wojciech was answered with a swift kick to the face.

Within minutes, the four members of the murder party had rounded up the other occupants of the home and brought them into the living room. Out of fear and confusion, the people staying in the house complied with their captors. Wojciech Frykowski remained on the couch, sitting beside his girlfriend, a petite twenty-five-year-old brunette named Abigail Folger, also a house guest. Nearby was a third house guest, thirty-five-year-old Jay Sebring, a tall, handsome Hollywood hairdresser. Closest to Jay was the only person who actually lived in the

4

house, a gorgeous twenty-six-year-old movie star named Sharon Tate. With blonde flowing hair and dark eyes, she was stunningly beautiful, and noticeably in the late stages of pregnancy.

With all assembled in the living room, the Manson Family went about using towels and pillowcases to tie up and blindfold their intended prey. The improvisation of the night was self-evident; armed with dull buck knives and a vintage revolver, they hadn't brought the proper tools to butcher several people. The women tracked dirt through the house leaving footprints with their bare feet. The large band of rope they'd brought was not used to bind the hands of their victims; instead, they tied the rope in a frantic noose around the neck of Sharon Tate, then looped it over a large beam that ran across the ceiling, tying the other end around the neck of Jay Sebring. The rope was given enough slack so they could both move several feet, or even lie down, without it becoming tight. Sharon Tate and Jay Sebring were panic-stricken but co-operative amongst the pleas of their friends for some sort of explanation. "Who are you people? What do you want with us?"

They were answered by Tex. "I am the devil and I'm here to do the devil's business," he told them plainly, his voice devoid of emotion due to the drugs racing through his brain.

Tex ordered Sharon Tate and Jay Sebring to lie down on their stomachs, still bound with the rope slung over the beam above and fastened around their necks. In a state of desperation, Jay Sebring pleaded with Tex, saying that Sharon Tate should be allowed to sit given that she was almost nine-months pregnant. Even while terrified himself, Sebring was valiant in continuing to challenge Tex, who was barking orders and directing the victims with the gun. Sebring grew more agitated moving closer to Tex, causing the noose to pull tighter around his neck. Tex responded with a mix of threats and transient apathy brought on by the wavering levels of drugs coursing through his body. Tex shook his head, attempting to focus on the task at hand, when the confrontation with Jay Sebring exploded into a fist fight. The two men wrestled violently toward the front door, the noose pulling tighter around Jay's neck, causing him to sputter and cough. Tex gripped the gun tightly in a growing rage; the girls yelled and laughed, threatening the other captives to keep still.

Jay used his free hand to tug at the rope, freeing enough slack to catch his breath and allowing both men to spill out of the entryway onto the porch. Tex caught Sebring in the nose with a right hook. Blood poured down Jay's face, giving Tex enough time to aim the gun and pull the trigger.

The deafening sound of a .22 calibre long-barrelled pistol echoed back into the house. Sebring followed the noise, stumbling back into the living room amidst the screams and panic of Sharon Tate and the others. The captives' hopes of escaping unharmed had evaporated—their friend was dying in front of them. Their captors were gleeful.

Jay collapsed onto his right side with blood pouring down his purple button-up shirt. The bullet had torn through the left side of his body, coming out of his chest. Tex pounced, stabbing wildly, and Sebring had just enough energy to try and fight off the attack with his left hand while covering the gunshot with his right. The fight ended with Tex plunging his knife deep into the centre of Sebring's chest—the blow causing Jay to drop his guard. The knife lodged deep, slicing Jay's aorta, the major source of blood to the body. Blood sprayed from the wound, forced out from the final pumps of Jay's heart. Tex continued to thrust the knife into Jay's back even though he was clearly dead. Sharon Tate screamed and cried, still bound to Jay.

Watching Jay's murder, Wojciech Frykowski and Abigail Folger were subdued by fear more than physical restraints—their hands were poorly tied with towels. With a rush of adrenaline, Wojciech jumped off the couch in a bid to escape. He was immediately tackled by one of the girls, and they wrestled onto the floor in a screaming chaotic display. Both Wojciech and his attacker screamed for help, prompting Tex to intervene. Using the butt of the revolver, Tex hit Wojciech across the face, breaking Wojciech's skin and smashing the handle to pieces. Wojciech was momentarily stunned, while the girl slashed wildly, the blade catching Wojciech's legs with superficial cuts. Wojciech ignored the pain and the blood that streamed down his legs, somehow managing to partially free himself from the altercation. Moving closer to the exit, Wojciech towed the girl and Tex up the hallway. Blood poured from Wojciech's forehead, smearing the walls.

At the same time, another of the Manson Family girls attempted to stab Abigail Folger from behind. The knife caught Abigail in the neck and the shock prompted her to free herself and run for her life. Abigail fled down the hallway with blood pouring from her neck. She reached the master bedroom, which contained a shuttered exit that opened to the pool. Abigail slammed into the shutters and frantically opened the door with her attacker seconds behind. Abigail fell through the door, quickly losing blood that smeared the shutter and pooled onto the floor. The girl tried to stab her but fell on top of her, and they both rolled out onto the grass. Abigail freed herself again and ran toward the guest house.

The girl lunged at Abigail slashing wildly with a knife, once again catching Abigail in the neck and stabbing her in the lower back. The latter broke Abigail's stride, and she slammed into the lawn face first and flipped onto her back only to be straddled by the knife-wielding young woman. The girl slashed at Abigail who raised her hands to shield herself from the blade frantically coming toward her. The knife shredded her hands, spraying blood. Abigail turned her head to her right and closed her eyes. The knife made progress past her arms slashing at her face. Out of shock and exhaustion, Abigail became unable to defend herself. Losing blood rapidly, she looked her attacker in the eye, ceasing to struggle. Her last words were, "I give up. Take me." Her arms dropped and the girl planted the knife into Abigail's chest, pulling the knife in and out until Abigail's crisp, full-length white nightgown became so saturated with blood it appeared red.

Hearing the screams of her friends being slaughtered on her front lawn, Sharon Tate composed herself enough to speak to the lone Manson Family girl left guarding her—a twenty-year-old skinny brunette with wild eyes. Sobbing and panic-stricken, Sharon begged for her life and for the life of her unborn child. The girl's response was plain and full of bravado as she knelt down to whisper in Sharon Tate's ear. "Look, bitch," she said, "you're going to die tonight, and I don't feel a thing behind it."

When the chaos subsided from the escaping house guests who now lay dead on the lawn, the Manson Family reconvened in the living room. They taunted and stabbed at Sharon Tate, who was still restrained by the neck to the middle of the room. The rope had enough give to allow them to struggle to the porch, at which point Sharon was stabbed in the back repeatedly before being dragged back into the living room. As she struggled, the rope around her neck pulled tight, hanging her as she fought against the knives piercing her skin, covering her in her own blood. Sharon guarded her pregnant belly as the women stabbed at her chest, planting a knife into her heart. Blood gushed from the wound, ending Sharon's struggle.

The attackers were not finished. The wild-eyed brunette proposed cutting the baby out of her but decided against it. Instead, they used their hands to smear Sharon Tate's blood all over her body, grotesquely painting her pregnant belly red. They played with her corpse, staging it to their liking. In a final display of savagery, the wild-eyed girl dipped a towel in Sharon Tate's blood and crouched by a large white door to write "PIG" in bold red letters.

At the same time, Charles Manson was on a ranch, looking into the sky and strumming his guitar; nowhere near the murders, unable to communicate with the murderers, having no idea who had just been killed.

I've always wondered what Manson was thinking, sitting forty miles away from the events that would come to define his life and change America forever.

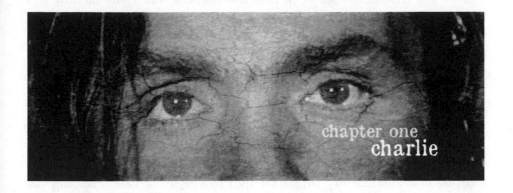

## Charlie

*"You eat meat with your teeth and you kill things that are better than you are, and in the same respect you say how 'bad,' and even 'killers' that your children are. You made your children what they are. I am just a reflection of every one of you."*

*- Charles Manson, November 20, 1970, addressing the court outside the presence of the jury.*

      Charles Manson died on Nov 19, 2017. At the time, he was still an inmate in the custody of the California Department of Corrections, though his passing completed his life sentence. Before his death he was transferred from California State Prison in Corcoran California, to Bakersfield Hospital where he took his last breath on a Sunday evening, dying from complications associated with cancer.

      Early the next morning my phone lit up with text messages. Still groggy I rolled over, reading the messages popping up and deciphering that Manson had died. I quickly got out of bed and made my way to work, attempting to respond to whatever I could. I listened to the news recount Manson's life and speculate over the circumstances of his death, knowing that I had a long day in front of me. What the media didn't know was that I had been working with Charles Manson on a documentary during what turned out to be the last year of his life.

The first time I spoke to Charles Manson was a Monday night. I was in Florida, filming a TV show called *The Shocking Truth* for REELZChannel (a true crime series about famous movies and the murders that inspired them). The cinematographer, Nate Harper, and I were in the midst of driving across the state retracing the footsteps of the female serial killer Aileen Wuornos, seeking out people who knew her. It was late in the evening and we were enjoying some cheap Florida beer and wings at Applebee's.

*Monday Night Football* was blaring from the flat screens overhead, but I could feel my iPhone jumping in my pocket. I grabbed it before it was too late and cleaned my finger enough to catch the call. Pressing the phone tightly to my right ear, I stuck my thumb in my left to block the restaurant noise and heard a robotic female voice that would soon become eerily familiar, "You have a collect call from Charles Manson, an inmate at the California State Prison in Corcoran, California. To accept this call, say or dial 5 now—beep."

"Holy shit," I said to Nate, "I think *Charles Manson* is actually calling me on my cell." My hands trembling from a rush of excitement, I managed to accept the call, and we both ran outside. The waitress—catching our escape from the corner of her eye—ran from behind the bar believing we were running out on our tab. Nate met her at the door and hurriedly gave her his wallet as collateral saying, "Sorry, we'll be right back. Charles Manson is calling my friend and he has to take it."

As we ran to the parking lot a second recording clicked in saying, "This call and your phone number are being monitored and recorded." To this day I'm not sure if that means all calls are reviewed, or someone is eavesdropping in real time—either way I've long since decided to disregard. At the time, my prison calls were coming from the most famous inmate in the United States, and the sheer number of calls going in and out of the prison combined with the bizarreness of Charles Manson's speech must have caused the monitors to throw up their hands in frustration years before I met him.

Within a few seconds Manson's distinct voice came over the line, "Hello."

"Charlie?" I said.

Manson responded, "Hey man, how you doing?"

"Pretty good, you?" I said.

"Groovy man," Charlie paused, "I got your letter."

Months before Charlie called me for the first time, I had been speaking with many people involved with or researching notorious crimes, and I had met a few who claimed they had actually spoken with the infamous Charles Manson at one time or another. One person suggested that I write him, so on whim I sent him a couple of letters.

In the letters, I explained that I was a documentary producer, and I wanted to know if he would consider being interviewed for an in-depth documentary. I included my personal phone number and was fairly certain that he would never call. At the time it didn't occur to me that handing out my cellphone number to the most infamous convicted mass murderer of all time might be unwise. When Manson called me that first time, I was shocked.

The inmate phone system only allows calls to be fifteen minutes or less. That, combined with the demand to use the phone and the prison-restricted phone time, makes connecting with outsiders challenging. When Charlie initiated a call, it came collect. Both my phone and I are from Canada, which at the time meant I had to set up a prepaid account to receive Charlie's calls.

On that very first phone call, I could only speak with Charlie for a few minutes—just long enough to get the basic instructions on how to set up my phone to receive his calls. This proved difficult and resulted in numerous calls with the customer service desk, e-mails back and forth to get the complex instructions, and ultimately driving around the state of Florida to find a specific type of Western Union that would process the required money transfer to set up my account. After several days, I managed to get a confirmation e-mail while I was in northern Florida. We finished filming for the day and drove ten miles to the nearest post office, which was a one-room building on a rural road between counties. I used some hotel stationery and wrote out a quick letter to let Charlie know my phone was good to go. I wondered if the one time Charles Manson called me would just turn out to be a story I could tell at parties.

I remember reading *Helter Skelter* when I was a teenager, the bestselling true crime book of all time and the bible in terms of all things Charles Manson. My mother was an aspiring author and true crime fanatic, so we had a house full of books about murder, and I took to them immediately. Throughout my formative years I would spend my time on the bus commuting to school devouring books about kidnapping, homicides, massacres, and above all else, serial killers. My interest in serial killers blossomed as I grew older, and I read everything I could get my hands on. I went so far as to write a letter to the Milwaukee police department and request a copy of Jeffery Dahmer's confession for a term paper. I recall paying a menial processing fee of ten dollars and receiving hundreds of photocopied pages in the mail, opening it like a Christmas present. This was long before the internet made such reading material readily available. I later pursued my interests in psychopathic violence academically, working on a post-graduate degree in counselling psychology.

As an adult, my fascination with crime evolved into a career as a documentary producer and director. I've had the unique opportunity to travel across America more than a few times curating stories about disturbing cases. I've met victims, attorneys, inmates, and everyone in between. I've heard some incredible accounts and met some really bad people. Through all the years of preoccupation with real-life monsters, one particular fiend always stuck with me: Charles Manson, the charismatic psychopath who, as legend has it, turned Sunday school teachers and librarians into bloodthirsty killers.

I was fascinated by the idea of the Manson Family, a sixties-era cult fuelled by sex and drugs in which the members would abandon their personalities and take nicknames like "Squeaky," "Tex," and "Lulu." The idea that Charles Manson was an insatiable genius who could get into the minds of his followers and bend them to his will was haunting. *Helter Skelter* was written by Vincent Bugliosi, the Manson Family lead prosecutor, and told a bizarre story of sex, drugs, and an apocalyptic cult set against the backdrop of civil unrest in Los Angeles.

It was a great story.

About a month went by before Manson called me a second time. The automated voice came on the line first, "You have a pre-paid call from Charles Manson, an inmate at the California State Prison in Corcoran, California. To accept this call, say or dial 5 now—beep."

I eagerly pressed 5 and heard his raspy voice say, "Hello, hello, hello."

I was astonished Manson had taken the time to call me back. *Why? What does he want?* I thought. *What do you say to the most infamous mass murderer of all time if given the chance?* I knew what I wanted: to hear Manson's story in his own words and to get his permission to make a documentary based on that story. Manson's response was blunt, "I don't give a fuck about telling my story. That's not what's in play here. My story has already been all over the world a thousand times. I'm interested in results. Can you get me a cellphone between you and I so we can communicate?"

I knew enough to know that cellphones are not permitted in prison, and that our phone calls were ostensibly being monitored and recorded by prison officials. I was taken aback that Manson, who I barely knew, would ask me in no uncertain terms, on a recorded line, to commit what I assumed was a federal crime. I told him I didn't think that was possible and even if it was, I had no idea how to do it.

"You're the man-jam," Manson said. "You're the one that's got the revolution money-bunny-back-door-rabbit-jack. In other words, I'm the one that's locked up." Manson's point of view was that I could find a way to get him a cellphone—I was on the outside, where anything is possible. He was in prison so all he could do was ask.

I told Manson I didn't want to join him in prison, so I wasn't going to smuggle him in a cellphone, but he was undeterred.

"I can't even get the chicken shit door open," Manson said, offering me an ultimatum. "Give me a cellphone so I can communicate with the world. And get me a door, so I can get some air once more, or stay away from me!"

I pressed on, "Don't you care about all the movies, books, and TV shows that have been made about you? Don't you want to set the record straight?"

Manson was keenly aware of the decades of stories that had been told about him—he didn't care if I told another one, "No crap is different than the other crap, it's all crap. You're just looking to make some money," he said.

I was blunt in my initial reply and wanted to sound open to his perspective, "I want to know the true story. Not that *Helter Skelter* crap." I was bluffing of course. I had no idea if *Helter Skelter* was crap, but I had seen enough on TV about Manson to know that he saw himself as wrongfully accused. I also selfishly thought a documentary about Charles Manson being innocent would be a must-watch if nothing else.

Charlie replied, "They don't want to tell the truth about nothing. They would rather die and destroy the planet and burn all the trees down and kill everybody. Hopefully they'll do it. I mean you can understand that if I was a tree, I certainly wouldn't like people." Manson pivoted to an environmental analogy using it as a metaphor for himself. "They're using me every day man, you cut me down making furniture out of me. Poor tree don't have a chance. He's got nobody to help him."

13

"So you do care about all that's been said about you? You want to set the record straight?" I asked.

"People don't want to look at it from the point of view that brings them to something they don't like, what they want reality to be," Manson replied. "They don't give reality a thought. They don't care about nothin'. All they care about is food."

"Then what is reality?" I asked, trying to keep pace with Manson's stream of consciousness. "All the things that have been said about you? I mean, what is the truth?"

He replied quickly, "The truth? I was born in it!"

*What does that mean?* I thought. "I want to know the truth. What really happened, not what everyone else thinks they know," I said. I was looking for a way in, trying to relate in a way other journalists had not. I wanted to express that I thought Manson's story could be untold and re-told, yet not sound as if I was completely siding with him. I was grasping at straws trying to go toe-to-toe with a mind-controlling serial killer, and to my surprise it was working.

"That's good," Manson said. "If I could just get out of this stupid fuckin' polly-parrot cage. They got me in a cage and everybody's shooting at me in their own way." Manson took a long pause. I was about to speak when suddenly he said, "I didn't have nothing to do with killing those people."

*Holy shit,* I thought. A shiver went down my spine; the surreal conversation had escalated. I was speaking with *the* Charles Manson and he had, unprompted, brought up his infamous murder spree.

Manson continued, "They knew I didn't have anything to do with it. They didn't want to hear it. I didn't get a defence; I didn't get to put on a trial."

I thought, *what the hell is he talking about?* My heart rate was picking up. It occurred to me that I would probably never get another opportunity to speak to Manson again. I decided to be blunt, "If you didn't kill those people, then who did?" It was a good strategy, Manson liked that I was willing to challenge him.

Manson yelled, "The people that told you they killed them. They stood on the witness stand and said 'yeah I killed 'em.'" Charlie paused, and I thought for a moment that he had hung up, but his voice came back almost meekly. "Everybody at that ranch did what they wanted to do."

The ranch was the nickname for the commune where the Manson Family lived back in the sixties. Charlie was subtly telling me he didn't

14

order the murders—people on the ranch did whatever they wanted, regardless of him.

For a second, I thought, *If Manson didn't order the murders then who did?* Before immediately asking myself, *Why would you believe anything Charles Manson has to say? Of course he's going to tell you he's innocent. What did you expect?* I was aware that the time limit on the call was nearing the end, and I had hundreds of questions swirling around my brain. I decided to ask the obvious, "Why do people blame you then? Why does everyone think you're the boogeyman if you didn't kill anyone?"

Charlie said quietly, "They still don't believe me."

*Charles Manson is innocent*, I thought, *who on earth would believe that?*

The automated voice came on the line abruptly, "You have thirty seconds remaining."

"Can you call me again?" I asked.
Charlie took another long pause, "I don't know, man."

"But if no one knows the truth, we can't set the record straight," I attempted to reason.

Charlie said, "Everybody is for money. Everybody hates me for a dollar." Charlie's way of saying, I don't trust you, you're just looking to make money off me.

The call abruptly cut out, leaving me to guess if I would ever speak to Manson again. I doubted that I would, as he seemed skeptical of my motives, and I had no intention of smuggling him in a cellphone. I imagined that he was inundated with requests like mine. I wondered why he had now taken the time to call me twice.

To my surprise, he called me again the next night, and over the next month we kept talking.

Sometimes we would talk about things of significance, other times I would just listen to him ramble. In those initial calls, I was incredibly naïve about the specifics of his story. Manson would reference obscure details about his life, and I would say, "I'll have to look that up." To which he would reply, "You don't have to look it up, you just have to look at it." But after those first conversations with Charles Manson, I did have to look up a lot of things. I watched every documentary and read every article I could get my hands on, and I re-read *Helter Skelter* carefully.

I had hours of conversations with Charlie and speaking to him over time gave me a fleeting glimpse into how his mind worked. He thought fast and changed subjects at the speed of no one else I've ever encountered. At times, he'd begin by talking about prison, then seamlessly transition into his take on the Mexican pyramids, then a quick anecdote about 1969, or a spider he'd watched for days while in solitary confinement, or his views on the environment, race relations, or the very nature of reality. To complicate matters, he referred to everything in context, as though I should already understand. For example, Charlie never explained to me what "Spahn Ranch" was, he simply talked about "The Ranch." He expected me to know that Spahn Ranch was the de facto home of the Manson Family. He referred to everyone by the nickname he'd invented for them and he often had more than one name for each person. I had to have those names memorized because Manson would get frustrated if I'd ask him to explain. He expected me to know exactly what he was talking about; he was, after all, *the* Charles Manson. As he once sharply reminded me, "When I say something you don't have to look it up. You already know it, 'cause I said it."

Charlie often made quick digressions embedded in the context of his own life, and in Charlie's case, every aspect of his life was overflowing with infamy. As a friend and fellow acquaintance of Charlie's once told me, "You have to really put some time into Manson before you can know what he's talking about," which I learned was absolutely true. Listening to Charlie was its own art form.

What I selfishly wanted from Manson was the ultimate opportunity to be able to speak to a man convicted as a serial killer about his crimes—the immeasurable opportunity to gain insight into the mind of a madman and tell a phenomenal story in the process. Charlie's story began with his insistence that the truth about him remained untold and that the system was out to get him. "When they lose control, they don't admit that they lost control; they just lost face and they make another movie like you're doing," he told me.

"Don't you want someone to make a movie about you that's truthful, at least once?" I asked.

Charlie paused, and replied, "Now they're bringing Patty Hurst back online trying to cover that up some more. She was the cover-up to start with. She was working with the government all the way down the line. They wouldn't accept the truth and won't admit the truth about it. She wasn't kidnapped that was an act."

16

Manson's answers were often complicated, but he insisted that he'd been the victim of some sort of cover-up. An accusation I found laughable at first, although I told him I was open to telling his story—whatever it was. Charlie was skeptical that this could be achieved. "If you can find a way to [tell my story] the way you want to, as soon as you get there you're gonna have fifteen thousand people who are covering up what they've been doing," he said.

Despite this warning, I was eager to try, and after lengthy conversations Charlie agreed to help me—with the caveat, "All I'm looking for is for you to help me," Charlie said. "I've always been by myself alone. That's why nobody testified against me, because I've always been alone."

After a couple of months, Charlie and I had reached a rudimentary understanding. I would make a documentary to tell his story and he would help. As we embarked on this journey, I had no idea that I would be documenting the final year of his life. For Manson's part, he had almost no conditions for our pact—to this day I'm still uncertain as to why he agreed to it. The one thing he asked of me (other than a cellphone) was that I be truthful. Tell his story, the true story, and not the bullshit—in his words—that had plagued him for his entire life. At the time he requested this I had no idea what he was talking about. I highly doubted the idea that Charles Manson was some sort of misunderstood patsy. Regardless, I agreed and gave Manson my word that I would tell his true story to the best of my ability.

"That's good," Charlie said, "I'm not opposed to doing something but not a lie. Lying's what fucked everything up."

# Helter Skelter

*"On the afternoon of August 8th, 1969...[Charles Manson] came out and said, 'Now is the time for Helter Skelter.'"*
*- Vincent Bugliosi, January 15, 1971*
*Lead prosecutor in the People v. Manson et al., closing arguments.*

It was a Saturday evening, and I was engaged in an intense debate with my seven-year-old son over who would win in a fight, Superman or Thor. I felt the answer was obvious—Superman—but he was countering with a strong argument, "No Dad. You're wrong," he said.

I was boiling water for hot dogs in the hopes that feeding him his favourite meal would quell the debate. I dropped the dogs in the pot and watched them sink to the bottom of the boiling water. As I set the element to simmer, my phone began buzzing on the kitchen counter. Using my other hand to reach for the phone, I accepted the call with my thumb and looked quickly at the number, recognizing it was coming from the California Department of Corrections. The automated recording kicked in, "You have a call from Charles Manson, an inmate from California State Prison, Corcoran."

"Who is it Dad?" My son asked.

"Just a guy from work," I said. "Don't worry about it." Luckily, my son had become invested in his iPad seconds after he posed the question so did not ask a follow-up. I called to my wife to finish his dinner and ducked into a spare bedroom in time to hear Charlie come on the line, "Good day, man," he said, sounding to be in good spirits.

"How you doing?" I said.

Charlie replied, "Hanging on, hanging on."

I was still getting used to the fact that a man most would call a serial killer was calling me at home—not that he had any idea where I lived. When I'd written to him, I had used my work address, but I was still nervous, excited, and uncertain as to whether I should even be talking to him. After all, he was considered the most evil man on the planet, capable of convincing people to murder at his behest. I had a strange feeling every time we spoke, as though the FBI was going to show up at my front door and demand to know what Manson had told me. I had fleeting visions of Manson corrupting my mind or tricking me into telling him something I shouldn't. At the time, I had never spoken to an actual inmate before, let alone an infamous inmate calling from a supermax prison. It felt like my own personal *Silence of the Lambs*.

Manson's voice was raspy with a Midwestern twang. His tone sounded exactly like the rambling monster shown on TV, but his speech was nothing like the screaming and ranting mass murderer I expected. In fact, for the most part he was an easy conversationalist. He talked about friends he had in prison or other people he'd been speaking with recently.

I asked him what it was like to be Charles Manson, curious to understand if the man I was getting to know was anything like the devil he had been portrayed as. "Do you find that people are afraid of you?" I asked.

"Well," Charlie said, laughing, "Yeah, I would imagine so."

"Is that because you're *the* Charles Manson?" I said, emphasizing the evil commonly attributed to his name.

"Not only that," said Charlie, "but I lived quite a life in the underworld." Charlie was downright proud of being a part of the criminal subculture he often referred to as the "underworld." According to Charlie, the underworld was a kill or be killed existence where a person was only was as good as their word. All of Charlie's evil deeds took place in this underworld and only made sense in that context. When I asked him directly about why members of the Manson Family had butchered Sharon Tate, Manson said, "Episodes like that happen every day in the

20

underworld. There is always someone getting shot and killed for doing something, or lying about something, or playing some sort of stupid game with the devil."

*What game did Sharon Tate play with Manson?* I thought. *Is Charlie telling me he's the devil?* Large questions that I would get answers to in due time.

Despite Manson's personal notoriety and the fact that he was widely understood as being evil, I found that the average person knew very little about his actual crimes. Because of my work on Manson, I'm often asked questions like, "Didn't he want to start a race war or something?" This is sort of true, but to put it simply, the State of California convicted Charles Manson of committing nine murders.

Wanting to understand these crimes, I arranged to meet Stephen Kay, an attorney who spent his entire career as one of the Los Angeles co-prosecutors of Charles Manson and his Family. Stephen was a tall, well-spoken LA lawyer with short white hair who looked more like a computer programmer. When we met, he was dressed in a well-fitted black suit and wearing horn-rimmed glasses. He was likeable, and had a tendency to smile often, even when describing his incredible knowledge of the Manson Family's gruesome crimes.

Stephen first joined the team of prosecutors as part of Charles Manson's original trial in the early seventies before taking over as lead prosecutor in the subsequent trials of Manson and his followers. After spending decades in court with the Manson Family, Stephen Kay fully embraced being associated with the murders that defined his career. He did countless talks, interviews, and public appearances long after he retired. Despite his willingness to engage others in his knowledge of the crimes, Stephen shared an anecdote that reflected the public's ignorance surrounding the specifics.

Stephen had spoken to a group of about a hundred law clerks only a few years before I met him, and he wanted to begin his lecture by talking about a record producer named Terry Melcher. For those who are not familiar with the details of the Manson Family murders, sixties-era record producer Terry Melcher was an integral piece of the puzzle and was also, incidentally, the son of fifties-era movie starlet Doris Day.

In front of his captive audience of eager students, Stephen Kay asked, "How many of you know who Doris Day is?" To Stephen's shock not one person raised their hand. When Stephen was a child he was obsessed with Doris Day. Stephen's father had even worked for Warner

Brothers and had gotten him an autographed picture, which read: "Hi Stevie! From Doris Day." Stephen had proudly hung the photo in his bedroom. This fact only intensified Stephen's disappointment in the law clerks' lack of Manson-related knowledge. "If they don't know who Doris Day is, then they don't know the facts of the most famous crime in the history of Los Angeles," Stephen told me.

It's hard to appreciate just how massive the Manson case was back in the late sixties; it was front page news in California for years. "I mean these were summer law clerks that had just been hired," Stephen said. "Most of them were finished law school and they had no idea what I was talking about." Stephen's outrage was not just that his students had not done their homework. From his perspective, people had not appreciated the depth of Manson's depravity. Manson became a sort of folklore, a cartoon villain from a forgotten age. This, in Stephen's mind, ignored the reality of a truly evil man. "You know the problem is that Manson is famous," he said. "The kids nowadays don't look into the case to see exactly what he did, and what he was saying. When members joined the Manson Family, Charles Manson was telling them how Adolph Hitler was his hero, because of what he was able to do to the Jews. Manson was a follower of Nietzsche. You know it was just sick stuff."

Manson's alleged murder spree took place in the summer of 1969. It was the peak of the Vietnam war and a time of civil unrest. It's been widely reported that Charles Manson was the leader of a religious cult called the Manson Family. They supposedly lived a bleak existence on the fringes of society, indulging in a constant stream of drugs and sex. Manson never denied the sex part of these stories. According to Manson, the group "went where nobody ever went before," referring to the undeniable hedonism and sexual experimentation that he often recalled fondly. Manson once said, "All I was, was fucking everybody I could. The sexual revolution everybody was doing I was just getting my share, that's all."

The first murder was discovered on July 31, 1969. Police were called to the home of Gary Allen Hinman after two of his friends reported that he had not been seen or heard from for a week. Gary was a college student with friends throughout the area, a skinny thirty-four-year-old who practised Buddhism at a temple in North Hollywood.

When police arrived at Gary's Topanga Canyon home, they noticed flies buzzing around an open window from his second-floor apartment. They pounded on the door but couldn't find Gary or his landlord, so they searched the exterior of the house finding an old ladder in the backyard. The responding officer made use of the ladder by climbing up to the open window, but when he reached it, he realized the few flies visible from the ground were just the tip of the iceberg. The deafening noise of buzzing insects and the overwhelming smell of decay poured out from the room, almost sending the officer falling two storeys. The apartment was dark, but enough sunlight had hit the windows to worsen the rot of whatever lay inside. The officer held his breath and forced his head through the opening just enough to see a dead body decomposing in the middle of the room. It was the peak of summer in California. The corpse was festering and crawling with maggots, and a black, dried fluid covered the floor.

The body was almost completely covered with a blanket and pillow leaving only part of the face exposed. When the coroner and detectives arrived, they confirmed the corpse was Gary Hinman. He'd been dead for at least four days and left to decompose in the midst of a sweltering California heat wave. Police discovered that Gary owned two cars, which were normally parked out front but were missing. It seemed possible that Gary had been the victim of a home invasion and robbery, but the apartment didn't appear to be ransacked and there was no sign of forced entry. Mail from one of Gary's old roommates, some kid named Bobby, was on a counter, and clean dishes were neatly stacked beside the sink. Otherwise the apartment was the usual state of mess you'd expect from a college student. The coroner concluded that Gary had been tortured before being stabbed to death, but the most glaring clue was above Gary's body where someone had used his blood to write the words "Politically Piggy" beside a bloody handprint on the wall. The message at this time was absolutely meaningless to investigators.

Manson and three members of the Manson Family were later convicted of a devious plot to kill Gary as part of an alleged attempt to extort money from him. The prosecutors claimed that Gary was a friendly ex-hippie who had come across the Manson Family at the wrong time, before being callously targeted. According to the prosecution, Charles Manson erroneously believed Gary Hinman had come into a large inheritance, which Manson wanted for himself. An open-and-shut case of home invasion and robbery that escalated into murder. Why the Manson Family had used Gary's blood to write a message on the wall was part of a bigger overall motive that would become clear after their next victims were discovered.

A week later on August 8, 1969, movie star Sharon Tate and a group of three friends ate a late dinner at the the El Coyote Café, a Mexican restaurant on the edge of Beverly Hills that's so authentic it almost feels cliché. They sat in the back corner tucked into a classic green leather booth. Sharon was eight-months pregnant and accompanied by a common-law couple named Abigail Folger and Wojciech Frykowski. Abigail's last name has become synonymous with coffee because she was the granddaughter of J.A. Folger, the founder of Folgers Coffee, making her the heiress to the Folgers Coffee fortune. Sharon Tate's close friend and ex-boyfriend Jay Sebring was also with them. Sharon's husband, film director Roman Polanski, was out of the country preparing a film.

After Sharon Tate and her friends finished their meal, they headed home into the hills that overlook Hollywood. At the same time, Charles Manson and his so-called cult were living at a ranch across town and had allegedly decided they would venture to Sharon Tate's house and kill whoever they came across. Charles Manson had never formally met Sharon Tate but was familiar with her estate located at 10050 Cielo Drive in Beverly Hills, California. According to the case against the Manson Family presented at trial, Charles Manson sent out four members of his cult with orders to invade the home and kill everyone. In closing arguments, Vincent Bugliosi stated, "On the hot summer night of August the 8th, 1969, Charles Manson, the Mephistophelian guru who raped and bastardized the minds of all those who gave themselves so totally to him, sent out from the fires of hell at Spahn Ranch...heartless, bloodthirsty robots."

On the morning of August 9, the bodies of Sharon Tate, her three houseguests, and Steven Parent were found strewn around the property on Cielo Drive by a housekeeper.

The resulting news coverage and investigation sent Los Angeles into a full-blown panic. The murder consumed the news cycle, gun sales spiked, and celebrities went into hiding believing that Sharon Tate had been murdered as part of a bizarre religious ritual targeting famous people. A Los Angeles resident who lived through the terror told me, "The fright in the town was gigantic, people were scared to death for months. I mean people were buying Gatling guns!" The Tate murders, as they are commonly referred to, took place in August of 1969, but Manson and his followers' involvement was not discovered until December of that year, leaving five months of speculation and fear running rampant through Los Angeles.

The day after the slaughter of Sharon Tate and four others, the Manson Family committed two more murders. They broke into the home of Leno and Rosemary LaBianca, an affluent couple who owned a chain of grocery stores called Gateway Markets. Allegedly, Manson picked their house at random and ordered his brainwashed followers to brutally murder a couple they had never met. The LaBiancas were found by their stepson the next day. They were beaten, stabbed, and Rosemary was blindfolded with a pillowcase. Leno had a knife and carving fork protruding from his corpse. One of the killers had taken the time to carve the word "WAR" into his belly, leaving the bleeding capital letters to be discovered by investigators. Continuing their fascination with writing in blood, another one of the assailants wrote "Rise" and "Death to Pigs" over the family artwork that hung on the LaBiancas' off-white walls. In the kitchen "Healter Skelter" [*sic*] was misspelled in large red letters painted in blood on the fridge.

A month later, Manson and his followers murdered their final victim, a ranch hand named Donald "Shorty" Shae. Shorty was a stuntman who worked on the ranch where the Manson Family lived. Allegedly, Manson didn't get along with Shorty and believed he was a police informant, so ordered him to be killed. Shortly thereafter the Family went into hiding. Shorty's body was not discovered for almost twenty years, buried in an embankment off a side road near the ranch.

Though these nine murders are attributed to the Manson Family, the original trial and most of the subsequent fascination only concerns the murders of August 8 and 10, while ignoring the killings of Gary Hinman and Donald Shae. The August 8 and 10 murders have become collectively known as the Tate-LaBianca murders.

When Charles Manson and the Manson Family were arrested and charged, it became the longest and most expensive trial in the history of Los Angeles. Gary Fleischman, an attorney for one of the members of the Manson Family, told me, "Charlie looked like the devil sitting in court. That trial was like a circus. I mean it was *insanity*." Like the murders themselves, the trial took Los Angeles by storm—it was covered daily in local and national newspapers for years. It's not an overstatement to say it captivated the nation. A documentary about the Manson Family won the Academy Award, and even President Richard Nixon personally weighed in. At a press event in 1970 President Nixon referred to Charles Manson saying, "Here is a man who was guilty, directly or indirectly, of eight murders without reason." The remarks were controversial at the time, as Manson was in the midst of trial and therefore presumed innocent under the law.

Manson and his followers' insane behaviour during the trial only spurred public fascination and fed into his growing legend. His female co-defendants would sing in the hallways as they were led into the courtroom, giggling and smirking during a trial in which they faced the death penalty. Manson spoke to the media frequently with bizarre rants, statements, and nonsensical ramblings about life and death. His other followers held vigils outside the courthouse, sitting on the corner of Broadway and Temple. Made up of mostly young women dressed in homemade clothing, they proselytized Manson's gospel to anyone who would listen and mimicked whatever he did in court. During the sentencing phase, Manson shaved off all of his hair, and his followers both in and out of the courtroom did the same. Soon afterwards he carved an "X" into his forehead, which he said was a symbol of his desire to be discarded from society. His followers all predictably followed suit. Manson finally turned the "X" into a swastika, a symbol he proudly displayed between his eyes for the rest of his life. If you look closely at that swastika, you'll notice that it was originally backwards. During his incarceration, the scar diminished, and Manson darkened it with a pen or prison tattoo gun, reversing its direction to the same symbol used by white nationalists and the Third Reich. Whether out of shared ideology or a need for protection, Manson went on to use the racist calling card on his forehead—aligning himself with white supremacists while in supermax prisons.

I met a trial witness named Phil Kaufman while filming our documentary who said, "Every time I went to court every day they'd be out there singing 'Charlie, Charlie,' with those swastikas on their heads, shaving off all their hair. You know, that's not normal. That's *looney tunes* right there."

When the dust settled after years of litigation, Manson was sentenced to serve two life sentences and eight death sentences. The California Supreme Court abolished the death penalty in 1972, so his death sentences were commuted to additional life terms. For almost half a century, Charles Manson's bizarre behaviour continued, and speculation over his unspeakable crimes only intensified. Manson became known as the most evil, dangerous man in the world. The glaring question that always remained was, *how did Charles Manson get these people to kill for him*?

The answer that was first proposed at Manson's original trial in 1970 can be summed up in two words: Helter Skelter.

When I spoke with Manson, the topic of "Helter Skelter" came up frequently, and his take was always the same. He maintained that "Helter Skelter" was something invented by the prosecution and used to convict him. According to Charlie, "The precious point is that Helter Skelter is what the DA made up. It's all crap."

"Helter Skelter" is the name of a song recorded and released by The Beatles in 1968. It's an uncharacteristic hard rock anthem intentionally filled with screaming vocals and distorted guitars. The song is about the rise and fall of society using the metaphor of a children's amusement park slide. In the United Kingdom, a "helter skelter" is a tall winding slide found at fairgrounds. Amidst a piercing guitar, Paul McCartney screams, "When I get to the bottom I go back to the top of the slide, where I stop and I turn and I go for a ride, 'till I get to the bottom and I see you again." It's a great song, with amazing guitar riffs that capture the sound of chaos and control all at once. Since its release, "Helter Skelter" has become one of The Beatles' more frequently covered compositions; there have been great versions put out by Motley Crüe, Aerosmith, Soundgarden, Oasis, and Rob Zombie with Marilyn Manson, among many others. I also recommend one of The Beatles' original recordings of "Helter Skelter," which runs for over twenty-seven minutes.

According to the State of California, Charles Manson was obsessed with the song "Helter Skelter" and believed that it prophesied the end of days—a belief that was the motive for his Family's murder spree.

The Manson Family's convictions were led by Vincent Bugliosi who co-wrote the book *Helter Skelter*, which became the bestselling true crime book of all time. According to Bugliosi, "Helter Skelter" was the name Charles Manson gave to his own bizarre philosophy—derived from The Beatles song. Bugliosi's theory, presented at trial, was that Manson became infatuated with The Beatles' *White Album,* listening to it obsessively. This led Manson to become convinced that there were hidden meanings in the songs, specifically "Helter Skelter," which

Manson believed predicted a black versus white race war that would consume Los Angeles.

Manson allegedly prophesied that he and his religious cult could survive the race war by hiding in a secret cave, which Manson believed was located in Death Valley. In order to procure the money to buy the necessary provisions for this trip, Manson ordered his followers to rob and kill Gary Hinman. After this, Manson allegedly became frustrated that the race war wasn't developing as quickly as he had hoped, so he sent his followers to the posh home of Sharon Tate under orders to slaughter her and anyone else they came across. Manson's evil plot was to stage Tate's murder to make it look like black people had killed her, thus fueling the growing racial tensions and speeding up the onset of the inevitable race war that The Beatles had predicted.

The next night, according to the prosecution's theory, Manson picked another house at random, ordered his followers to kill all who were inside, and once again had them stage the crime scene to make it appear as though black people had committed the murders. By Manson's supposed logic, these murders would further terrorize the white people of Los Angeles and motivate the black people of Los Angeles to continue killing them.

The Manson Family's writings on the walls in blood were supposedly all a peculiar attempt to further this plot. Allegedly, they were using lyrics from The Beatles' *White Album* to communicate the onset of the revolution to black people. "Pig" and "Political Piggy" were theorized to be references to the song "Piggies," which appears on side two of *The White Album,* and "Rise" was a reference to the song "Blackbird," also from *The White Album*. According to prosecutors, the Manson Family believed a black person would see these words, understand they were Beatles references, and tell other black people of their significance.

It was a bizarre theory in 1969, and it remains one today. A convoluted plot to instigate a seemingly unbelievable prophesy, all inspired by The Beatles. It generates many questions: *How did Manson actually come to believe The Beatles could predict the future? How did he convince anyone this was true?* And, *why would anyone listen to him?*

In our conversations, Manson generally wasn't forthcoming about any aspects of his story, with the exception of "Helter Skelter." Manson was adamant that "Helter Skelter" was complete bullshit. "It's all underworld, soldier. Who do you think the president is? Not me," he said, implying that he wasn't the one in charge. "Where you think his office is? In my cell?" Charlie said that he never believed in some bullshit race war, and he certainly never ordered any murders because of a bullshit race war. He insisted that didn't even really like The Beatles. He maintained Vincent Bugliosi had made it all up. "They still won't admit the truth," Charlie said. "They had no evidence against me. None."

*That can't be true,* I thought. *Surely there was a mountain of evidence against Charles Manson.* By that point, I had re-read the book *Helter Skelter* and was very familiar with the case itself, but I had not delved deeply into the actual evidence for myself.

When speaking to Charles Manson, the most famous mind-controlling mass murderer of all time, I knew I couldn't take him solely at his word. This did not go over well with Charlie. In Charlie's underworld his word was everything. He'd been in prison for almost fifty years and his word was one of his most valuable possessions. He made it clear that what he was telling me was not only true, but of value. "You're telling me 'I don't trust what you say,'" Charlie said. "If you tell me something, then I *know* that. It's 'cause I know you won't lie to me. And, how could I know that? 'cause I got a .357 magnum and you know what I'll do to people that lie to me." Charlie's tone was forceful and direct, and although I knew he was in prison and was speaking in metaphor it sent a shiver up my spine. "When you're in the *know* with somebody that's in the *know,* you don't play games with them." Charlie's message was clear: don't fuck with me. I'll tell you the truth but you better fucking listen.

After months of conversations with Charlie, in-depth research, and speaking with others who were involved in the case at the time, questions began to emerge. In making the documentary I strived to speak with authors, researchers, and people who knew Manson directly. Charlie began to personally put me in contact with people who knew him; others my team and I found on our own. I sought to speak to anyone who was there when the crimes took place, all to unravel what actually happened.

What I found was something I never expected.

# Survival

*"My life has never been important to anyone, not even in the*
*understanding of the way you fear the things that you fear, and the*
*things that you do."*
        *- Charles Manson, 1970*

I'm told that time passes differently in prison, so even though Charlie had not called in many weeks he spoke as if we were still in the middle of a conversation.

"Hello," I said. "Charlie?"

"Do you realize I've been locked up forty-eight years in a cell?" Charlie began.

"Yes, I know," I said, trying to sound somewhat understanding.

"You know how impossible that is?"

"How did you manage to survive?" I asked.

"It's all a movie. It's a big show. It's a big act. It's not real," Charlie explained. "The only thing that's real is death." Charlie often spoke about life, telling me it was a fleeting masquerade of reality. He said that "you" is the only thing that exists. "*You* are *me. I* am *you. Me* is all there is," he reasoned, in a way that seemed to make sense only because Charles Manson was saying it.

I could see how a solipsistic philosophy or reasoning that one's own mind is the only thing that surely exists, would be helpful if one spent most of their life trying to cope with the brutality of prison. Manson

31

oozed prison, as if being an inmate was pouring out of him uncontrollably. Charlie said that every day he woke up in hell and realized that "the day was too fuckin' fierce." For Charlie, the world was made of concrete and steel. The only lens in which you could truly understand Manson was prison. There's no doubt in my mind that the infamous killer we've come to know as Charles Manson was born and bred in prison.

Manson spent the majority of his life in a small farming town called Corcoran, California, which is a little over a two-hour drive north of Los Angeles. There's not much to Corcoran. Its population is a meagre 22,000 people, and that includes the 10,000 men who live on the corner of Paris and King, the location of the two California State Prisons. The prisons are collectively called California State Prison, Corcoran, and in addition to housing almost half of Corcoran's residents, they also employ most of the town. Corcoran is the epitome of America's prison industrial complex; the sheer size of these buildings is staggering—you can see them for miles.

The combined prison is split into two separate and equally massive complexes colloquially called Corcoran One and Corcoran Two. Charlie was housed in the more decrepit Corcoran Two, which at first glance appears as if it was designed for a seventies prison skin flick. It's a stoic brick complex surrounded by razor wire and guard towers, which Charlie spent the majority of his life looking up at.

Before Corcoran, Charlie was at the state prison in Vacaville, California. Charlie recalled prison officials talking about building a special unit to house notorious inmates who are at risk for being harmed by the general prison population. As soon as the Protective Housing Unit (PHU) became a reality, Manson was sent to Corcoran, causing him to speculate that they built a prison (or at least part of one) just for him. Allegedly when Robert Blake and Michael Jackson both looked as if they might need to spend time in state prison the PHU was retrofitted to receive them. Michael Jackson's cell was to be directly beside Charlie's, leaving us all to speculate on what mind-bending conversations would have taken place inside California State Prison between Michael Jackson and Charles Manson.

Once transferred to Corcoran, Manson lived in a segregated unit where he was kept under guard at all times so that the other inmates wouldn't kill him. For any inmate, becoming the man who killed Charles

Manson would have helped their position on the inside. It was an honour no one was ever able to claim.

Prison is all about this daily battle for survival, so everything about Charlie was survival, and in prison he found a way to survive for almost five decades. It's hard to forget that he was sentenced to death nine times, and yet he lived well into his golden years in the care of the state. Charlie described his living conditions as a "cell with another cell in it." Being in prison for so long had made Charlie appreciate every nuance of his cell. "It's got these big beautiful doors. Two thousand or three-thousand-dollar doors," Charlie described proudly. "You could buy a car for what these doors are worth. Big iron doors."

In regard to his life spent in jail, Charlie told me, "You know you're coming back 'cause there ain't no getting out. All that's fantasy. Prison is a mind; the mind is prison. That's why they haven't been able to break me, because there's no such thing. They're in a fantasy. They don't have a reality; their reality is television." For Charlie, true prison was the outside world. Prison was the real world where things made sense to him. Things were black and white in prison but outside the world was in Technicolor. Charlie spoke in terms of life or death, because that's what it's like in prison. I'm not the first person to make this observation.

On the road to Charlie Manson I met many travellers. Over the years a lot of people had gotten to know Charlie in one form or another, writing him letters and establishing some sort of relationship with him. While Manson was in prison, he cultivated a bizarre small group of pen pals who became exceptionally loyal to him. They all share the common narrative of writing him a letter on a whim, being surprised that he wrote back, then proceeding to establish a relationship with him through additional letters, phone calls, and visits. Most of these relationships have gone on for decades, and all claim to be Manson's best friend in a surreal high school-like competition in which they fight over who Manson liked best. Most of this animosity spills out through various online forums, text messages, and emails in an intense back and forth where the stakes could not be lower. I can rationalize my own desire to speak with Manson as journalistic intent, but I struggle to understand why someone would go out of their way to be associated with him. I've put this question to the men who compete for the title of Manson's closest confidant. When I started to become known for my work on Manson, many of them reached out to me, and Manson himself would tell me about them.

John Michael Jones is a larger-than-life character who speaks with a gravelly voice and is the human embodiment of Boston. He claims to have known, and been extremely close with, Manson for about seventeen years. Ben Gurecki is John Michael's Midwestern equivalent, having known Manson for approximately the same amount of time. Stoner Van Houten is the pseudonym of a YouTuber in California who claims to be a confidant of the remaining Manson Family members and spews his Manson opinions online to the few who will actually listen to him. There are many others, and all share a common view of Manson as a "warrior" persecuted by the system—a true humanitarian who was wrongfully accused, unjustly convicted, and mischaracterized by a malicious media. They each claim to be some sort of truth seeker, part of a special club that knows the secret reality of Charles Manson. I've spoken to all of these people, who collectively refer to themselves as "The Manson Community." They'll talk for hours about Manson innocence, and you can challenge them ad nauseam about the facts of the case, but you will get nothing even close to a satisfying answer. The truth is they are not the Manson experts they claim to be; instead, they are a group of individuals who all have a deep void that is somehow filled by being associated with Charles Manson. Even if they learned some undeniable piece of evidence that exonerated Manson, they each went into a relationship with him in the knowledge that they were seeking out a convicted mass murderer and avowed racist. A fascination with serial killers and the way their minds work is not hard to understand, but to become enamoured and to align yourself with a person whose actions are so shameful seems disturbed. The best I can tell is that this community is like a flat earth society or those who don't believe in the moon landing—they believe they're privy to some elite information about Charles Manson, a position that gives them meaning.

What did Charlie get out of all of this? Charlie was in maximum security, and anyone in maximum security needs help to survive. Friends on the outside were of enormous benefit to Charlie; they'd fill up his commissary account, visit him, bring others to visit him, and help him get messages to people on the outside. His friends would go so far as to call other prisons to pass around messages between inmates, giving Charlie vast connections and therefore power. John Michael Jones would even pay off other inmates to protect Charlie. They would all buy Charlie any number of personal and luxury items and call the prison to complain on his behalf. All Charlie had to do was write a letter or make a phone call now and then telling them that they were his friends.

Some of these friends have written books or made documentaries like I did. Some thought they'd gained Charlie's trust, and many lied about what they knew or how they knew it. For the record, I don't think anyone has ever gained Charlie's trust, but a person who may have gotten very close is Michael Channels. Michael did a brief media tour shortly after Charlie's death when he filed to be named the executor of Charlie's estate and claim his remains. He lost the case to Manson's grandson who was named his next of kin.

Michael is truly unique among the travellers. He knows more about Charlie than I thought humanly possible, and I believe he has spent more time interacting with Charlie than almost anyone who ever lived. Michael grew up on the Ohio River, thirty-two miles away from where Charli̶̶ ̶̶̶ ̶̶ ̶ ̶̶ ̶ 1. As a young adult Michael learned that rs if he was able to somehow obtain an harles Manson, so he took the initiative st letter grew into a friendship that lasted ear, the word friendship is how I classify ld be the first to tell you that the term ss to Charlie. According to Michael, a sentiment that included Michael. he could spit," Michael said. ded over commonalities in their Ohio nder a strict and religious grandmother, eir families converted to Nazarene hin about thirty minutes of each other. hael could relate to Charlie's self- carry a conversation in a way that was

first met Michael over the phone and was taken by that first conversation. His manner of speaking is infectious. He was incredibly passionate no matter the subject. He spoke with intensity regardless of whether he was describing the intricate details of Charlie's life or sharing the location of the nearest gas station. The first time we met in person was aptly on the Santa Susana Pass, directly across from the remains of Spahn Ranch. The ranch was the former home to Charlie and his commune at the time of the murders and burned down in 1971. Michael was an imposing figure; his natural intensity matched by his wild eyes and hair that's unusually long for a man well into his sixties. He moved quickly and used grand gestures to get his point across. All his vigour could easily be misconstrued as aggression but actually came from a place of wanting to be understood.

Michael was a self-made Charles Manson historian who had also acted as both Charlie's quasi executive assistant and confidant for lack of a better description. Michael did not claim to be an expert on the murders (although he'd share his opinion if asked) but did know absolutely all there is to know about Charlie's life. He knew every detail and could tell you how he knew—he'd show you the paperwork and tell you what Manson himself had to say about it.

Michael met me near Spahn Ranch with a small film crew and a guide from the California Department of Parks to take us on a private tour. Little remained of the original structures but for those who knew their way around there were still things to see. Michael spent twenty years seeking out the exact locations associated with the ranch and has seen much of it disappear. Since the arrival of the internet the ranch has become easier to locate, and almost everything that remained on the property has been destroyed or pilfered.

Michael showed me a large boulder that had been hacked to pieces buried deep in the back country of the property. In 1969, the boulder would have been on the edge of the creek that ran behind the northern row of structures that flanked Spahn Ranch. He explained that he'd found a picture of Charlie sitting on that very boulder playing guitar, as Charlie often did. The spot carried significance as Charlie had carved his initials "CM" into the side. It sat that way for decades. Michael spent years exploring the grounds until he stumbled upon it completely overgrown by foliage. Years later, he came to visit the boulder again and discovered that a neighbouring church group had taken a high-pressure saw to the boulder, carving out Manson's initials to destroy any remnants of the devil incarnate. It's this disrespect for the significance of Manson artifacts, regardless of what evil they may represent, which sends Michael into a rage. "It just fuckin' pisses me off," he yelled. "Those fuckin' people who carved up this rock are more evil than fuckin' Charles Manson. This was history! You can't change it. You can't ignore what happened here just because you don't fuckin' like it."

I couldn't help but agree with his point of view; sometimes the worst parts of history are the ones that need to be responsibly preserved the most.

Michael wasn't naive about who Charlie was when they first met. "I went into this knowing that the dude was Charlie Manson," he said. "For all I knew every horrible thing that was ever said about him was true. So, when I walked into the prison visiting room for the first time, if he had jumped across the table and stabbed me in the head with a knife, I would've deserved it because I should've known what I was in for. It was nothing like that." According to Michael, Charlie wasn't a crazed Svengali with murder in his eyes, he was just a regular man.

Over the next twenty years, Michael spent hours and hours visiting with Charlie and speaking with him on the phone. I asked Michael what the best way to understand Charlie was. His answer was simple: prison. Charles Manson was prison. Michael told me, "Charlie's world was a different world than ours, man. He woke up in evil every single day of the week. When he woke up in the morning, he opened his eyes to see that he was in hell. It was all about life or death for him. He had to watch his back every day because the guy next to him might be looking to kill him just to eat a Cup-a-Soup that he had in his cell. That's how little life is worth in prison. It's worth nothing."

Michael's insights resonated with me because I'd heard Manson himself echo these sentiments. At his 1992 parole hearing, Manson chided the parole board for not understanding what life was like in prison. Charlie said, "I have to deal with every kind of psychotic maniac you got in the world trying to burn me up, trying to beat me up, trying to get some attention to get me in any kind of direction he can. And I have to propose a certain image and keep a certain kind of guy stuck up there to keep those bullies off of me. Because if I show any weakness, if I fall down in any perspective, I get ate up because I run with a pack of wolves and I've got to be a wolf."

Years later, Manson still held these strong feelings. He brought up his prison experiences to me often, saying that they shaped his entire experience of life. "You don't spend years in prison and not learn a lot," Charlie said. "You learn the mind; you learn the day. You learn how to get up and live for the day. If you live for the day and in an enclosure with five thousand people—that's five thousand days."

Michael showed me a grainy green Polaroid that Manson had given him of his cell inside Corcoran. A small room with a toilet and a low protruding wall on which Charlie stashed all his worldly belongings. This room, where Manson lived most of his life, was so small and desolate. It made me realize how much he came to rely on people on the

37

outside. As Michael got to know Manson, he began running errands for him, coordinated visitors if needed, and spoke to other inmates to relay messages. Michael even helped Manson sell personal items when eBay came along.

Michael made no secret of the fact that he gave Charlie a significant amount of money over the years. The prison had a system in which anyone could send money to any inmate, for any reason. Michael took that opportunity to give money to Charlie. In an unspoken partnership over the years, Charlie had given Michael things like artwork, prison documents, or personal items, and what Michael didn't keep he sold online. Authentic Charles Manson memorabilia continues to thrive in the internet marketplace, a practice often referred to as murderabilia. Some people will pay a premium to own a picture drawn by a serial killer, or a blood-spattered piece of carpet from a famous murder, or, in Michael's case, a personal item belonging to Charles Manson. The money Michael made he split with Charlie.

There's something that feels insidious about murderabilia, especially when it comes to Charles Manson. Michael Channels was certainly not alone when it came to selling all sorts of Manson items. Charlie's artwork, hair, glasses, dentures, flip-flops, and every other personal item he ever owned can still be found for sale online. Many of the Manson friends I mentioned are also Manson death dealers who all give different excuses for why they partook in this macabre trade. Their most common justification is that Manson was victimized by the media who misrepresented him as the boogeyman, so they—and Manson—had a right to profit from it in some sense. I can understand the dark fascination with wanting to own something that belonged to a famous killer, but I can't help but feel that murderabilia is a violation of an unspoken expectation of social empathy. I'm less concerned that selling the proverbial bloody glove or owning a piece of a serial killer glorifies their actions (all manner of media already achieves this), but actively selling or seeking an item that derives its value solely because of the misery associated with it, feels equivalent to blood diamonds.

Lawmakers have been trying to curb the ability of criminals to profit from their crimes ever since New York serial killer David Burkowitz tried to sell the rights to his life's story to the highest bidder in 1977. These Son of Sam laws were named after his notorious moniker. The California supreme court struck down their Son of Sam law in 2002 in favour of criminals' right to free speech, leaving the door open for

Charles Manson to sell some artwork here and there, although this didn't prevent the prison from trying to stop him.

The prison shut down an art program Charlie participated in when it was discovered that his creations were being sold online and that the money was making its way back to him. Prison officials even went so far as to investigate Michael for money laundering, but nothing ever came of it. Michael showed me the documentation he received from the prison that detailed the investigation. He expressed that he was ecstatic when he'd received it, because it was an official document in which his name and the name Charles Manson appeared together.

None of these attempts to stop him prevented Charlie from establishing a small Charles Manson industry from his cell in the Protective Housing Unit. He understood his name had value, which he used to garner favour, debts with other inmates, and money from those on the outside. Many people have shown me a letter they've supposedly received from Charles Manson, and many people have been disappointed to learn that it's fake. Over the years if someone wrote Charlie a letter, he would turn it over to another inmate who would write back under Charlie's name, corresponding with their new pen pal to gain favour and money for themselves.

Co-prosecutor Stephen Kay was continually amazed by what Manson got away with in prison. "He got on average four fan letters a day, and people would get responses signed Charles Manson and they'd think, 'Oh, this is great. I got an autographed letter from Manson. I'll sell it on eBay and make lots of money.' But Manson is a con artist so what he did was pass the letters out to other prisoners and say, 'You answer the letter however you want,' and they sign it Charles Manson."

If the con was successful the inmate would owe Charlie a debt, a concept that is vital to understanding prison and who Charlie was. Manson would collect the debts and cash when he needed money—or more often protection. Money can only get you so far inside prison, and there's a pretty limited monetary system between the inmates, so interpersonal interactions carry significant weight. If you owe someone, you truly owe them something significant: contraband, sex, beating someone, protection. When Charlie said, "You owe me," to anyone, he meant it literally.

At one point, prison officials attempted to curtail the open market trade of Charlie's name by telling him that he couldn't send out any letters that were signed by him. This strategy was short-lived when

Charlie began refusing to sign anything the prison presented him with. This caused numerous headaches for officials when the prison would require Charlie's signature on reprimands, incident reports, or hearings. Prison officials would tell Charlie he had to sign these documents and Charlie would tell them to fuck off. Not being able to cope with the unsigned official documents, they relented, and Manson was once again allowed to sign his name to whatever he wanted. After this, Manson's foray into murderabilia only grew. Charlie befriended a number of individuals like Michael who set up websites selling anything from Manson's artwork to his hair and everything in between. Because of the internet, this macabre trade went completely unregulated throughout Charlie's life, so it's unclear who he was working with, and who was selling items without his knowledge. It's also unclear what money actually made it back to him, but there's no doubt that small fortunes were made exploiting the victims of his crimes.

The stark truth is that Charles Manson was incredibly famous—and he knew it. Charlie once told Michael, "I'm the most famous human being that is alive, the most famous human being that ever lived and I'm not even dead yet. What the fuck you think is going to happen when I die and all these youngsters are raised up to see all those people that lied and misused me and beat me and drugged me and set me on fire. Where do you think that's coming back to?" The infamy of Charles Manson not only attracts a unique sort of fan, but it's also made anything associated with his name into something of value.

Michael told me that Charlie talked a good game, but that the talk was a "prison thing" as well. In prison, it's to your advantage to convince the other inmates that you're not only tough, but also perhaps a little bit crazy. Michael said, "In prison you have to convince a lot of people that you might just go off the rocker right now and take you out. If people think you're a bit like that, which is the show that Manson gave them a lot of times, they stay away from you. If people don't bother you, then you're safe. Charlie even took that kind of stuff out into the real world with him too."

Michael reiterated the theme I'd heard from Charlie himself— Manson was about survival. Michael said, "It's all about survival. Everything in Manson's life was survival. If you base it on that then it's a little easier to understand where he was coming from, the things that came out of his mouth, and his basic life. It's just waking up and staying alive."

I'd heard Charlie speak about this is audio recordings from the investigations. In a recording from 1977 Charlie said, "I'm an animal and I'll do anything it takes to survive. It's that simple, and I look out for this guy right here, number one. I've always been that way and explained that to all the people I was with. I said you be for yourself and the world that you live in."

This is where most people go wrong in really understanding who Manson was—they misconstrue what was coming out of his mouth. People looked at Manson as if he were capable of some sort of mind control, as if he had some supernatural genius that gave him the power to talk people into doing whatever he wanted. Nothing could be further from the truth.

Manson was about survival, and in order to survive in prison he had to get to know people very quickly so he could determine their intentions. Manson wasn't a great speaker, but he was a great listener. He would take in everything people gave him. Early on, Manson came to believe there were only about thirteen different types of people and if he could figure them out, he would understand the entire world. Charlie's trick was listening to people and lumping them into one of his thirteen categories, making it seem like he had some sort of unique ability to understand that person. "The mind is powerful,' Manson said. But he wasn't talking about his mind, he was talking about the minds of others. What he was doing was a parlour trick, but the effect it had on people was profound. "It's like you being a producer, you gotta get into the heads of everybody," Manson said, attempting to relate to me.

*Do I really want to get into the head of Charles Manson?* I asked myself. *Well, I've gone this far.*

As I continued talking to Manson, I questioned his true motives in continuing to call. He clearly knew that I was interviewing him and using our calls to make a documentary, so I wondered what he was getting out of our conversations. I thought perhaps he wanted to get the truth out—his truth at least—or maybe he just wanted a break from the monotony of prison or simply enjoyed the attention. None of these reasons seemed satisfying to me because, from what I could gather, there had been hundreds of books, movies, and documentaries already made about Manson, and mine was one of the only projects he truly collaborated on during his life. I asked Charlie, "What do you want people to know when they see this documentary?"

"I don't want them to know anything," he replied, almost laughing, before quickly changing his mind. "You know what, I want them to know ATWA."

ATWA was Charlie's mantra, an anagram meaning Air Water Trees Animals—an environmental manifesto going back to the sixties. Charlie said that he was an environmentalist at heart. He loved nature and was never happier than when sleeping under a tree. As a young man when he'd go to prison and then be released, he'd see that his favourite creek had been turned into a restaurant, or a forest had been turned into a shopping mall. Going in and out of prison gave Manson a unique appreciation for nature and a distinct view on development's encroachment on the natural world. Over the years he turned this point of view into a saying, Air Trees Water Animals or ATWA, which Charlie turned into a word, ATWA (pronounced At-wah). Charlie turned ATWA into a sort-of code word by giving it a different meaning, only known to those who Manson considered friends: All The Way Alive. While filming interviews for the documentary, one of Manson's friends had told me the code word, so by the time Manson asked me about it, I was well-prepared.

"You know ATWA?" Charlie asked.

"Oh yeah," I said. "I'm All The Way Alive."

"Ha!" Manson laughed joyfully. "That's it, Jack! You can't live without that. They say well what about Jesus? What about prayer? I say there ain't no prayer if you got no air. How you gonna pray if you ain't breathing man?"

Over the years, Air Trees Water Animals was incorporated into an official California-based charity, trying to give Manson's mantra a more official designation and website.

"You ever look up ATWA on the dot com?" Manson asked.

"I've seen it," I said.

"ATWA is all there is, man. If you don't have air you don't exist," Charlie said emphatically. "Without ATWA we're all gone."

Believe it or not, Charlie truly spoke passionately about the environment—something about nature resonated with him. I suspect it had to do with spending fifty years removed from it. I read a quote from Manson Family member Lynette "Squeaky" Fromme, in which she said, "If a person had been locked up for a long time, every little bit of the outside world is like a special treat."[1] I felt like this was some version of Manson wisdom that greatly reminded me of how Charlie would talk about nature.

The man behind the contemporary version of ATWA was a long-time Manson supporter who went by the name Gray Wolf. I first met Gray Wolf in Corcoran, California to interview him for the documentary. It wasn't hard to see where Gray Wolf got his name— he's a tall imposing figure with an intense stare and a long grey beard. His intense look was offset by his welcoming affect. In my interactions with him, he spoke thoughtfully and was incredibly gracious. Everyone who knew Charlie seemed to see something different in him, and Gray Wolf saw an environmental warrior—a truth teller who pained over the destruction of the planet.

A man after Gray Wolf's own heart.

During Manson's life, Gray Wolf lived near Corcoran to be closer to Charlie, visiting him for years. "I *named* him Gray Wolf," Manson told me proudly. As the story goes, Manson started out calling Gray Wolf, "Coyote," which over the years Charlie morphed into "Gray Wolf" as his friend developed his characteristic grey beard. Continuing this theme, Manson named two of his other supporters Black Wolf and Red Wolf. I've had the opportunity to meet the entire Wolf Pack, who were all uniquely dedicated in their own feelings toward Charlie, and their names symbolized their connection to him.

Black Wolf was Charlie's main connection to the outside world—he visited Charlie hundreds of times and supported him in prison. Charlie said that because he relied on Black Wolf so much, he had advised him to stay in the shadows, away from the public eye—thus the name "Black Wolf." Red Wolf was tasked with looking after Charlie's best girl, Squeaky, who Charlie was barred from having contact with. Charlie referred to Squeaky as "Red," thus her protector was "Red Wolf." Gray Wolf had the biggest responsibility of the three wolves. He was to look after the planet while Charlie was in prison.

Gray Wolf told me, "ATWA as a word came into being after Charlie was convicted, but that concept is what Charlie was all about. It goes back to his uncle in the thirties and forties." According to Gray

---

[1] State of California v Manson Et al. 175, Cal Supp. 22,232 (1971, February 2).

Wolf, Manson began his deep connection to the environment when the government brought electricity into the Ohio River Basin when Charlie was a child. Charlie's rural family saw the benefit from electricity but also the destruction that the infrastructure brought to local rivers and creeks. "That's when Charlie invented that word," Gray Wolf said. "ATWA means a lot of different things. It's a tool for meditation, but it's also a tool for illuminating what's really going on. It covers all the bases. It's kind of a magic word. You can put an 'R' on the end and it means AT WAR."

"At war with what?" I asked Gray Wolf.

"At war with pollution," he responded.

In 1970, when Gray Wolf was twenty-one years old, he became disenchanted with the status quo and dropped out of college. He ventured out to California from his home state of Florida where, while hitchhiking in Los Angeles, he met the Manson Family's Squeaky and Sandy. They invited him to Spahn Ranch, and he didn't leave for six months. At Spahn Ranch, Gray Wolf found everything he was looking for—a unique "awareness" as he called it. People living in harmony with each other and with nature, spiritually enlightened away from the grinding machine of society. He remembered the women bringing him up to speed on the fact that their so-called leader and their friends were facing the death penalty for the most infamous murders in the history of Los Angeles. Gray Wolf saw all of that as background noise—a series of misconceptions and lies proliferated by the media who resented the Manson Family's spiritual awareness and way of life. "The ranch was the most beautiful place I'd ever been," he recalled, almost losing himself in the memory.

Soon after his arrival at the ranch, Gray Wolf joined the women at the courthouse and saw Charlie for the first time. "The courtroom was upside down," Gray Wolf recalled. "What I mean by that is, in a normal courtroom everyone looks to the judge, but at the [Manson Family] trial, everyone was looking at Charlie. They didn't like that, man."

Gray Wolf was so enamoured with this first impression that he joined the vigil on the corner outside of the trial. While the rest of the world was perplexed and horrified by the Manson Family murderesses, Gray Wolf admired them. "The girls used to sing songs in the hallways of the courtroom. They had such beautiful voices," Gray Wolf recalled fondly.

During the trial, Squeaky and Sandy took Gray Wolf into the holding cells to meet Charlie, and the encounter changed Gray Wolf's life forever. He realized immediately that Manson was a "truth talker," capable of seeing the world on a different level. The next day, Gray Wolf returned to his place on the corner of Temple and Broadway (the intersection of the LA County courthouse), sitting next to Squeaky and Sandy, where he was arrested as a member of the group.

Gray Wolf remembered Charlie talking about the environment even when he was on trial for murder. "He was talking about the ecosystem ATWA as soon as he hit the ground. [The Manson Family] was saying, 'We wanted to stop this war, we want to stop this pollution.' That's what they stood up for."

In 2013, Gray Wolf was arrested for allegedly trying to smuggle a cellphone in to Charlie. Since then, he'd been unable to speak with Charlie directly. After his release, Gray Wolf took up the cause of promoting Manson's ATWA philosophy. "Charlie, he was talking about that as soon as he got out," Gray Wolf told me. "We are being overwhelmed by the concrete; we're being overwhelmed by the corporations. We just can't get away from it."

When I met Gray Wolf the first time, to interview him for our documentary, he asked if we could conduct the interview outside to ensure nature would be part of the filming. It took me a while to convince him otherwise, and he reluctantly agreed to meet at a house we'd rented in Corcoran.

During the interview, Gray Wolf read a quote from Charlie he'd brought with him: "Crime is anything that's done against your survival. Any sin that's against your life is a crime. The law is the will of god. The law should be respected as god's will, not something to be toyed and played with and used for bureaucratical bullshit. The problem is the atmosphere is dying, anything that sins against the air is a sin against your life. Anybody that sins against the air should be considered a criminal."

"So you listen to that," Gray Wolf said, "and you say I've never heard a man talk like that, and then you say the media shows Charlie as someone who's crazy and evil but that's not a crazy man talking unless you look at him as a prophet—but all prophets are crazy."

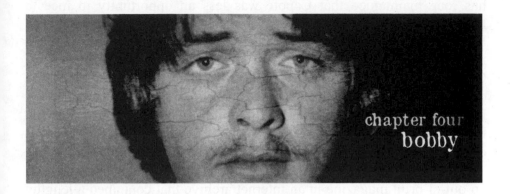

chapter four
bobby

# Bobby

*"I'm trying to be honest with you in terms of my participation, and what those factors were that led up to my situation with Gary and with the other people that were involved. That's all I can do. I can't really speak to the, you know, I don't even—the Manson mythology thing that's developed. A lot of that came afterwards."*
*- Bobby Beausoleil, 2016 Parole Hearing*

The first person arrested and accused of being a member of the Manson Family was Bobby Beausoleil. In 1969 Bobby was a twenty-one-year-old handsome young man with dark, shaggy hair and intense eyes. By all accounts he was charismatic, ambitious, and fiercely independent. In putting together a picture of what truly happened, I knew Bobby Beausoleil's perspective would be an essential piece of the puzzle. Before the murders began, Bobby was a soon-to-be father living in Topanga Canyon—a talented musician with a bright future. By the end of 1969, he was on trial, facing the death penalty for the murder of Gary Hinman.

In 1973, while serving his sentence in San Quentin, Bobby became the fascination of American cultural icon Truman Capote, who interviewed Bobby in prison. Capote published his account of their interaction as part of his 1980 collection *Music for Chameleons*. Bobby has long maintained that Capote was less an opportunity to meet a literary genius, and more a hindrance than anything else. According to Bobby, Capote did not record their conversation, took few notes, and yet managed to publish a lengthy transcript years later. A re-reading of Capote's work from a modern true crime perspective leaves a lot to be desired. Though beautifully written, it's full of factual errors about Bobby, Manson, and the crimes in question; inaccuracies that may not have called attention to themselves in 1973 but are now obvious because of online access to crime scene photos, interviews, and police reports.

In my initial research for the documentary, I found an article from an out-of-print magazine in an internet archive that contained a lengthy interview with Bobby. The article expressed a point of view that hinted at an alternative explanation for the murders and contained seeds of ideas that I was slowly gleaning from my phone calls with Manson. I sought out the author of the article, who by that time was a freelance journalist living in New York. After a few weeks I got him on the phone and explained what I was up to. I told the journalist that I wanted to interview him for our documentary, as he could help me understand Bobby's point of view. He immediately refused saying, "I would never speak for Bobby." Before I could try to sway him, he asked why I had not spoken to Bobby myself. Up until that moment, I had not considered that an option. I didn't know Bobby, nor did I know anyone in the California State prison system (expect for Charlie Manson). I didn't think it even plausible that Bobby Beausoleil would have any desire to talk to me. The journalist suggested that I try and offered to reach out to Bobby on my behalf.

A week later while driving through Beverly Hills, my phone rang with a call from the California Department of Corrections. I assumed it was Charlie but instead heard, "This is Global Tel Link. You have a pre-paid called from Bobby, an inmate in the California Medical Facility, Vacaville, California. To accept this call, say or dial 5 now—beep." To my surprise, Bobby was downright annoyed that I hadn't called him sooner. I learned that he had curated a solid online presence based around his artwork and music, which I had somehow completely missed. Despite being in prison since 1969, Bobby had become an accomplished artist and musician. Bobby was well-spoken, thoughtful, and had an incredible perspective on his life—and the greater context of the Manson story.

According to Bobby, what Charlie had been telling me was true—at least from the perspective that what happened in 1969 was misunderstood. "It's the same regurgitated Helter Skelter nonsense," Bobby said. "That is so far away from the truth. I don't care, I will never say what Vincent Bugliosi said was true, to get parole. Never! I'd rather die in prison than get out on a lie." I was fascinated by Bobby's take. He was a convicted murderer and alleged Manson Family member—a first-hand witness to Charles Manson circa 1969. I felt Bobby's perspective would be the perfect complement to the conversations I was having with Manson.

Bobby met Manson while both were part of the hippie scene in Topanga Canyon. Bobby was a rebellious kid who grew up in Santa Barbara. His tendencies for acting out pushed his parents to send him to reform school when he was fifteen, after which he left for Los Angeles to hang out, smoke pot, and play music. Bobby was creative, handsome, and good with women, a skill set that allowed him to fit easily into the relaxed bohemian culture of Topanga Canyon in the late sixties.

In 1967, Bobby got a brief gig behind the scenes for a low-budget western soft-core porn movie called *The Ramrodder*. The film is an almost satirical and over-the-top cowboys and Indians story in which an ample number of the female cast bathe naked in spring water or have sex with anyone they come across. While making the movie, a producer met Bobby and liked his look, casting him in a bit role. In his pinnacle scene Bobby played a toothless outlaw trying to abduct a pretty, young Indian woman played by another aspiring actress named Catherine Share. "I'm overacting. I've got a frown on my face the whole time because I'm a badass Indian Outlaw," Bobby recalled with a laugh. "I was living in Topanga Canyon and I got recruited to work on the sets and ended up in the movie. It was a lark." Catherine and Bobby remained friends after the movie, and both became associated with the Manson Family. Catherine's nickname within the group was "Gypsy," and Bobby's was "Cupid." Catherine borrowed the name "Gypsy" from a male friend she felt was her look-alike, and Bobby's nickname was related to his way with women.

Beyond infrequent acting work, Bobby was more interested in music—he was a great guitarist and played in several informal local bands. In one such pick-up session he met Charlie Manson. I asked Bobby what Manson was like back then—did he see anything in Charlie that would foreshadow the monster the world later saw? Bobby said, "As far as Charlie's character, he was first of all a fool, a narcissist, and a consummate conman. You combine those, and things like this are going to happen." Bobby laughed nervously. "I mean, he was charismatic and there were qualities about him that were good." Bobby's take on the events of 1969 was straightforward in a way that enabled me to challenge Manson with real insider information. At the time, Bobby was also the first person I spoke to who could corroborate what Manson had been saying about "Helter Skelter."

"It's extremely important that people understand what happened," Bobby said. "If we don't want the same things to happen again, we have to understand them, and we can't understand them in the context of Vincent Bugliosi's little horror story. He did more to victimize Sharon Tate than Charlie Manson ever did."

I was taken aback by this direct assertion, as it was something I had not yet considered. If the Helter Skelter theory put forth by Vincent Bugliosi was fabricated, it would mean that the prosecution revictimized Sharon Tate and others by creating a false narrative to gain a conviction. But why would they need to fabricate a narrative around Manson? Wasn't there overwhelming evidence of the chaos he had orchestrated?

More questions, and at that time, few answers.

The next time I spoke with Charlie I asked him about Bobby. "Hey Charlie, I've been talking to Bobby a lot. Do you remember him?"

"I remember him, yes," Charlie said.

"He's been calling me," I replied.

"Yeah he would, he rides with Satan."

I thought this was a strange statement but brushed it off as one of Manson's bizarre metaphors. I would later understand that a lot of what Manson said only sounded bizarre because I didn't understand the context.

Is [Bobby] in prison?" Charlie asked.

"Yeah, he's in Vacaville. He's in prison for the Gary Hinman murder," I said.

"I was there for a long time," Manson said. Charlie had spent time in Vacaville State Prison in California in the late seventies and early eighties when he was often transferred around the state for a variety of reasons. "[Bobby] wouldn't declare himself in the family," Charlie said.

Manson couldn't recall exactly how he met Bobby but remembered they bonded over their mutual love of music, "At night we'd all play music together and Beausoleil was a part of that. But Bobby was a strong individual and he wouldn't submit to helping us." Both Bobby and Charlie agreed that Bobby was generally mischaracterized as a member of the Manson family; however, Charlie hinted that Bobby was a key to understanding why the murders took place.

Charlie said, "Bobby was the brother in that episode, he was staying with us, we were driving his truck." Another riddle, but one that I would eventually solve.

Bobby was a little more direct when explaining what had happened. "Part of it was the times and the desperation that had set in, in 1969. The events got out of hand," Bobby said.

Bobby maintained that to truly understand what happened, one needed to first understand who Manson really was. A good place to begin was Charlie's childhood. "A lot of the attitudes and beliefs that Charlie had in 1969 became over-expressed," Bobby said. "And again, I'm not defending him, he was a psychopath for sure. Not genetic, but this was something that had been developed. Charlie's compassion and empathy had been beaten out of him by the system that he grew up in, which was the juvenile justice and criminal justice system."

Taking a cue from Bobby, I decided to start at the beginning and ask Manson about his childhood. I read everything I could find and made notes in preparation for our next call, but for the following few weeks my phone remained silent.

Becoming anxious to talk to Charlie again, I picked up a postcard, addressed it to him, and wrote on it with a black Sharpie, "Hey Charlie, need to talk, call me."

Five more weeks went by.

Nothing.

And then, while doing the dishes, a call came in from the California Department of Corrections. "Charlie?" I said.

Charlie's raspy voice came on the line, "Hello brother-man."

Having waited weeks to ask my questions, I took a breath and dove in headfirst. Taking a page from Freud I said, "Hey Charlie, tell me about your mother."

Manson Born

*"You've got a juvenile. You lock him up in juvenile hall, you don't
know anything. He's got no parents. He's got nobody telling him the
truth. Everybody's lying to him. So the only thing he can do is run
away. So that's all I did."*
  *- Charles Manson, 1992, Parole Hearing*

Manson's childhood is fascinating if only for the sole reason that
it's incredibly difficult to know what is actually true. His birth certificate
from 1934 identifies his mother as Kathleen Maddox. The documents list
Kathleen's age as eighteen, but, based on her own public records, she
was undeniably sixteen when Charlie was born, and most likely lied
when questioned at the hospital. Charlie was born on either November
11 or November 12, 1934, depending on who you ask. His birth
certificate lists his date of birth as November 12, but his death certificate
claims he was born the day before. Manson told me that he was born on
November 11. I've been told by Manson supporters that being born on
November 11 romanticized the day of his birth; the idea being that he
was a *warrior*, and therefore born on Veteran's Day. A friend of
Manson's I met later, told me that the government attempted to *steal*
Manson's birthday by moving it to the twelfth, which is why Manson

fought to have it recognized as the eleventh. It's unclear why they would conspire to do this.

If Manson was born on November 11, then we coincidentally shared the same birthday. "You and I have the same birthday," I once told Manson, thinking it would be something he would appreciate.
Charlie laughed, "That's not opening this door." His way of telling me that he didn't give a *fuck* if we had anything in common. I later discovered that November 11 was also Manson's mother's birthday, leaving me to speculate whether the date was important to Charlie because it connected him to her.

Manson's mother has often been described as a teenage prostitute who struggled with alcohol and men. She allegedly beat and robbed men she picked up in riverfront bars while roaming the Ohio River Basin, namely, Ohio, West Virginia, and Kentucky. As the story goes, Kathleen was cruel and indifferent, abandoning Charlie at her leisure, trading him for pitchers of beer, or callously betting him in card games. This caricature made Manson the product of an abusive and neglectful childhood, which allegedly shaped him into the monster he became. But, like a lot of things with Manson, many aspects of his life have become more legend than fact.

For her part, Kathleen seldom went on record; however, after Manson's conviction in 1971, she disputed many of these facts to the *LA Times*. According to Kathleen, she was a wild teenager who became involved with an older man and got pregnant. She was shipped out of town by her mother, meeting another man named William Manson. William became Charlie's de facto father, at least while Charlie was an infant. Not long into their marriage, William and Kathleen divorced, and she moved home to her mother's with Charlie. For that time, Charlie was by some accounts raised in a loving home and would see his birth father regularly.[2]

As best as I can tell, the truth about Manson's upbringing seems to be a mixture of these accounts. There's ample documentation to show that, as both an adult and a child, Manson was nomadic. He was born in Ohio but often roamed Kentucky and West Virginia with his mother or other relatives. Manson told people that when he was three years old, his

---

[2] Smith, D. (1971, January 26). Mother tells life of Manson as a boy. *The Los Angeles Times*, pp. 1, 11.

mother was briefly hired by the department of corrections to clean the inside of a state penitentiary. At one point, Kathleen was assigned to the death tower, which housed four small cells leading to the archaic-looking electric chair—literally called "old sparky." With no child care, Charlie's mother would bring him along as a toddler, and he would stumble around exploring the same type of electric chair he would later be sentenced to. I later found out that West Virginia executed prisoners by hanging until 1951, leading me to believe this was a "memory" Manson made up.

In 1939, when Manson was five years old, Kathleen was implicated with her brother in a robbery. They allegedly used a ketchup bottle to mimic a gun and were sentenced to five years in West Virginia State Penitentiary. The prison closed in 1995 but still sits as a tourist attraction in the middle of a small West Virginia town called Moundsville. The prison itself is a massive castle-like structure that looks like it should be sitting on the side of a mountain in Transylvania. While Kathleen was serving time, Manson was sent to live with his aunt and uncle in nearby McMechen. His family would take him inside the castle-like structure, amidst the screaming of inmates whose windows looked out onto a cement walkway leading into the main entrance. Charlie would sign in and be led into a concrete and metal visiting area to see his mother, who would tell him about the horrid conditions. When I met Charlie, he couldn't recall exactly why his mother went to prison but remembered clearly that she did. Manson also reasoned that his prison sentence was related to being raised by a single mother. "The only reason I'm here, in this position, is because my mother didn't get married," Charlie said, making little sense.

"Your mother was Kathleen, right?" I asked.

"Right, she went to prison and so did my uncle," Charlie replied.

In the seventies, when Manson was sentenced to life in prison, he wrote a letter to the warden of the West Virginia State Penitentiary in Moundsville, the same prison that once housed his mother, asking to be transferred there. In the letter, now hanging in the prison gift shop, Manson wrote, "I got 9 life's [sentences] and don't want out no more." Manson complained that California authorities had made him out to be a monster and pleaded with the warden to let him serve out his life in the countryside he remembered fondly from his childhood. "I can't seem to get no mercy from California," Manson wrote.

After a few years of his mother's imprisonment, Manson continued to live with his aunt and uncle until his uncle contracted tuberculosis. By then Kathleen was on probation and Manson was returned to her, at which point she remarried. Kathleen's second husband was an abusive alcoholic, and at age ten Manson started to act out, running away frequently and committing petty crimes. Around this time, Manson was caught robbing a grocery store and breaking into a car dealership. In March of 1949, the *Indianapolis News* featured an article about a fourteen-year-old Charles Manson. In the article, Charlie's mother is described as a careless, drunken adulterer who often abandoned him and didn't care if he ran away. We don't know if this is accurate or something Manson told authorities to avoid going to prison at the time. Whatever the reality, it garnered sympathy for Charlie from the judge, and Charlie managed to avoid juvenile detention by agreeing to be sent to Boys Town, the famous home for abandoned and homeless boys in Omaha, Nebraska. The article was written as the uplifting story of a desolate young man who is given the chance to turn his life around. Manson is quoted as saying, "I think I could be happy working around cows and horses. I like animals."[3]

    Manson told me that Boys Town was the beginning of an evolution of violence—a series of escalating confrontations that taught him how to be a man. Charlie said, speaking in the second person, "In Boys Town you're a juvenile. You go in when you're ten years old and you play ping pong and if someone beats you, you gotta give the table up to them, unless you want to fight them. You see, everything is about fight. If you don't fight, they'll fuck you in the ass. They'll take everything you got, and you're raised up like that." After Boys Town, Charlie spent the majority of his youth in different boys' homes. It's safe to say that it was a miserable existence, filled with prison-like conditions, harsh discipline, and little affection. It's not surprising that Manson created his particular version of a family later in life, as he was abandoned by his own during his formative years. While his peers were fishing with their fathers and learning geometry in school, Manson was trying to survive. He ran away frequently and showed little regard for the strict rules caretakers would try to impose on him. This led to Manson being shuffled around often, always having to establish himself with the other boys who were also fighting for dominance within the social order.

---

[3] Newell, R. (1949, March 7). Dream comes true for lad; He's going to Boys Town. *The Indianapolis News*, pp. 1, 8.

"So, you learn how to box and you learn how to fight," Charlie said, continuing his autobiography in the second person. "Then some guy gets a dagger, or a knife, or an ice pick, and then it's a different kind of fight. You graduate and you grow up, and your dick is getting hard and you're learning how to suck and fuck, and you learn what girls are."

Arrest records that I've seen for Charlie only go back as far as 1951, when Manson was arrested at the age of sixteen for stealing a car and driving it across state lines. As a young man, this became one of Manson's favourite pastimes; he was arrested for that particular offence numerous times into adulthood. Grand Theft Auto is made exceptionally worse when the stolen car crosses state lines because of a federal law called the Dyer Act, passed in 1919, designed to curb interstate vehicle theft by making it a federal crime. Manson's police records reflect that by the time he was twenty-four years old, he'd been arrested more than thirty times. In addition to continually driving stolen cars across state lines, he'd been picked up, and in some cases convicted, for probation violations, escaping from a federal prison, cheque forgery, mail theft, and even pimping. These numerous offences became a blur to Charlie, though he seemed to look back on them fondly. "I've been in and out of jail all across the county—Ohio, Kentucky, West Virginia," he told me proudly.

The Dyer Act earned Manson some real prison time in 1952, but he was paroled in March of 1954 and moved back to West Virginia to live with his grandmother. Around this time, he met a woman named Rosalie Jean Willis, a tall, pretty brunette with bright eyes. As a teenager, Rosalie often accompanied her father to a local racetrack—she'd met Manson there, and they began dating. Rosalie was an optimist, and though she knew about Charlie's criminal history she thought she could change him. They were married in a quaint ceremony in West Virginia— a youthful-looking, clean-cut Charlie Manson was dressed in a well-fitted suit and tie. Charlie convinced Rosalie to move out west but was once again arrested for driving a stolen car over state lines and jailed in California. Rosalie, now pregnant, returned to West Virginia and was sent to live with family in another state. She gave birth to their child, Charles Manson Junior, after which she filed for divorce and never saw Charlie again.

Charlie was released from prison, given five years probation, and instead of seeking out his wife and child, decided to stay in California. To my knowledge Manson never met his son, who later committed suicide after his father became the most infamous criminal on earth.

In the late fifties, Charlie's mother joined him in California and the two lived in a small apartment in Culver City. Though he did nothing to reconcile with his wife and child, Manson was depressed and lonely after Rosalie left him, and he sought solace with this mother. Around this time, Charlie began wandering California. He met and married another woman named Leona "Candy" Stevens. Candy was a beautiful and spirited young woman who bore Manson's second child, Charles Luther. It's unknown what became of Charlie's second son—he lived his life in obscurity, managing to stay hidden from the public.

It was at that time that Manson allegedly forged a US Department of Treasury check and tried to cash it at Ralphs, a southern California supermarket. Manson denied the forgery and claimed he'd won the check in a poker game. He was arrested almost immediately and handed over to the FBI. Manson found himself in a windowless room with an FBI agent dressed in a sharp black suit, white shirt, and black tie. Charlie took one look at the generic FBI agent and thought he could most definitely outsmart him. The FBI agent slammed the forged check down on the table in front of Manson giving him the classic, "Tell us everything and we'll make sure the judge goes easy on you," routine. Manson kept his mouth shut and let the FBI agent do all the talking, keeping his eye on the check sitting on the table in front of him. "They left the check on the table," Manson recalled. "I picked it up when they wasn't looking and ate it."

When the FBI agent realized what Manson had done, he was both furious and embarrassed. Since Manson had ingested the key piece of evidence against him, he was released pending trial. Charlie figured that without the check he was home free, which probably would have been the case, except he was arrested again, this time for driving prostitutes across state lines from California to New Mexico.

It's conceivable that Charles Manson's life would have turned out completely different if he had committed his crimes within California, instead of continually crossing state lines before getting arrested. He stole old cars, which would have been only a state felony, but drove them across state lines, which made it an interstate federal crime. He drove women around as a pimp, which was a state misdemeanour, but because he drove them to New Mexico it became human trafficking. Manson's New Mexico arrest was perfect timing for the FBI who still wished to prosecute him for the check forgery. Manson had given them a new crime to compensate for the missing evidence they knew he had eaten. Feeling the walls crashing down around him, Charlie made bail and fled the country.

"Do you remember that time you went down to Mexico?" I asked Manson.

Charlie said, "Yeah man, I've been to the Mexican Pyramids." He then recalled, "I stole some cars, and some gold and some guns and I took off and I went to the jungle on mushrooms. That was in 1959."

About a month after sneaking across the border, Manson was discovered by the Mexican authorities. Charlie was confused and disoriented having been on mushrooms the entire time he was a fugitive. He was classified as an undesirable alien and driven to the border in Laredo, Texas, where he was met by the FBI and taken back to California to stand trial.

Classified as a federal fugitive and facing human trafficking charges, the FBI had Manson dead to rights; though as Charlie remembered it, he felt he was unjustly prosecuted because they couldn't recover the check he had eaten. In Charlie's opinion, the other crimes didn't really matter—the FBI was pissed off that he had outsmarted them and wanted revenge.

"I went inside for ten years for a check they didn't even have," Charlie said.

"Oh really," I laughed.

"Yeah," Charlie chuckled. "They said I hurt the FBI agent's career, so they gave me ten years. I did seven years for it, in McNeil Island."

Because he was a federal inmate, Charlie landed in McNeil Island Corrections Center, a Washington State prison, which at the time was run by the Federal Bureau of Prisons. Candy Stevens filed for divorce, took their child, and never saw Manson again. Charlie's sentence in McNeil Island was hard time. The prison closed in 2011 but was home to many notable inmates including Robert Stroud, a.k.a. The Birdman of Alcatraz, and depression-era gangster Alvin Karpis, who was still there when Manson arrived.

"Alvin Karpis was in Alcatraz for twenty-six years," Charlie said. "I used to be honoured to walk around the yard with him and listen to him because he had many things that he'd experienced that I had no information about. I learned a lot." Charlie was captivated by Alvin Karpis and listened intently to his views on life, crime, and how the government had been built on his back.

Karpis was a ruthless gangster in the twenties, engaging in bootlegging, gambling, robberies, and even shootouts with police. In the mid-thirties, Karpis had an underworld doctor remove his fingerprints to make himself more difficult to catch. During a brief stint in prison, Karpis met a like-minded inmate named Fred Barker. When they were both released, they met up with Fred's family, which included his mother, Ma Barker, and together formed the "Ma Barker Gang." The group plundered Missouri, Oklahoma, and Kansas, murdering anyone who got in their way. Their downfall was kidnapping a banker whose father was friends with President Franklin D. Roosevelt. This made Karpis and the Barkers public enemies, leading to the FBI killing Fred and Ma Barker. Karpis was enraged by the murders of his associates and personally threatened to kill J. Edgar Hoover. After a lengthy pursuit, J. Edgar Hoover personally arrested Karpis in New Orleans in 1936.

Charlie would listen to Karpis recount these stories, hanging on every word. Over five decades later they still stuck with him. "J. Edgar Hoover, he *creepy crawled* Alvin Karpis for forty-five years for being in the Ma Barker Gang. That was a lie to save the face of the government. The government killed Ma Barker and her three sons to save the economy. They started the FBI, that's what they did man," Charlie recalled in a rant. It amazed me that Manson described Hoover's relentless pursuit of Karpis by saying he "creepy crawled." When the Manson Family girls were arrested in 1969, they described their home invasions as "creepy crawling." Before the murders, they allegedly dressed in black and broke into people's homes while they slept, moving furniture to freak them out. Mattel's bug-themed crafts called Creepy Crawlers were a popular children's toy at the time, which is probably where the Manson Family heard the term and appropriated it to mean a sort of nighttime raid.

Manson was transferred out of McNeil Island and back to California to serve out his sentence in Terminal Island Prison, located in the port of Los Angeles. If you drive across the Vincent Thomas Bridge, you get an overview of the port, which is made up of thousands upon thousands of shipping containers. Drive past these containers and you'll reach the infamous medium security prison where, in 1968, Manson was last incarcerated before his infamous murder spree.

While inside Terminal Island, Charlie met a fellow inmate named Phil Kaufman. We tracked Phil down and flew him to Los Angeles to be interviewed for the documentary, meeting him at the house we'd rented in Venice. The house featured multicoloured walls, furniture that spanned decades, and taxidermy mash-ups like a rabbit with large antlers. We thought it would make the perfect backdrop to a bizarre story.

When I met him, Phil walked with a cane because of a life-threatening motorcycle accident he'd been involved in two years prior. Despite this, he was a force of nature. He had a big white moustache, dark sunglasses (which never came off), and a baseball hat pulled down. He spoke quickly with a witty, dry humour that was charming—coupled with a compelling dose of irreverence. He swore liberally and had the air of someone you just don't fuck with. At the same time, he was incredibly likeable and presented me with a signed copy of his memoir *Road Mangler Deluxe.*

In the years after he was released from the prison he'd shared with Charlie, Phil excelled in the music industry as legendary road manager for The Rolling Stones, Frank Zappa, The Flying Burrito Brothers, and Gram Parsons. Kaufman infamously stole Gram Parsons' body from LAX after Parsons died from a drug overdose. Phil drove the body to the Joshua Tree and cremated it, fulfilling a pact the two had made before Parsons' death. Phil was played by Johnny Knoxville in a 2003 movie about the incident, brilliantly titled *Grand Theft Parsons.*

When Phil walked in at the start of filming, I handed him a brown paper bag of cash. As a documentary filmmaker, it's a harsh reality that you sometimes have to compensate people for their time—simply to get them to meet with you. It's not something I make a habit of, but it's also not something I necessarily have a problem with. I don't feel the integrity of the story is compromised just because you throw someone a few bucks. Phil's compensation was a special case, however, because the payment method was something that I had never encountered before. Phil insisted on being paid in cash—in a brown paper bag—instead of the customary cheque. He even called before the interview to emphasize that this was something he was very serious about.

When I handed him the bag he chuckled and put it in his jacket. Later, he pulled me aside and admitted that when he'd received the call to be interviewed, he thought if he asked us for money and demanded a brown paper bag cash payment, we would certainly refuse—and he wouldn't have to do the interview. To his disappointment we said, "no problem."

"Where do you want to start?" Phil began, settling into a chair across from me. "Where I first met Charlie?"

I was eager to speak to Phil about his time in prison with Charlie—in a stroke of luck, he turned out to be incredibly candid. Phil began, "I was a marijuana felon…"

In 1967, Phil was an aspiring actor who got busted trying to smuggle a couple pounds of weed into the US from Mexico. As Phil remembers it, if you were caught importing marijuana the only option was a prison term without the possibility of parole. Probation was off the table. Knowing this, when Phil found himself in a car with two friends— and it was clear that his amateur smuggling operation was going to end in his arrest—he wrote a quick confession to clear his friends of any wrongdoing, left it in the car, and ran.
He didn't stop running until he got to Europe.

Knowing that the police might be looking for him, Phil called a close friend, a UCLA graduate student named Harold True. "Harold had never gotten a passport, so I was able to get a passport in Harold's name," Phil recalled.

Phil spent his time overseas under the name Harold True, but he longed to return to the US and resume being Phil Kaufman. He waited until the government changed the law allowing for parole eligibility for marijuana offences, and surrendered in Tucson, Arizona. As part of his conviction he told the judge he was a marijuana addict, which earned him a pass to Springfield Federal Hospital in Missouri. From there he bounced around to Leavenworth before ending his sentence in Terminal Island Prison in California.

According to Phil, "I had just gone through the A&O (Admission and Orientation), before I was allowed out in the yard. Before you go anywhere in the prison, they give you a test." As a new inmate, Phil was called into a small room with a prison psychologist to determine what job he would be assigned while serving time. Phil was put through a battery of now outdated tests, after which the psychologist sat him down for a serious conversation.

"Mr. Kaufman," the doctor said. "What in your heart of hearts would you like to do with your life?"

Phil paused and replied, "I'd like to be an ex-convict sir."

The psychologist was taken aback before he laughed and said, "Son, you'll do fine here."

Phil was assigned to the education department. When he walked in, he saw a short, skinny, long-haired man who introduced himself as Charlie, taking Dale Carnegie classes. Dale Carnegie was a self-help guru who developed a series of personal leadership and sales training courses after he wrote the still popular book *How to Win Friends and Influence People.*

In Terminal Island, Charlie took the courses to heart and studied them at length. Phil described Charlie's take on what he learned as, "How to Win Friends and Influence People...then Kill Them."

Some of Phil's first interactions with Charlie involved hearing him play guitar. Aspiring to be in the music industry, Phil immediately identified with Charlie's talent and spent hours talking to him. "Charlie was small in stature, for one thing, but he really had this charisma. He was just really a non-conformist," Phil told me.

Phil recalled a time when a guard approached Charlie, who was playing his guitar in a section of the prison where instruments were not allowed.

"Manson, you can't play guitar here," the guard said. "You have to play guitar over there with the musicians, that's the rules." Much to the guard's frustration, Charlie continued to strum his guitar, singing to himself, seemingly unaware the guard even existed.

"Manson! Manson!" The guard yelled, growing increasingly frustrated. "Manson, you ain't never gonna get out of here!"

"Out of where, man?" Manson asked the guard casually, without missing a beat.

According to Phil, this was the perfect way to understand Charlie. A prison inmate who didn't seem to appreciate that he was in prison.

Then and now, the prison system is built around incentives. A prison needs its inmates to behave, as there isn't the manpower to beat everyone into submission. Prisons offer inmates incentives, like special privileges or time off for good behaviour. This way, the inmates have a reason to behave, the guards can control them more easily, and the prison can maintain high inmate turnover, making more money. Charlie never fit into this model. Throughout his life he received countless reprimands from prison officials. Charlie was so apathetic to reprimands that other inmates gave him things to hold, like drugs or other contraband items, because he didn't care if he got caught. One of Charlie's long-time friends once told me, "He'd get put into solitary confinement for any reason. He really didn't give a fuck."

As Phil Kaufman recalled, "Charlie didn't program well." Phil explained that even in the late sixties the inmates knew they could earn time off their sentences for good behaviour but, "Charlie didn't do that, he did all the time. He didn't program. If he got five years, Charlie did five years. I didn't see any wisdom in that at all."

Refusing to curb his behaviour in any way, Manson completed his sentence in Terminal Island and was released on March 21, 1967. Charlie related to me that he looked back on his release from Terminal Island proudly because he had done nothing to earn it, yet they had no choice but to let him go. Charlie said, "I was a federal prisoner. I was dead when I got out of Terminal Island. Can you understand that? In other words, it's like I had played that game and won every pocket."

When Charlie walked out of prison and into the port of Los Angeles, Vietnam was at the forefront of the American consciousness. According to Charlie, the war was a flashpoint for people at that time, and he was definitely part of the anti-war sentiment, though he saw it as a hopeless cause. Charlie said, "Everybody wanted Nixon to stop the war. But the government didn't want the war stopped, they loved that war. That war was their fucking eternal, fucking dream man. You can't stop war."

Vietnam meant that many of the men were either at war or at school, and many of the women left behind were embracing what would become known as the "summer of love." This is when it's been reported that Charles Manson formed a cult called the Manson Family.

*How did he transform from a chronic petty criminal into a psychotic villain capable of mind control?* I wondered.

Until this point in his life, Charlie had never been charged with a violent crime, and no one had ever described him as a guru or spiritual leader, so something must have changed in the summer of 1967.

It was time to ask Charlie about his "Family."

"How did your family come together?" I asked Charlie.

"Well, what you think something is, is not necessarily what it is," Charlie said. "What you think, is what you've been led into thinking."

"What have I been led into thinking?"

Charlie paused, "This thing is so vast that, I'm not sure you can accept it."

chapter six
the family

# The Family

*"[Charlie] has more love to give the world than anybody I've ever met. He would give himself completely, completely to anybody."*
- **Susan Atkins, December 5, 1969, testifying to the grand jury.**

I hadn't heard from Charlie in a few weeks, so I sent him another postcard with my standard inscription, "Hey Charlie, Call me. Got more questions." The next week Charlie called again. I could tell that he was not in the mood for my questions. I had not smuggled him in the cellphone he'd requested, nor put any money in his account. He had no reason to call me other than that I was asking him to. I needed his help to unravel his story for the documentary, and I didn't have much to offer him in return.

"I'm not giving you any information," he yelled into the phone. "Unless I get, I'm not giving. You dig it?"

Even though he was thousands of miles away, my stomach turned. He was still Charles Manson, and I had no idea what he was capable of. *Unless I get?* I thought. *Is this about the cellphone? Money? Something else?*

In many ways Charlie was a stubborn man—something I knew I could use to my advantage. He hated telling people what to do, so I thought if I pushed him for specifics on what he wanted me to "get" for him, he might become frustrated.

"What do you want me to get for you, Charlie?" I asked directly.

The automated recording kicked in, "This call is being monitored and recorded." A reminder of why Charlie was wisely being coy. Charlie backed off. I'd anticipated that he wouldn't come out and tell me what he wanted, and I'd been right. He began to hint at things but wouldn't say anything specific, prolonging our conversation and allowing me to pry.

"What am I giving you information for anyway," Charlie said. "Anything I say can be used against me. You're in a gigantic media that's controlling the world and any information I give you can be used against me. That's an amendment."

"We both know the phone call is recorded," I said. "Are you worried about saying something that's going to get us both in trouble?"

"No!" Charlie screamed. "I'm not worried about anything. I understand everything."

I asked Manson, if he understood everything, why not tell me the truth that has eluded everyone except for him. This seemed to momentarily quell his anger. It's hard to know what brought it on in the first place. Someone could have tried to murder him when he woke up that morning for all I knew.

Charlie's tone adjusted noticeably as he reversed course. "I don't know anything man," Charlie said. "I'm locked up in a cell." He began to sound more reasonable. "They're hiding me away, man. They're covering me up, man. I'm held hostage." There was frustration in his voice. "There's no honour, trust or truth in this bullshit. It's all a bunch of garbage. Everything's on the run, man." The more we spoke, the more I found myself really beginning to feel like we were talking. I was beginning to see Charlie as an old convict, perhaps just trying to be understood.

*Is that what I have to offer him?* I asked myself. *Am I beginning to bond with Charles Manson? Am I becoming part of his Family?*

I asked Charlie if he remembered getting out of prison for what would be the final time in 1967. Charlie said that his release from Terminal Island was his final *run*, "You see in prison they call it a 'run.' When I get out of prison I *run* until I'm back in prison again." Manson explained.

This short exchange gave me a big insight into how Manson saw the world. He'd been in prison so frequently throughout his life that he saw freedom as a temporary situation—this was the unavoidable consequence of life in the underworld.

One fascinating aspect of Manson was his impeccable timing. When he went to prison in the late fifties, he was an outlaw. He had long hair, played music, and spoke in philosophical terms about life and death. He was a stark contrast to the clean-cut, square-jawed men of the era. When Manson got out of prison in the late sixties, the world had changed drastically. Civil unrest and the Vietnam War had reshaped America. Men were no longer expected to be well-dressed with a classic hair part. Long hair, beards, and free expression were rampant. Everything about Manson that made him undesirable in the fifties, made him cool in the sixties. It was a completely different world. On top of this shift in the zeitgeist, Manson found himself in a place of incredible opportunity for someone like him.

According to Manson, he spent the first year after prison going back and forth between Haight Ashbury in San Francisco and Topanga Canyon in Los Angeles. Within months of Manson's release, the Haight-Ashbury district of San Francisco saw an influx of hundreds of thousands of people flocking to be part of the "summer of love." People were handing out marijuana, hash, and LSD on the street corners, and free love was the norm. Everything Manson had been denied in prison—sex, drugs, and music—was in overwhelming supply. In the fifties, Charlie couldn't get a job because he was a *greasy ex-convict*; in the sixties he didn't need one because he was a *groovy hippy,* even though nothing about him had really changed. The fact that he had been an inmate gave him even more appeal—the world was a prisoner's dream come true.

"I went to 'Frisco," Charlie said. "I was talking to this supposedly great holy guy. You dig? And he's telling me when you can sit and be comfortable and at peace with yourself that you're just in harmony, you dig? Now check this out. I figured a lot of things out. I figured this out. I figured it would be easier not to understand anything and keep your mind open and never make your mind up about nothing."

From what's been reported, this is when Charlie allegedly formed the Manson Family—supposedly a sinister religious cult with evil intentions. The so-called cult was primarily made up of young women who adopted cute nicknames that offset their supposedly wicked personalities. At first glance, names like Squeaky, Darling, Sadie, Snake, Lulu, Mother Mary, and Gypsy seemed like such a contrast to the horrific deeds I knew some of them had committed. It reminded me of how the notorious serial killer John Wayne Gacy would dress up as a clown named Pogo for children's birthday parties before returning home to his victims' decomposing bodies, which he'd stuffed into his walls. I would come to learn that this contrast I'd assumed was reality couldn't actually be further from the truth, at least in the case of the Manson Family.

The media has characterized the women who participated in the murders as middle-class and virtuous. They've been described as girl scouts or good students or Sunday school teachers, who Manson transformed into serial killers. I wondered, *why would young women with good backgrounds leave their homes to live with an ex-convict who just wanted sex and death? Why would Manson choose to form a "cult" when he found himself in the sixties' cultural oasis?*

For Charlie's part, he said the answers are simple—he long maintained that he didn't form a cult. If this is true, if Manson didn't recruit the women that eventually became the Manson Family, then how did they come together? And what's with the creepy nicknames?

I came to learn that many of the nicknames actually had a fairly simple explanation. When the group was living in Topanga Canyon, they squatted in abandoned houses or crashed at pseudo hostels for hippies. During those times they were subject to many raids by the LAPD. Many of the girls were underage, hiding from their parents, or avoiding law enforcement for other reasons. To cope with authorities the group used fake IDs, adopting false names. When the LAPD showed up, all the girls would present fake IDs with false names and birthdays to satisfy the beat cops and avoid being taken downtown. The cops weren't stupid, they often knew the IDs they were getting were counterfeit, so once in a while they'd find a reason to arrest the girls and interrogate them. This backfired because it was decades before any sort of computer database, so the girls discovered that if they held firm the cops had no real way to identify them. This meant the girls would spend a few days in the county jail, and when they were released their false names would become part of their arrest record. The next time they were questioned or arrested, these names would seem legitimate—the police had inadvertently sanctioned them through paperwork.

Using nicknames not only allowed them to avoid police detection, but also to leave their pasts behind. For the same reason the army shaves the heads of new recruits to encourage them to adopt a military-provided self-perception, abandoning birth names was freeing for the girls, allowing each of them to become a new person within the group. But this doesn't answer the question of how the group actually came together in the first place. From the outset, I wondered whether Manson was some sort of hippie Jehovah's Witness, wandering around California recruiting people.

It's well established that while travelling through San Francisco in the spring of 1967, Manson first met a woman named Mary Brunner, often described as the first member of the Manson Family. Though Mary has been characterized as Manson's first "recruit," it's unclear how someone could become the first member of a group that didn't yet exist. Mary Brunner was a plain brunette with a square jaw whose petite look contrasted with her reputation as Charles Manson's favourite and strongest-willed woman. The exact details of how they came together are sketchy. As the legend goes, Mary was a wide-eyed innocent librarian who moved to California from Wisconsin to work at UC Berkley. When she met Manson, she fell under his hypnotic spell and gave up her life to follow him, relinquishing her inhibition to blindly follow this charismatic guru who recruited women into his thrill-kill cult.

Like many Manson stories, there's little evidence to support this version of events, but you can nevertheless find it reported in numerous reputable news outlets.

From what Mary has said publicly, when she was twenty-three years old, she did indeed work in some capacity in the library at UC Berkeley, though she was not an actual librarian. At the time, she longed to break from the routine she had fallen into and was eager to take part in the counterculture lifestyle that Manson and others had found. Meeting Manson was a combination of attraction and a desire for adventure. Charlie recalled Mary as a strong-willed woman, disputing her characterization as an innocent he manipulated and controlled. "Mary's a tremendous girl, man," Manson told me. "She delivered her own baby. Mary's a hell of a woman. She reminds me of a Viking woman, a tremendous person who would stand up and fight. She punched me out a couple times. You don't find too many women who will stand up in any kind of fight."

Manson and Mary began travelling around California together and were soon joined by another young woman named Lynette Fromme, who's since become known by her more infamous nickname, "Squeaky."

Of all the members in Manson's Family, Squeaky has captured my interest the most. In the sixties, she stood out because after Manson was arrested, she became the spokesperson for the group. Her bright red

71

hair, freckles, and natural beauty gave her a look of youthful innocence, yet in Charlie's absence she was supposedly the leader of the Manson Family. When she spoke, she did so with a characteristic manner of speech, a sort of aw shucks-type diction like she was in a *Leave It to Beaver* episode. This was in contrast with her obvious intelligence. You can see many interviews online with Lynette and read her self-published book *Reflexion*; it's clear that she has a natural and compelling way with words despite an extreme and passionate ideology. Lynette is an ardent defender of both Charlie and the environment—beliefs that drove her to attempt to assassinate the president of the United States.

In 1975, President Gerald Ford was taking a short walk from a Sacramento hotel to the state capitol building amidst a throng of reporters, en route to a meeting with the governor. At the time, Lynette was living in a small apartment with a fellow Manson devotee named Sandra Good. Seeing Ford on TV, Lynette decided it would be a good time to share her advocacy for the plight of the enormous California Redwood trees being decimated by the logging industry. Ford paused in the middle of the street, surrounded by hundreds of people as well as the secret service, and reached to his left to shake hands with the eager members of the public. As Ford looked down, Lynette appeared to his right, ready to explain her views on the environment and armed with a Colt .45 pistol she had strapped to her leg. Though small in stature, Lynette stood out—she was dressed in homemade red robes with a matching nun's habit. As she came up alongside President Ford, she drew the gun, putting the barrel to his temple. The crowd flew into a panic, and the secret service tackled Lynette, jogging President Ford into the state capitol building. Lynette pleaded not guilty to the alleged assassination attempt claiming she ensured there was no round in the chamber. She also explained that she thought her arrest would be an opportunity to call the Manson Family as defence witnesses, thus giving her a platform to re-try their cases in some sense. Her plea was unsuccessful, and the incident landed Fromme a thirty-four-year prison sentence.

In the spring of 1967, Lynette was eighteen, the daughter of an aeronautical engineer named William Fromme. In many California news articles from the early seventies, Lynette described her upbringing as a "typical middle-class home," however her relationship with her father was strained. According to Lynette, "On that particular night I was kicked out of the house by my father. I didn't have too many friends. I hitchhiked, got on the freeway and went to Venice Beach, where I had seen people living kind of freely."[4]

In the late fifties and early sixties, Venice Beach was the home of beatnik poetry, full of coffee houses and literary street performance. By 1965, only one coffee house remained, and Venice had been transformed into an undesirable neighbourhood. Bombarded by tourists, the residents had responded by offering strange performances and displays of inhibition. This in turn attracted crime, increased homelessness, and biker gangs like the notorious Straight Satans. The Satans became a fixture of Venice Beach, wearing black denim vests with a red caricature of Lucifer on the back. They took over a local hot dog stand to declare their territory and established a clubhouse across the street.

After leaving home, Lynette found herself a few blocks away from the Satans' clubhouse, wandering Venice Beach with no destination in mind. She sat on the edge of the deserted beach, soaking in her depression and looking out over the ocean. Suddenly, a complete stranger seemed to appear out of nowhere beside her. She looked at him and heard him say, "Your father kicked you out of the house, did he?"[5] The man, of course, was Charles Manson.

"You met Lynette in Venice, right?" I asked Manson.

"That's right. She's been righteous all the way down the line," Charlie said. Manson never spoke about people who were close to him— in fairness there weren't very many people in the world he was actually close to—but I could tell by his tone that Lynette was special to him. He spoke about her in a way I never heard him speak about anyone else. He told me he missed her and was upset that they were barred from speaking—because of her assassination attempt on the president. Lynette was prevented from contacting Manson after her conviction and subsequent probation, which lasted well beyond his death.

During their fateful meeting on Venice Beach, Lynette developed an immediate bond with Manson. He spoke to her about life and was able to articulate exactly what she was thinking. As part of Manson's penalty

---

[4] State of California v Manson et al. 175, Cal Supp. 22,219 (1971, February 2).

[5] State of California v Manson et al. 175, Cal Supp. 22,219 (1971, February 2).

phase Lynette testified, "Nobody ever treated me like that before. Nobody ever didn't push me; you know what I mean? So, I just picked up everything I had and left [with Charlie] then never went back."

"[Lynette] was one of my best angels," Charlie told me. "She was from LA. Her father was a rocket scientist. He invented some of the planes that you're flying around in. She believed in the constitution. She was raised up to believe in it, so I know she did."

By September 1967, Manson, Lynette, and Mary had returned to Venice where they met a fourth member of their party.

Patricia Krenwinkel, who would later take the nickname "Katie," was unique among the original Manson women as she was the only one who later participated in the Tate-LaBianca murders. What I found surprising was that Katie was far from a girl scout before she met Manson; in fact, quite the opposite. Katie grew up in a troubled home in Southern California. Her half-sister, Charlene, who was seven years her senior, was a drug addict who became pregnant as a teenager. Both of these facts caused enormous tension in the Krenwinkel family. By the time Katie was fifteen her parents were divorced, and Katie was a confused teenager living with her mother and switching high schools every year. Katie followed her sister into drugs and alcohol, starting with marijuana and progressing to Benzedrine, commonly referred to as bennies or speed. Katie was first prescribed Benzedrine by a family doctor for weight loss, but she soon discovered the value of their illicit use.

When she was nineteen, Katie's family broke up even further. Her mother left California to be closer to her family in Mobile, Alabama. Katie's father took up residence in the Krenwinkel family home, and Katie and Charlene relocated to a small apartment near Venice Beach. Katie's life near the ocean turned more and more chaotic as her sister became increasingly dependent on drugs. On an otherwise nondescript day, Charlene introduced Katie to a friend named Billy, who had recently been released from Terminal Island Prison. In turn, Billy introduced Katie to his friend Charlie, a fellow ex-con who was looking for a place to crash. Katie spent the next three days having sex with Charlie and bonding with Mary and Lynette. At the time, Katie was desolate—her home life had fallen apart and life with her sister wasn't much better. Two years later, in June of 1970, Charlene was skinny dipping with her boyfriend in a local creek while they were both high. Her boyfriend passed out and when he woke up the next morning, he discovered

Charlene had drowned. Her body was recovered from the creek by authorities who were accompanied by Katie's uncle.

Katie had struggled with self-confidence her entire life and sought a feeling of self-worth. Meeting Charlie was fortuitous for Katie—not so much that she was recruited into his group, but rather that he came along precisely at a time when she sought to escape her situation. At a 2011 parole hearing Katie said, "This seemed like a way out. [Charlie] he was a boyfriend, he seemed like the answer. He seemed like my salvation at that time."

Three days after meeting Katie, Charlie told her he planned to continue on with Lynette and Mary and invited Katie to join them. Together, the four drove around in a beat-up Volkswagen Bus for the better part of nine months. At first, they exhausted Katie's father's credit card for food and gas before doing odd jobs or convincing people to give them money. At every stop they would somehow find a way to get the bus down the road a bit further. During this time, they operated as any small group would—there was jealousy, anger, love, and everything in between. They travelled together and met hundreds of people, often visiting with men Charlie had met in prison and parking the bus at any vacant beach they could find.

After nine months, they found themselves back in San Francisco where they met Susan Atkins. Susan has always fascinated me. I've struggled to understand whether she was a true sociopath or playing some sort of role she thought could gain her sympathy. It's possible the answer is a little of both.

Susan Atkins was a California native who grew up in Santa Clara, north of Los Angeles. When Susan was fourteen her mother died from cancer, and the treatment costs bankrupted her family. Susan's father descended into alcoholism, and Susan attempted to care for her young brother, Steven, who at the time was only nine years old. Her older brother, Michael, had enlisted in the navy and had left the family prior to their mother's death.

We managed to contact Steven for the documentary, and he agreed to be interviewed but cancelled prior to meeting. He called in tears, explaining that the family had gone through so much tragedy that he couldn't bear to relive it.

After Susan's mother passed, Susan began working and struggled to keep pace in school, eventually dropping out. Her father abandoned both her and Steven, but they managed to stay with their grandparents for a short period of time. Susan was able to contact her older brother, Michael, who had recently married, and he took Steven in. At that point Susan Atkins was truly alone in the world. At the age of fourteen she'd been living the life of an average middle-class teenager; by nineteen she was abandoned and homeless.

Susan began hitchhiking anywhere that she could get a ride. One ride in particular ended with her being arrested for Grand Theft Auto. Susan claimed that she had hitched a ride and had no knowledge that the car she found herself in was stolen. In a 2005 parole hearing, this incident was referenced as one that planted a mistrust of police in Susan. She ended up in the Haight-Ashbury district of San Francisco, and it was there that she was introduced to marijuana and acid. In a 1976 interview Susan said, "I used to think that you came down off an acid trip after twelve hours. That's not true. Every time you take LSD the moral fibre of your character—your mind expands beyond these moral characteristics, your concepts of right and wrong. So, you step out beyond those bounds."

In 1967, Susan found work as a topless dancer at a San Francisco club called GiGi. She was recruited to perform in a show called Witches Sabbeth [*sic*]. The show was put on by cultural phenom Anton LaVey, the man who dubbed himself "the first priest of the Satanic Church." A topless Susan Atkins paraded around the stage aiding the display of so-called satanic rituals to the delight of the audience. It was around that time that Susan met Charlie. Susan was briefly living in a dilapidated house in San Francisco with a group of drug dealers when Charlie wandered in, playing music for them on his guitar. In a recorded interview with her attorney from 1969, which was leaked to the media during her trial, Susan recalled meeting Charlie. "A little man came in with a guitar and started singing for a group of us that were together— his voice, his manner, just more or less hypnotized me." According to Susan's recollection in front of a grand jury in 1969, she was instantly enamoured with Charlie, falling to the ground and kissing his feet. "I don't know what it was," Susan recalled. "It was exactly what I was looking for, he just represented something to me inside, and I went down and kissed his feet. I don't know why I kissed his feet; I just kissed his feet."

Two days later, Charlie took Susan to have sex in a house he was crashing at. He asked her to stand naked in front of a full-length mirror saying, "Look at this body form. You were born perfect and everything that has happened to you from the time you were a child all the way up to this moment, has happened perfectly. You have made no mistakes, the only mistakes you have made are the mistakes that you thought you made, but they were not mistakes."

Before they had sex, Charlie said, "I want to make love to you."

Susan readily agreed and Charlie asked, "Have you ever made love to your father?"

"No," Susan replied.

"Have you ever thought about it?" Charlie continued.

"Yeah," Susan responded with embarrassment, "two or three times."

After this exchange, Charlie made Susan examine herself in the mirror before having sex with her, challenging her to imagine that he was her father while he climaxed. According to Susan the sex was "better than I'd ever had it before. It was the most beautiful experience, I'd ever experienced."

The next time Susan met Charlie he was accompanied by Lynette, Mary, and Katie. Susan packed what little belongings she had and joined them, travelling around California and finding a new sense of self-confidence.

I asked Charlie what he remembered about Susan.

"I create people," Charlie told me.

"You created a lot of people," I replied.

"Yeah I know, I got a whole list of them, but Susan she's..." Charlie took a moment to find the right words. "She's *me* actually."

According to Charlie, he and Susan were almost the same person—conflicted individuals capable of both immense charity and hurt. "Susan was an angel," Charlie said. "She'd give you everything she had. Susan was the most giving person at the ranch. Her love was just so abounding that it wasn't even a joke. It hurt. But she'd also get serious and she'd steal everything I had, man. Take all my tools. Get my music, give it to the outside."

Phil Kaufman also remembered Susan and recalled that when he got out of prison in 1968, he stayed in Los Angeles and sought out a friend he'd made while inside Terminal Island. Phil's friend was living near Topanga Canyon forging fake IDs for acquaintances in order to scrape together enough cash to get back on his feet. The forger told Phil that he'd been making fake driver's licences for a group of women living in an abandoned house in nearby Topanga Canyon. At the time, Topanga

Canyon was known as a hippie enclave and music community, similar to the Haight-Ashbury district in San Francisco. The forger told Phil that the women were living with Charlie Manson—both Phil and the forger had met Charlie in prison. Charlie's girls were good fake ID customers—they were arrested often and were constantly changing their names. This, combined with Charlie's habit of welcoming underage girls to stay with the group, had created a steady demand for new IDs.

The forger told Phil that he'd made one particular fake ID for a tall, free-spirited brunette named Susan, recalling that she had an unforgettable killer body but, despite her looks, was exceedingly full of herself. "She was really the hot broad on board," Phil recalled. "Her real name had been Susan Atkins, but they had changed it to Sadie Mae Glutz," Phil said. "A very unromantic name to knock her down a peg."

The name stuck, and unlike many of the other girls who used their names and nicknames interchangeably, Susan became Sadie, using it as her sole moniker until her birth name was rediscovered by authorities after her final arrest in 1969.

While testifying in front of a grand jury in 1969, Sadie was asked if she was in love with Charlie, to which she replied, "I was in love with the reflection and the reflection I speak of is Charlie Manson's." This is crucial insight into the understanding of Charles Manson, at least as I came to understand him. Manson, it seemed, was not a master of mind control; rather, he long ago figured out that people feel understood when you reflect their ideas back to them. Michael Channels, Manson's long-time friend, told me that he had discussed this with Manson at length. According to Michael, "Charlie would be whatever you wanted him to be. He would say that all the time. People didn't listen to him. If they would've listened to him, they would've understood him a little more. He was just a mirror, a reflection of you. Whatever you'd come with, that's what he was going to come with."

As Susan Atkins said in her grand jury testimony, "Charlie Manson changes from second to second. He can be anybody he wants to be. He can put on any face he wants to put on, at any given moment." From Charlie's perspective, if you were looking for a father figure or a best friend or a soulmate that's what he would give you. In his later years, if you were a reporter looking for a madman or a serial killer or a hippie cult leader, he'd happily give you that as well. In a recovered audio recording from the Los Angeles District Attorney archives, I discovered a cassette tape of Manson actually talking about his strategy for dealing with people. "What you see in me is you," Manson said. "If what you see in me is a decent sort-a-fella, hey I'll wave, we'll have a beer, we'll be decent sort-a-fellas. If you see me as a bad guy, then I'll reflect bad guy to you." Breaking it down simply, Charlie said, "To me it's just a part of existence."

Within a few months, the group made up of Charlie, Mary, Katie, Squeaky, and Sadie had grown to about fifteen people. They moved around California, up to Oregon, over to Washington State, and back. The formation of the group was very gradual. They'd meet someone looking for a place to crash and invite them to stay. Charlie absolutely bonded them together, but no one described him as a guru or cult leader during that time. Instead it was an ad hoc, roaming commune, made possible by Charlie's nomadic spirit and gifts of personality. Charlie talked all the time. He had a specific point of view that he'd learned in prison—one that was especially appealing in the sixties. The people he met liked him and the small welcoming community of women that he lived with. The biggest problem the group had, as they grew larger and kept moving, was how to get everyone from place to place.

On or close to April 11, 1968, a school bus was reported stolen from the Haight-Ashbury district in San Francisco. Eleven days later the bus was spotted nearly four hundred miles down the coast by a sheriff's deputy in Oxnard, California. The deputy approached the bus, which was seemingly abandoned by the side of the road, and saw a mass of bodies scattered on the ground. The deputy reportedly became alarmed, believing he had come upon the scene of a massive accident, only to realize that it was a group of hippies sleeping in the nude after their bus had become stuck in a ditch. Seven members of the group were taken into custody for producing false identification, and three were booked on suspicion of disorderly conduct. Mary was found inside the bus caring for a shivering newborn infant.

When questioned, Mary claimed that she had given birth to Charlie's child at some point in the previous week, while on the bus trip. She said the baby had been born breach, a complication that was somehow navigated by Sadie who delivered the baby instinctually. The baby's official name was Michael Manson, although Charlie and Mary called him "Son-stone." Others in the group took to affectionately calling him "Pooh Bear." Mary was booked on suspicion of endangering the health and wellness of a child, and though the baby was taken to hospital he was soon returned to her. Son-stone lived with the Family up until the murders, after which he was raised by Mary's grandparents in Wisconsin who changed his named to Mike Brunner. I got to know Mike long after the documentary and was surprised to learn how well-adjusted he was. He'd escaped all the negatives associated with his birth father, maintaining a lifelong relationship with Mary. I asked him what Mary had told him about the entire Manson Family story, and he surprised me by saying they had rarely, if ever, spoken about it. Mike had a healthy curiosity about Manson, whom he'd never met—at least not that he remembered as a child, and not later as an adult.

The story of nude hippies being arrested on the side of the road made the rounds in local California newspapers. What's interesting is that, at the time the stories were published, numerous outlets reported that "a man named Charles W. Manson" identified himself as the "self-proclaimed leader of the group." At the time, Manson was completely unknown to the media and the world at large, which explains the misspelling of his name as Charles *W.* Manson as opposed to Charles *M.* Manson. Regardless, the description of Manson is interesting because he often described the group as a loose band of individuals living in complete freedom—and always disputed that he was in charge. "I was no leader," Manson told me. "Do what you want, if you're with me then you're free like me. I do what I want to do. You do what you want to do. That's me baby."

Months later I was reading the trial transcripts from 1969 and came across testimony that was almost verbatim what Charlie had often told me. Susan Atkins is recorded as saying, "I want you to understand that Charlie always told us, 'you do what you want to do. If you do not want to do it, do not do it.' But, when he would ask me to do something, I felt I had to go ahead and do it because I knew he would do the same thing for me otherwise he wouldn't ask me to do it."

It seems Manson's message had stayed consistent over the nearly fifty years since he formed the commune. Bearing this in mind, the news accounts of his arrest for stealing the school bus still present pretty clear evidence that Charlie did indeed view himself as the leader of the group. On the other hand, the self-appointed leader of a nomadic group of hippies is *not* the same as a Svengali cult leader, brainwashing people to murder for him.

I asked Stephen Kay, the Manson Family co-prosecutor, about this discrepancy, to which he replied, "These weren't ordinary people. I get upset with the historians that refer to this group as hippies. They weren't hippies. Hippies were flower children, they believed in 'make love, not war.' The Family referred to themselves as 'Slippies.' They said they were going to *slip* under the awareness of society—that society would think they were peace-loving hippies because they dressed like hippies, but they weren't. They were very violent. It was a religious cult. Manson said he was once Jesus Christ but became the devil. We didn't know a lot about Satanism at the time—I mean if we had to do the trial all over again, probably there would be some Satanic part of it, because I think that was part of who they were."

During the Manson Family trial, the prosecution unequivocally painted a stark picture of the group as a cult devoted to Manson. In his closing arguments lead prosecutor Vincent Bugliosi said, "The Family—was nothing more than a closely knit band of vagabond robots who were slavishly obedient to one man and one man only, their master, their leader, their God, Charles Manson. Within his domain, his authority and power were unlimited. He was the doctoral maharajah, if you will, of a tribe of bootlicking slaves who were only too happy to do his bidding for him." This visceral depiction of the group is terrifying and difficult to understand, and it's something authorities continually asked Manson about well after he was incarcerated in 1969. In a recovered interview with a prison psychiatrist in 1977, Manson replied to these questions saying, "I influenced those people, most assuredly I influenced them. I influenced them in a totally negative way compared to what you would call positive. In my mind, it was a positive way." Even back in the seventies, Charlie maintained it wasn't a cult saying, "The words positive and negative are relative to the value system that you live under."

The psychiatrist countered Manson, saying, "Well what do you mean when you say you had a negative influence on them from society's viewpoint?"

"Negative in the respect that I was truthful and honest with them," Manson said. "And society's not truthful and honest, they don't want no truth and they don't want no honesty."

In order to get a legitimate perspective on the true dynamics of the group, I did everything I could to speak to the people who were there. I managed to track down several Manson Family members who I spoke to on the phone, via e-mail, text, or some combination. Using old public property records, I was able to find a home once owned by Nancy Pitman, who went by the nickname Brenda and was an integral part of the group in 1968. I was then able to match the records to a wedding registry and match the registry to a charity, which got me an e-mail address of the homeowner. After connecting with the young couple who owned the home and explaining the house once belonged to a member of the Manson Family, they eagerly searched their appliance documents and sent me a plumbing receipt that contained Brenda's cell number. After some back and forth we exchanged e-mails, but she was reluctant to talk, expressing that she had drank the Kool-Aid and survived.

I had similar conversations with many of the other women in the Family. Using contacts given to me by Manson, I connected with Catherine Gillies, who adopted the nickname "Capistrano" or "Cappi" after falling in with Manson in the spring of 1968. I was able to track Cappi down living in Oregon, and after several long conversations she was willing to go on the record.

Cappi was adamant that life with the group was misrepresented at trial and continues to be misconstrued by the media. "We didn't have stabbing practice on Saturday and hang Charlie from a cross on Sunday," she said sarcastically. "I mean none of those things are real. We didn't call ourselves The Manson Family, that was the press. We called ourselves *a family,* but we meant that because we were brothers and sisters, not because we were The Family, we were *a* family."

I've heard this sentiment echoed by several people who were part of the group, and it appears to be supported by the trial transcripts. In many instances Vincent Bugliosi says clearly that the group called themselves "The Family," but no witness ever referred to them as the "Manson Family," the label so often reported. This is counter to the thought that Charlie was actively recruiting people to set up some kind of organization to carry out his homicidal aims. Charlie maintained that the label the "Manson Family" was only used by the press and not consistent with how they interacted or viewed themselves at that time. Manson himself even addressed this at his trial when he was given an opportunity to speak in open court, outside the presence of the jury. "Most of the people at the ranch, that you call "The Family," were just people that you did not want, people that were alongside the road, that their parents had kicked them out, or did not want to go to juvenile hall. So, I did the best I could, and I took them up on my garbage dump and I told them this: In love, there is no wrong."

The first time the group was ever referred to as "The Family" was on the first day of the grand jury testimony, which was convened as part of the original trial. It was Vincent Bugliosi himself who coined the term.

During Susan Atkins' initial testimony on day one, Bugliosi asks plainly, "Did you call your group by any name, Susan?"

Susan responded by saying, "Among ourselves we called ourselves the family, a family like no other family."

In her testimony, it's clear that Susan Atkins' use of the word *family* is in the context of the group's relationship to each other. However, Bugliosi turned Susan's description into a proper name, as if the group was not *a* family but an organization called "The Family." Bugliosi asked Susan, "In terms of love or hate, how would you describe The Family?" Oblivious to Bugliosi's semantics, Susan responded by describing her feelings toward the people in the group, saying "love completely."

It was this exchange that forever turned the group's continued self-reference as a tight-knit family into an organization known as The Manson Family—at least in the media. "The media has the power," Charlie told me. "Nobody can refuse the BBC. When the BBC tells the King of England, you talk to us, he has to do it. The media has the power of the press and the power of the press is the power. You don't know that?"

I admitted to Charlie that I did not know that; at the same time, I was beginning to wonder how much of what has been reported about the Manson Family was real.

"Saddam Hussein was hung by the media," Charlie continued.

I struggled to comprehend his meaning. "So, you mean you were hung by the media as well?" I asked.

"I know it," Charlie said. Apparently, I had guessed correctly.

Charlie continued, "I understand the media. Every time I gave something it came back to lock this damn door."

I took all this as support of the so-called Manson Family's assertions that there was, in fact, no Manson Family. There was unquestionably a group of young men and women living in a commune, and Charlie was absolutely the group's leader—for lack of a better term—but groups can have leadership without being a cult.

Was this a commune working toward a shared purpose? Or a religious sect devoted to a living deity?

Cappi lived with the group in the two years leading up to the murders, seeing all the people that came and went, so I asked her directly, "Was it a cult?"

"A cult? Horseshit. It wasn't a cult to begin with, it was a commune and there were tons of them at that time," Cappi insisted.

"So, people were allowed to leave?" I asked.

"Yeah!" Cappi yelled back at me. From her point of view, the summer she spent at Spahn Ranch had been mischaracterized for years. "You could do anything you wanted. It was like, just be your own person. It was that kind of thing."

"So, to be clear, no one was being held against their will?" I asked.

"No," Cappi said sternly. "No one. Ever. No." Cappi was insistent. "I was there, and I didn't kill anybody."

I asked Bobby who, up until the murder of Gary Hinman, was a first-hand witness to the formation of the group. He backed up Cappi's claim unequivocally. "They were always free to leave," Bobby said. Bobby was insistent that the notion of a religious cult was complete horseshit. "It was a commune like many others in the area," Bobby said. "You know most of those people were inexperienced with communes prior to joining that one. So, their only experience with communes would have been with Charlie."

The group was made up primarily of young women. Contrary to the common picture of Manson being a master manipulator who recruited them and controlled their minds, Bobby related that they came together much differently. "What most people don't understand is that it wasn't Charlie's charisma that attracted more women," Bobby began, "it was once he had two women together, the women attracted the women. Women who like a community of women, and that was the attraction in that group."

In addition to Bobby and Cappi's assertions, there is other evidence that people often came and went from the commune. In April of 1969, four months before the murders, Leslie Van Houten was arrested for hitchhiking. After she was arraigned and released, she went to her parents' house in Southern California and spent the night. This instance demonstrates that Leslie was seemingly travelling freely and had ample opportunity to escape if she was being held hostage by a cult. Instead, the next day she bid her parents farewell, left of her own accord, and returned to the group, having never mentioned anything about Charlie or the others to her parents.

According to Charlie, he truly believed in the ideals of communal living and often preached that to the others. I asked Charlie how this all worked. He said, "In here they're all working to keep you locked up, but outside they got all kinds of little games that they play, did you know that? Jealousy is a power. Jealousy is a gigantic power man. It will just suck all the energy out of you. People will put the bad mouth on somebody for all kinds of psychological reasons. Jealousy is a big reason that people maneuver."

I replied, "There must have been a lot of jealousy when you were with all those girls? How did you get away from it?"

Charlie paused and replied curtly, "I killed it." After another moment, he paused and explained, "You see, when I'm out and I'm not locked up, I'm the emperor. I'm the boss, everything comes under me. It's my horse. I'm the pharaoh."

"I get that," I said. "But if it wasn't a cult, then why did they all listen to you?"

"Because my mother never had a husband," Charlie replied, as if this was an obvious answer to my question.

Not understanding what he meant, I attempted to relate it back to him. "So, you're saying that you are your own man?"     Of course, that is not what he meant. He paused again before explaining that what he meant was that his mother never had a husband, which made him Jesus-like.

Charlie said, "My father never married my mother. It was the same thing as the Mother Mary. Mother Mary didn't have no husband, she had that baby in the barn." According to Charlie, these pseudo philosophical ramblings, in which he would not so subtly compare himself to the Christian messiah, went a long way with the ladies in 1967.

"You know it's weird man," Charlie said. "It's like you see a bunch of people and they're coming along in your life and they're doing what you've already done. I noticed this about people when they think I'm a hippie cult leader." [6]

How the group came together and viewed themselves genuinely matters because it's the first part of understanding whether Manson and the others were a hippy commune or a religious cult. The Helter Skelter theory is dependent upon Charles Manson being a brainwashing cult leader, but people who were part of the group deny that dynamic.

---

[6] Quote from Manson is from a taped phone call provided to me from a Manson supporter, recorded in approximately 2010.

*Is there another explanation for their heinous acts other than Manson dictating that they murder on his behalf?* With the context of the group in hand, I had to question what I thought I knew about the so-called Manson Family and explore those implications.

*If these were not perfect young women plucked from society and corrupted solely by Charles Manson, did he actually brainwash them or were they working alongside him with a common motive?*

*What was going on inside the group the year leading up to the murders?*

# The Summer of 1968

*"All that shit was already going on before Charlie got out. You can dump it on Charlie, and lock Charlie in the cell, but that doesn't alleviate the situation. That's only compounding it and making it worse. You brought it down to another level."*
*- Charles Manson, 1977, speaking in the third person.*

In the summer of 1968, Phil Kaufman was released from prison and sought out his old friend Charlie Manson. He found him living in a dilapidated, abandoned house in Topanga Canyon with a group of young women. Seeing how good Charlie had it, Phil decided to stay. "I lived with them for almost a month—it was like sex on demand," Phil recalled gleefully. As a horny ex-con, Phil was on board with Charlie's meaning of love, saying, "His interpretation of love, you know, was sex. But love was the key word." According to Phil, Charlie would announce to the group, "Everybody has to make love," or "spread the love," meaning it was time to get busy.

As Phil recalled, the evening ritual would begin shortly after dark. Charlie would play his guitar and they would all sing along, signalling that it was time to pair off. "It wasn't like, night-night let's fuck," Phil said. "It was a little subtler than that." The group would all come together in the living room, and the women would take the men into a corner or the bathroom or out to the front lawn and pleasure them.

According to Manson, this reflected the idea that he was not a cult leader. In a phone call Michael Channels recorded with Manson, they talked sex. Michael played the recording for me and Manson says, "Those are your kids, not my kids. I wasn't their *leader*. I was a *beater*. I was just following that pussy, that's all I was after. I just wanted to suck on them titties."

Charlie had a keen interest in making everyone complicit. This is a theme that comes up time and again. It's the prison mentality—if you're not with us, you're against us. Phil told me, "If someone was getting laid more than someone else, or a girl wasn't getting, you know, serviced, Charlie would come up and pat you on the head and say, 'Hey, you know Patty Krenwinkel needs some lovin.'" Meaning, Hey Phil, go over and fuck Krenwinkel, right now.

I've always wondered why the women would go along with this. It's obvious that Charlie benefited from their continual sexual freedom. Not only did he get laid whenever he wanted, but he could also entice other men into the group and use the women to barter for almost anything. Meanwhile, the women had to deal with the emotional fallout, pregnancies, and continual sexually transmitted infections. Perhaps it was the culture of the time, the overall mentality of the commune, or something else entirely. I asked Charlie but he had little insight.

I talked to Phil Kaufman about which of the girls stuck out in his memory from the time he spent with the Family. Phil said he would never forget Sandra Good. Sandy was a twenty-four-year-old affluent young woman at the time, and like many of the others she was a lost soul.

Sandy grew up suffering from numerous respiratory conditions requiring multiple surgeries. Her mother resented having to care for an ill child and would often say—right to Sandy—that she wished Sandy had died. Sandy's father raised her to believe that the only path to self-worth was through higher education, a goal that made Sandy, who had a learning disability, feel worthless. In 1968, Sandy met Manson and the group in Los Angeles, while on vacation from San Francisco. Manson's philosophy and the group's counterculture lifestyle was the exact opposite of everything she had been told was important. She soaked up every word, quit her job over the phone, and told her roommates to sell all her belongings, deciding to stay with Manson and the group indefinitely.

Phil's first meeting with Sandy was etched in his memory as follows, "When Sandra Good came, I nailed her." Phil recalled being won over by Sandy's eagerness to become part of the group and took it upon himself to hook up with her. When Charlie saw Sandy, he had a similar thought. "He was right behind me," Phil said. "Charlie was thinking the same thing, but I was just a little bit quicker." Phil laughed as he recalled undressing Sandy, explaining that even though he was clearly about to have sex with her, Charlie was undeterred. "I thought he was going to stick his dick in my back," Phil said.

Not all the women were into Charlie's free love mantra. Phil recalled trying to sleep with Squeaky, whom he described as "Charlie's Ace." Phil said, "I mean she wasn't in on the murders *allegedly*, and she was frigid. But Charlie said that 'Sex is love and love is sex, if you love me, you'll have sex with me.' So, she went along with it. But let me tell you, whenever you had sex with her man, it was like sticking your dick in a snowbank. I mean that girl was not having it. She wasn't having a good time."

A seventeen-year-old young woman named Barbara Hoyt joined the group that same summer. During the trial, she turned state's witness and later relocated to Idaho, which is where we met to film an interview for our documentary. Barbara was good-natured and still looked remarkably like her teenage Manson Family pictures, despite it being nearly fifty years later. She had the same round face, bright smile, and dark-rimmed glasses that had set her apart from the other girls in the commune.

Barbara recalled joining the group after spontaneously running away from her nearby home. "I had planned to just go back home," Barbara told me, pausing to consider the reason she joined the Manson Family in the first place. After a moment, she said sternly, "I had planned to go home, and didn't." Barbara had grown up in the San Fernando Valley, a stone's throw away from where the group was living at the time. Her mother was a master's degree librarian, and her father was a psychologist who worked on top-secret projects for the government. "I think he did experiments on other countries' troops or something," Barbara said laughing. "I don't know."

Growing up, Barbara was obsessed with the ocean and aspired to work in the field. By the time she was twelve, she began submitting unsolicited reports to companies who published books on marine animals. At fourteen she became the youngest certified scuba diver in LA County, and in junior high school she even taught a self-made course on oceanography. There's no question Barbara would have continued into a career in the open ocean if not for a fateful day in 1968 when she had an argument with her father. "I wanted to go to spring break with some friends and he wouldn't let me go," she told me.

Before this point, Barbara's relationship with her father had been tumultuous. "My dad was pretty mean to us," she said. Her father's aggressive personality had always been offset by her mother's ability to calm the waters. Barbara had fond memories of her mother taking her and her brother on outings to Disney movies and to the beach once a week. Despite her mother's influence, Barbara was often forced to cope with an aggressive father. Barbara recalled that her father was incredibly difficult to deal with, to the point that her brother, seven years her senior, had run away at sixteen. For Barbara, once things reached a boiling point with her father, she quickly packed a sandwich and cupcake in a brown paper bag and walked out of the house. She told me, "I thought I understood things my parents didn't, they were from the wrong generation, you know."

Barbara recalled, "I took a bus up from Canoga Park, up through to Devonshire." After this, she made her way north before turning west, walking down the Santa Susana Pass. Sitting by the side of the road with the sun beating down, Barbara contemplated returning home. She opened her brown paper bag and began to eat her hastily made lunch, still unsure of her destination. Soon after, a rusted-out Volkswagen bus fought its way toward her. The bus was being driven by two young women looking at her through the gaping hole in the front of the vehicle where the windshield should have been. The bus seemed to sigh with relief as it came to a stop beside her. Barbara made her way toward the vehicle as the side door opened. Inside was Stephanie Schramm, who at the time was Charlie's teenage girlfriend, and Deidre Lansbury, the young daughter of actress Angela Lansbury. Both girls were staying with Charlie and the group. Like Barbara, Stephanie had also run away.

Deidre had used her more affluent home life to help provide for the commune, making her more than welcome. Phil Kaufman remembered Deidre, saying, "We used to pick her up at school and she'd go out with her credit card and buy us things." Phil Kaufman laughed to himself saying, "She was getting laid as much as anyone else."

The girls playfully offered Barbara a ride, and, with no place else to go, Barbara made a fateful decision that would change her life forever.

She got into the bus.

The girls went to a local farmers' market, laughed, talked, and made Barbara feel welcome and accepted at a time when she felt completely alone in the world. As the afternoon wound down, the girls told Barbara they were living with a larger group inside an abandoned house in the valley. The house was on Gresham Street in Canoga Park and was once painted a vibrant canary yellow, though by the time Barbara arrived the upkeep on the exterior was an afterthought.

Soon after arriving, Barbara met Squeaky. "She was very motherly," Barbara said. Sandra Good, who was pregnant with Bobby's child at the time, also welcomed Barbara. After meeting several others, Barbara met Sadie, who took a special interest in her. "We went and climbed a tree and sat in it and talked about life," Barbara recalled. At dinner time, the group sat in a circle and ate a big pot of soul food. Later in the evening, Charlie arrived, to the excitement of the group, and they sang songs and passed around a couple of joints.

Barbara recalled Charlie giving one of the girls a task, and the girl replied, "I can't do it."

"You can't?" Charlie asked. "Well you can't, can't."

The girl paused, trying to comprehend Charlie's logic.

Charlie said, "Repeat after me, I can't can't and I can can. I can't can't, and I can can..."

After several minutes the girl decided she could.

It was that intensity that first attracted Barbara to Charlie. The vibe of a teacher, and the spirit of a poet. "I really liked him," she recalled. "The next morning, we took off on a motorcycle together and bought donuts. I don't know what our trip was for originally, but I paid for the donuts and he kept the change. He had no problems taking my money. The little bit I had."

Though Barbara elected to stay with the group full-time, many others came and went. Deidre didn't live with the group full-time, nor did Bobby. Phil Kaufman left after about a month. Around that time, two of the women from the group were hitchhiking when they were picked up by a handsome, long-haired hippie with a bushy beard. The driver's name was Dennis Wilson, one of the Wilson brothers who made up The Beach Boys.

It might be hard to appreciate now how popular The Beach Boys were in 1968. They were American icons as teenagers. In the mid-sixties they competed for dominance in the music industry with The Beatles. Dennis was one of three brothers who made up The Beach Boys plus their cousin Mike Love, and a friend named AJ Jardine. When not on stage The Beach Boys liked to party, and Dennis Wilson partied the hardest. He grew his hair long, had a bushy beard, and often wore dishevelled clothing while driving expensive cars. He smoked pot frequently, went on week-long cocaine binges, and engaged in the sexual exploits one would expect of a true rockstar. While his brothers were stressed about music, Dennis resolved to live life to the fullest.

Unfortunately, his life was also the shortest.

In 1983, Dennis threw on some cut-off jeans and convinced a friend to drink with him on a private yacht. While his friend lounged on deck, Dennis put on a scuba mask and dove into the ocean. He never surfaced, drowning at the age of thirty-nine.

Fifteen years before his untimely death, in the summer of 1968, Dennis was returning home from dropping acid with a friend and picked up Katie and another woman living with the group named Ella Jo Bailey, inviting them back to his house. They invited their friends, and within days Manson and the entire commune had moved in. Dennis was taken by Charlie; he like his style, and his music. Wilson and Manson became close friends. At one point, Wilson had even arranged for Charlie to play with The Beach Boys in Texas, but Manson couldn't go because of his parole restrictions. Because Dennis Wilson was rich, he could afford to fund a never-ending party for the group. People came and went frequently from his Pacific Palisades mansion, and Dennis paid an enormous sum of money for groceries—and penicillin.

While living with Dennis, Charles "Tex" Watson, the eventual leader of the murder parties, became a part of the group. Tex is undeniably a key to unravelling what really took place in the summer of 1968. Tex was either carrying out Charlie's orders, working alongside Charlie, or killing people for his own reasons. Vincent Bugliosi said unequivocally during the trial that Manson was in complete control. To the jury, Bugliosi described Tex as a mindless soldier killing at Charlie's behest. In his closing arguments Bugliosi said, "[Charlie had] total and complete domination over his family including the actual killer Tex Watson." This was a point of emphasis for the prosecution because Charlie wasn't actually present for any of the murders—Tex was the one who physically carried them out, with the exception of Gary Hinman. Bugliosi asked the jury rhetorically, "How complete was Manson's control over this family? Tex Watson couldn't even go to sleep at night before Charlie. He couldn't even go to sleep and lie down on the good earth without Charlie complaining and telling him to get up." Given the accounts of the group I'd received thus far I wondered, *how did Tex Watson truly come to be with Manson and perhaps fall under his control?*

Tex was a small-town boy who grew up in Copeville, Texas. At the time the population was around 150 people. In grade school, he excelled, and in high school his size made him a standout athlete. Tex was a tall, lanky kid who grew into a six-foot-two, strapping young man. By all accounts Tex was handsome, with an aw shucks kind of appeal. He was tall with an athletic build, laid-back personality, and just the right amount of a southern accent. Watson attended North Texas State and became a member of the Pi Kappa Alpha fraternity. In his senior year, he went to visit a fraternity brother in Los Angeles.

Tex's account of his life has tended to differ from time to time. In an account given as part of a 1978 parole hearing, Tex claimed that he became so captivated with LA that he transferred to Cal State. In an unearthed 1971 psychiatric report, submitted to Tex's defence team as part of his stand-alone trial, Tex claimed that he'd struggled at North Texas State after he'd joined the fraternity—instead of studying, he'd been dating and partying. He then chose to move to California to escape his controlling mother, who had ruined multiple serious relationships he'd attempted to have with women.

What's clear is that Tex found work at a Hollywood wig shop when he landed in California. At the same time, he partook in the drug subculture. In March of 1968 he was in a car accident and required knee surgery. Tex dropped out of school, began travelling, and was ultimately invited to stay at Dennis Wilson's house.

The short time that Charlie and his group lived with Dennis Wilson truly changed everything. Wilson was fascinated with Charlie and elevated him from a wandering teacher to a full-fledged guru with celebrity friends. The Beach Boys' fifteenth studio album *Twenty-Twenty*, features a song co-written by Charles Manson originally called "Cease to Exist," which The Beach Boys retitled as "Never Learn Not to Love." Incidentally, the 1993 Guns N' Roses' album *The Spaghetti Incident?* also features a song written by Manson called "Look at your Game Girl." By many accounts, Manson was a reasonably good singer-songwriter, and over the years he continued to find ways to compose music in prison. Twenty or more albums of these recordings have been released by numerous people who found a way to obtain the music from Manson while he was incarcerated.

Dennis Wilson, Charlie, and Tex all bonded during that time, playing music and having deep, drug-fueled philosophical discussions. Dennis and Tex found Charlie to be a source of ceaseless amusement, and Charlie's girls ensured they had all the sex they could handle. At one point, Dennis invited a friend named Terry Melcher to come by the house and experience the never-ending party with Manson and his women.

Terry Melcher was originally from Cincinnati where he was born Terry Jorden and primarily raised by his grandmother. By the time he was eight or nine years old, he had relocated to Los Angeles to be with his mother, Doris Day, who by then was a rising radio and film star. When Doris married her manager Martin Melcher in 1951, he adopted Terry, who changed his name.

My last name is also Day, which was something that Charlie once asked me about.

Charlie said, "With the last name Day—you're not related to Doris Day, are you?"

I laughed, assuring Charlie that I wasn't. "No, no," I said.

Charlie said, "Yeah, I used to hang around with her son."

"Terry, right?" I asked.

Charlie said, "Yeah, he was a pretty good dude, but he was too scared man. You know, he was like a little fly. He was always scared of everything."

To my knowledge, Charlie never met Doris Day but there is no question he did know Terry. In researching Terry's life prior to meeting Manson, I came across something that could be a key piece of the puzzle. When Terry was twenty-six his adoptive father, Martin, died unexpectedly from a heart attack, and Terry was left to be the executor of his estate. This was only a few months before he met Manson.

Backing up a bit further, it's important to understand that the marriage between Doris Day and Martin Melcher was not good. Martin ruthlessly drove Doris Day's career, which transformed her into an incredibly successful TV and film actress. In the process, he isolated and abused her. Terry was also physically beaten by Martin and shipped off to boarding schools before finally leaving home as a teenager. As a young man, Terry was ambitious, taking a fifty dollar per week job at the William Morris Agency and enrolling himself in a record executive training program. He was soon producing records for up-and-coming artists like The Byrds and Paul Revere & the Raiders. His skills as a junior record producer paid dividends, and within a few years he was making a lot of money and dating TV actress Candice Bergen, who would later become well-known for her title character role on *Murphy Brown*. Together they rented 10050 Cielo Drive, the same house where the Manson Family would later commit the Tate murders.

When Terry was named the executor of his late adoptive father's estate, he discovered to his shock and horror that Martin had squandered the millions of dollars both he and his mother had earned, leaving them both hopelessly bankrupt. Terry had to abandon his growing career as a record producer to undertake the massive burden of untangling his family's financial affairs. He spent months with lawyers and accountants trying to stave off creditors and find a way to recover the money.

By the fall of 1968, ten months before the murders, Terry was completely overwhelmed with overseeing his mother's career, trying to rectify their family estate, and handling lawsuits. It was at this time that Terry met Charles Manson and Tex at Dennis Wilson's house. The dynamic between Terry Melcher, Manson, and Tex is key.

Prosecutors claimed that Manson was an ambitious musician who aspired to be like The Beatles and The Beach Boys, so Dennis Wilson introduced him to Terry Melcher. Allegedly, Manson lobbied Melcher to help him realize his musical aspirations. At trial, Melcher testified that he saw Manson play music twice, once at Dennis Wilson's house and one other time thereafter. The prosecution claimed that Melcher rejected Manson, which sent Manson into a rage, so when Manson decided to begin a race war by killing random white people, he chose Terry Melcher's house. During his summation to the jury at Manson's trial, Bugliosi said, "On the evening of August the 8th, 1969, when Charles Manson sent his robots out on a mission of murder, since the only qualifications the victims had to have was that they be white and members of the establishment, obviously, it made immense sense to Charles Manson, so he may just as well select a residence that he was familiar with, particularly one where he had been treated rather shabbily and whose former occupant, Terry Melcher, had rejected him."

Manson told me definitively that this is patently untrue. "I'm not an entertainer," Charlie said. "I didn't want to be a rock-and-roll star. That's what the DA said."

Considering the state of Melcher's life at the time he met Manson, it seems strange that Manson and Melcher had any legitimate conversations about turning Manson into a recording artist. Melcher wasn't active in the music industry at the time he met Manson. He was in a great deal of turmoil due to the fallout from his adoptive father's death. Melcher became so unravelled that he broke up with Candice Bergen, moved out of Cielo Drive, and began therapy for his worsening anxiety and depression—all in the ten months prior to the murders during the time he knew Manson.

When Leslie Van Houten, one of the killers who later joined the group, was questioned in November of 1969 by an investigator from the Robbery Homicide Division of the LAPD, the investigator said to Leslie, "Tell me about Terry Melcher. Remember him?"

"Terry Marshmallow?" Leslie replied playfully. After some back and forth to establish that Terry Melcher was indeed called "Terry Marshmallow" by some of the girls, Leslie explained that the group would sit around a campfire in the back of Spahn Ranch, playing music and singing songs. In contrast to the prosecution's portrayal of Manson as a serious or dedicated musician, Leslie described a very lighthearted approach to music in which they would all sing and laugh. According to Leslie, there was talk about bringing a mobile recording studio to Spahn Ranch to capture the free-spirited campfire essence of the music. "Record the natural surroundings or something," Leslie said. "Get the echoes and all that stuff."

According to Leslie this was all just wishful banter—nothing ever came of it. After visiting Spahn Ranch, Terry and his friends didn't come around anymore and the talk of recording their music naturally ended.

"Was Charlie upset by that? the investigator asked.

"No," Leslie replied. "Charlie hardly ever got upset, as far as I could tell."

In another interview conducted in January 1970 by Aaron Stovitz, a Los Angeles Deputy District Attorney, Phil Kaufman was questioned about Charlie's ambitions as a musician. According to Kaufman, Charlie was a carefree musician, unconcerned with becoming any sort of professional artist, even though Kaufman and others had actually tried to convince him otherwise. "Being as transient as he was, he never stayed around long enough to consummate a record deal," Kaufman said. "No one could ever release his music because he'd never sign any contracts." Phil recalled that Manson didn't even really have conventional songs; instead, Kaufman described Manson as basically playing guitar and singing/speaking a sort of stream-of-consciousness poetry.

When I met Phil Kaufman, I asked him about these interviews, even playing him excerpts. He laughed remembering them, saying he recalled the DA fishing for this portrayal of Manson as a rejected ambitious musician, obsessed with his own philosophy. Kaufman said to me that as far as he was concerned, that's not what he saw. Manson couldn't care less about being recorded or making money from his music, and why would he? He had a great set-up. Phil told me, "[Manson] he had a good thing going for him you know. Money wasn't even involved in anything. He didn't have to earn a living, he had girls going out and getting him food, he was having sex, playing his music you know. Life was good for him."

According to Cappi, this is fundamental in understanding how the group worked—money was never an issue. "There were no robberies, or whatever, I mean none of that shit was real," she told me.

"We went through garbage cans," Cappi said. "Back then you could go through the garbage behind a store and they would have everything in there and it wasn't even out of date." Cappi was adamant on this point, countering one of the central ideas put forth by the DA at Manson's trial. "We weren't about money," Cappi told me. "It had nothing do with money or being a rockstar or anything like that."
What most people don't understand, according to Cappi, is that the group did have a clear goal, but it was the opposite of these material ambitions. "We were trying to step out of society," she said. "That's what we were trying to do. All the rules and regulations and shit. We just saw where the world was going, and we wanted out of it."

All of this is counter to the prosecution's unequivocal claim that Manson wanted to be a rockstar and was counting on Terry Melcher to help him achieve that goal. If Manson wasn't rejected by the music industry and Melcher's house didn't represent the establishment to him, then what was the real reason for Tex Watson taking three women over to Terry Melcher's house and killing five people?

According to Bobby Beausoleil, the answer is something else entirely. "Charlie was told that he would be compensated for the use of the song," he told me. That song was "Never Learn Not to Love." Recall that when Manson was staying with Dennis Wilson, Charlie gave Dennis a song. Charlie called the song "Cease to Exist," but it was recorded by

The Beach Boys, for their album *Twenty-Twenty,* as "Never Learn Not to Love."

According to Bobby, however Dennis Wilson and The Beach Boys actually came into possession of the song, they left Charlie with the impression that he would be paid five thousand dollars for its use. "Now, Charlie didn't care so much about the money," Bobby told me. "All Dennis had to say to Charlie was 'Oh, I thought you gave me that song,' and then Charlie would have said 'oh ok, yeah,' because Charlie wouldn't have restricted Dennis—he liked Dennis a lot. But the fact that Charlie was *told* that he was supposed to be paid for the use of the song, the fact that he didn't get paid, that was the problem. If you're in prison and you owe somebody, and you give your word, and you don't keep your word—that's a justification for being killed."

Bobby and I talked about this a lot, and I asked him how he knew this for certain. Bobby said he'd discussed it with Charlie at length while both were serving time together and that this motive is unequivocally the thing that has been missed when it comes to Manson. Bobby said that on August 8, 1969, the night of the Sharon Tate murders, Manson didn't give a shit about a race war—he was pissed at Terry Melcher. Contrary to the prosecution's theories though, Manson wasn't angry because Melcher refused to make him a rockstar. Manson was upset because he blamed Melcher for The Beach Boys' going back on their word. "[Charlie] sent Tex to kill Terry, not a house full of five people," Bobby said. "You see that's what's so critical here. Charlie wasn't picking a house full of innocent people; he was picking Terry Melcher. The people that were there are the ones that took the brunt of what Tex Watson brought there that night."

In an interview with investigators, Leslie Van Houten corroborated this idea, saying that the day after the Tate murders Katie told her, "that they had murdered five people, but they didn't know there were going to be that many at the house and they didn't know who the people were." After watching the news coverage, Katie was shocked to learn the identity of the people she had helped murder saying, "Oh my god, they were rich, they were famous people."

Charles Manson seeking retaliation on Terry Melcher for breaking his word about the five thousand dollars Charlie was promised contradicts the motive laid out by the prosecution. It changes Manson's intent from starting a race war to vengeance. According to the Helter Skelter theory, Charles Manson planned to inspire a race war by killing affluent whites, so he sent his followers to Terry Melcher's house. During the war, Manson would hide with his followers in a secret cave located in Death Valley. Afterwards, they would emerge, and Manson would lead the victorious black army.

The prosecution further claimed that Manson undoubtedly knew that Melcher had moved and also knew that Sharon Tate now lived at 10050 Cielo Drive. At trial the prosecution brought forth a witness named Shahrokh Hatami, a photographer and close friend to Sharon Tate, to testify about an encounter with Manson. Prosecutors claimed that Hatami was at Cielo Drive on March 23, 1969, four and a half months before the Tate murders, when Manson came to the house looking for Terry Melcher. Allegedly, Hatami had a confrontation with Manson in view of Sharon Tate before curtly telling Manson to leave through the back alley. In closing arguments, Vincent Buglisoi said, "It appears, ladies and gentlemen, that Charles Manson saw Sharon Tate, and Sharon Tate saw Charles Manson." Bugliosi continued reasoning that, "to Charles Manson the back alley is a place where they have garbage cans, it is the habitat of rats, and cats, and dogs. So I am sure he wasn't too happy when Hatami says to take the back alley. One doesn't have to stretch the imagination to realize that the Tate residence was symbolic to Charles Manson, and particularly the establishment's rejection of him."

There are two issues with this. First, Manson was an ex-con hippie who routinely ate discarded food, rarely showered, and embraced his reputation in the underworld. By March of 1969 he had been "rejected" by the establishment hundreds or perhaps thousands of times in his life going back to his days in Boys Town, through his years of incarceration, and finally with his embrace of the sixties counterculture upon his release from Terminal Island. Manson and almost every other member of the Family talked frequently about their collective desire to drop out of society. Given this, it's unclear why Manson would be so outraged after being asked to leave any house via the alley that he would feel the insatiable urge to murder everyone inside. Also, the main house at 10050 Cielo Drive was a sprawling property situated high above the road and didn't even have a back alley. When the description "back alley" was used, it was a figurative—and misleading—way to describe the path that connected the main house and the guest house and in fact ran in front of the property. So, when Bugliosi said Manson was upset about being banished to the back alley, he actually meant Manson was upset by the idea of having to walk through a figurative back alley—in reality he just left in plain view.

Second, when you dig into Hatami's actual account the entire story becomes suspect. When Shahrokh Hatami first testified, he claimed he wasn't sure if it even was Manson who came to the house, saying it was a man possibly "resembling" Manson. In regard to Manson asking about Terry Melcher, Hatami said he actually couldn't remember who the unknown man was asking about. Finally, Hatami wasn't even sure that the man did see Sharon Tate, explaining that the man was only there briefly and *may* have seen her. In another seemingly obvious omission, the prosecution never inquired whether the man could have been Tex.

The prosecution also presented witness testimony from Rudi Altobelli, the actual homeowner of 10050 Cielo Drive. Altobelli testified that after renting the property to Tate and Polanski, he was staying in the guest house prior to hiring Bill Garretson to look after the property and his dogs. According to Altobelli, on March 23, he was showering in the guest house when he heard his dogs bark, alerting him to an unexpected visitor. Altobelli got out of the shower and allegedly greeted Manson who had come by to inquire about Terry Melcher. According to his testimony, Rudi Altobelli knew Manson through Dennis Wilson. Altobelli claimed he told Charlie that Melcher had moved to his mother's house in Malibu.

The issue with this claim is also twofold. First, Rudi Altobelli was questioned by investigators and never mentioned this fleeting interaction with Manson, which is perhaps not unreasonable given Manson was not a suspect at that time. However, after Manson's arrest—when he was on the front page of every newspaper—Altobelli still didn't mention the encounter to anyone. It wasn't until the following year—when Altobelli was interviewed by Vincent Bugliosi—that Altobelli remembered the interaction and subsequently testified in suspicious detail. So, we are left to believe that while the world media was talking about Charles Manson daily, Altobelli had direct knowledge that Manson had been to 10050 Cielo Drive prior to murdering Altobelli's tenant and friend Sharon Tate, and he told no one.

Even if we somehow accept this, we would also have to ignore the prosecution's own timeline. In Bill Garretson's testimony for the prosecution, he described being hired by Altobelli as the groundskeeper and moving into the guest house in mid-March, to take care of the dogs. This directly contradicts Altobelli's testimony in which he states he was still using the guest house on March 23. So, not only did Altobelli not report the interaction with Manson until the following year, but he also didn't live in the guest house at the time the interaction is said to have taken place.

At best we can say that the prosecution relied on circumstantial evidence in an attempt to tie Manson directly to Cielo Drive; at worst we can say they lied. The question is, *why does it matter?*

It matters because all of these descrepancies and things that simply don't add up could be more evidence that the prosecution made up the Helter Skelter theory in order to more easily convict Charles Manson through a sensational conspiracy narrative. It was at this point that I developed another theory that can explain the murders without the race war motive. An alternate Manson theory.

I asked myself, *If the prosecution did construct the Helter Skelter theory, is convicting a man like Charles Manson so essential that any means of achieving that goal is acceptable?*

Near the end of a conversation with Charlie, I put this question to him.

"Everybody eats you up, they'll use you in all kinds of ways," Charlie said.

The automated recording kicked in, cutting Charlie off. "You have thirty seconds remaining."

"Have you ever trusted anyone?" Charlie asked.

Knowing the phone would cut out at any second, I turned the question back to Charlie, "Have you?"

"That's what I'm doing in here," Charlie said, slowly laughing to himself. "You have a good day, brother-man."

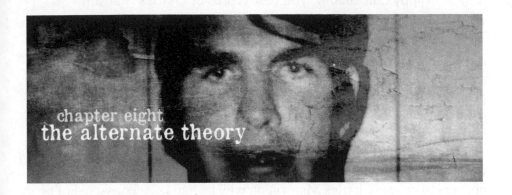

# The Alternate Theory

*"I've sat in solitary confinement and I've watched everything you guys do, and the truth is you're all lying to yourselves."*
*- Charles Manson, 1992, Parole Hearing*

It was Thanksgiving and I was at my parents' house for a large family dinner with my extended family. I had just filled my plate with turkey, mashed potatoes, stuffing, cranberry sauce, and a generous amount of gravy. My kids were running around between bites, and I was a few glasses of wine in, very much looking forward the meal. I sat at the table eagerly, with my napkin across my lap, knife and fork in hand. But before I could take my first bite, my phone vibrated in my pocket. I put down my utensils and retrieved the phone just enough to see the top of the screen, trying to make out the number. It was the familiar call centre that routes incoming calls from inmates of the California State prison system. I looked longingly at my food and up at my confused aunts and uncles, who wondered why I would even consider taking a call in the middle of Thanksgiving. "Sorry," I said. "I have to take this. It's Charles Manson." I didn't wait long enough to hear their replies, ducking out of the room with the phone to my ear.

"Hello, Charlie?" I said.

Charlie's familiar voice came on the line. "Yeah. Listen, I'm already all around the world. I tricked Vincent Bugliosi in that courtroom. I let him convict me for something I didn't do."

"Why did you do that?" I asked.

"I'd never grown up in that world," Charlie said, beginning a rhythmic freestyle as if he was a beat poet riffing at a coffee house, not someone calling from a communal phone in the hallway of a supermax prison. "I live in rock and roll. I live in the penitentiary. I live in the chain gangs. I live in the south-land. I live in the graveyards. I live in the tomb. Do you realize they're torturing people even today?"

Despite the ill-timed arrival of Charlie's call, I wanted to speak with him, and while my family stuffed themselves on turkey, I went upstairs to debate Charles Manson on why he had been convicted of nine murders he claimed he didn't commit. Based on all I had gathered for the documentary, and these ongoing conversations with Charlie, I wanted to propose an alternate theory that could explain the murders as a culmination of events centred around Charles Manson—with no mention of the Helter Skelter race war.

The theory begins in July of 1969. By that summer Charlie had fallen out with Dennis Wilson. The costs of feeding the group, along with the medical bills from the sexually transmitted infections they continually passed to each other, had all added up. To add insult to injury, the group had destroyed parts of Wilson's mansion and wrecked his car, all of which had pushed him to the edge. By July of 1969, Dennis asked them to leave, and the group was looking for a new place to stay. It was then that they settled into Spahn Ranch.

The ranch burned down on September 25, 1970, a little more than a year after the murders. Long before it was consumed by a brush fire or discovered by the Manson Family, it was situated just off the Santa Susana pass for almost a hundred years. Going back as far as 1885, the property was a working farm. As it was overtaken by the city of Los Angeles, it transformed into a working movie ranch. By the 1940s, it served as a backdrop for movies and then, with the invention of the medium, television. Howard Hughes had even spent time on the property filming his 1943 western film *The Outlaw*. In 1948, the ranch was purchased by a tall, Pennsylvania farmer named George Spahn. Spahn had left his wife and eleven children to move to the ranch with a younger woman named Ruby Pearl, who served as the ranch manger. By the time Manson and the group found Spahn Ranch, George was eighty-one years old and blind. George was known to dress in formal cowboy attire complete with a white hat and dark sunglasses, and he lived in a small house near a dirt road that served as an entrance to the ranch, sprouting off the main road. For George, the ranch was his refuge from the world, a secret piece of Americana, hidden in plain sight in the middle of Los Angeles.

Charlie talked about the ranch frequently. To him, the time on the ranch was one of the quintessential periods of his life, at least when the group first began to live there. Charlie felt at peace on the ranch. Life in prison had made him appreciate being outside. He often spoke about feeling the air, seeing the trees, and hearing the calming ambience of nature.

"Air Trees Water Animals," Charlie said, reciting his personal mantra.

"What do you remember about the ranch?" I asked.

"Everybody at the ranch was one," Charlie began. "There was only one moving thing on that ranch. That was George Spahn, the old blind man. Everybody served George. George was the boss." For Charlie, appeasing George was part of a philosophy that Manson had discovered in prison—true power is gained by those who are subordinate. "In other words," Charlie said, "it's like the horses ruled the ranch. We all served whatever was capable of service. A slave understands his master much better than the master understands his slave."

The Manson Family moved onto the ranch gradually, first staying at a nearby church sometime in 1967, then squatting in the empty shacks along the riding trails from time to time. After leaving Dennis Wilson's house in the summer of 1969, Charlie made a more formal arrangement—some of the women would look after George Spahn in exchange for room and board. Spahn's primary caregiver at that time was Squeaky, who coined her nickname from a noise she made when George would tickle her. In the book *Helter Skelter*, Squeaky is quoted as giving prosecutors a graphic description of sex with George, which Vincent Bugliosi admits was an obvious attempt to shock them. This caricature of Squeaky, using her youthful sexuality to control the eighty-one-year-old owner of the ranch, has permeated through the years. Bobby Beausoleil explained to me how Squeaky's motivations have been badly mischaracterized. "Squeaky didn't like having sex with other men, that's why she got into that," Bobby said. "She took care of George and that became her thing. She wanted to only have sex with Charlie, and so she put herself in that position where she wouldn't have to have sex with anyone else. She was George's caretaker."

Barbara Hoyt echoed this statement. "[Squeaky] she loved him," Barbara said, referring to George. "I think Charlie wanted George to will the ranch to Squeaky, after he died."

When the group began living at the ranch full-time, Charles Manson had been out of prison for a little more than two years. In the alternate theory I am proposing, at this point the Manson Family was a commune of lost souls looking for connection—not a fanatic religious cult centred around Charlie.

The first event in the alternate theory involves Charlie, Tex, and a drug deal gone wrong. Before delving into specifics, it's important to understand that there was a stark contrast between Charles Manson and Tex Watson when it came to money. Charlie Manson cared about people keeping their word, but he didn't give a shit about money; in fact, he would give money away to people to show the group it wasn't important. Cappi recalled a time when the group came into ten thousand dollars, donated by a wannabe member of the commune who wished to stay with them at the ranch. Charlie took the money, and within a few hours he had given it away to anyone he came across. He told members of the commune that he'd done this to show them there was more to life than the almighty dollar.

"Charlie was trying to illustrate that if you give it away it will come back to you," Cappi recalled. Manson would often tell the group that money was behind society's problems—a poison that they were trying to escape. Manson told me the same thing; he always spoke about money in a negative sense, saying things like, "everybody hates me for a dollar."

Tex was more of a capitalist. When Charlie would give money away, Cappi recalled that Tex would say, "Hey give me the money, man." As Cappi eloquently put it, "Tex was on his own trip."

Charlie was a lifelong convict, educated in the school of hard knocks; Tex was a college educated graduate of North Texas State. Charlie was abandoned by his mother who allegedly once traded him for a pitcher of beer; Tex was from a hard-working family who appreciated the value of money. When Charlie was released into the counterculture, he embraced free love and a nomadic lifestyle; when Tex landed in California, he got a part-time job and saw an opportunity to sell drugs.

According to court records, Tex reportedly eased into alcohol and marijuana while partying with his frat brothers at North Texas State. At numerous parole hearings Tex has recounted that when he moved to

California his drug use escalated. By the spring of 1969, Tex was heavy into LSD, methedrine (speed), and cocaine. On April 23, 1969, Tex was arrested for public intoxication in downtown Los Angeles. On that day, Tex told authorities that he'd been introduced to belladonna, a natural root that grew near Spahn Ranch. Belladona is a seemingly innocuous plant that looks like a small sycamore tree. It grows in limestone-rich areas, including patches found around the Santa Susana Pass where Spahn Ranch was once located. For those who know how to cook and ingest it, belladonna can be a potent substitute for more expensive hallucinogens like LSD.

On April 23, 1969, Brenda, a member of the commune with the proper know-how, prepared a batch for Tex, sending him into a full-blown psychotic episode. In a subsequent psychiatric assessment, Tex recalled, "I began talking to space people in space language." Tex left the ranch and was arrested in downtown Los Angeles, after which he was taken to a general lock-up. While in jail, Tex became enraged with a fellow prisoner. The incident devolved into a bloody fist fight, and Tex was further restrained by police. Tex was questioned, arraigned, and fingerprinted. His fingerprints from this event were kept and eventually used to tie him to the Tate-LaBianca murders.

Not only was Tex a heavy drug user at that time, but he was also a drug dealer. Over the years, Tex has admitted in numerous forums that he was dealing drugs from at least 1967 through 1969. According to a psychiatric report submitted to Tex's defence team in 1971, by December of 1968, Tex was growing unsettled with life at Spahn Ranch and reached out to his fraternity brother for a place to crash. Tex subsequently left the ranch and stayed with this frat brother, who enlisted in the army shortly thereafter. Not wanting to return to the ranch, Tex began staying with his frat brother's girlfriend, a young woman named Rosina, who also made a living as a small-time drug dealer. Tex began dating Rosina off and on. At this time Tex described "staying high constantly."

Tex and Rosina's relationship is key to understanding the first event in the alternate theory. It shows that Tex was not a prisoner of Charlie's, living under some kind of mind control. On the contrary, Tex had a life outside of Manson and the group. He would stay in the city with Rosina for significant periods of time, and she did not have a significant relationship with Manson or any other members of the commune at Spahn Ranch.

In the alternate theory, Tex's habit of dealing drugs with Rosina is the context for the inciting incident that led to the Tate-LaBianca murders.

In the first week of July 1969, Tex Watson became involved in a drug deal that went bad. It's difficult to piece together exactly what happened because, until now, Tex is the only one involved who has ever given a full account, and his version of events has shifted depending on who he was talking to. What we know for certain is that the drug deal involved Tex, Rosina, and another drug dealer named Bernard Crowe, who went by the nickname "Lotsapoppa." Crowe was a large African-American man with a well-groomed Afro, who was thought to be associated with the Black Panthers' political movement.

I asked Charlie, "Do you remember Bernard Crowe?"

"Bernard Crowe," Charlie repeated slowly.

I assumed he was pondering Crowe's name, trying to find the right words to describe a man who was once part of an essential moment in his life. I was completely wrong.

"Who the hell is that?" Charlie said.

"He was the Black Panther drug dealer that Tex got mixed up with," I said.

"Oh yeah," Charlie recalled. "I shot the Crowe."

There's no question that Charlie shot Bernard Crowe. This was established beyond a doubt during the Tate-LaBianca trial in 1970. As we talked, Charlie's memory of the event came flooding back, and he told me his version of what happened.

According to Charlie, the reason he shot Crowe had long been mischaracterized by Tex, who had been involved in numerous drug deals leading up to the summer of 1969. At the time of the drug deal in question, Tex and Rosina were low on cash. They had been burned by Crowe and his people during a previous drug deal—Tex and Rosina had paid for drugs they never received. On July 1, 1969, Tex and Rosina came up with a way to get their money back. They told Crowe that they could get a large amount of marijuana at a bargain price, as long as Crowe would pay up front. Somehow, they were able to sell Crowe on the deal, and he gave them about $2,500. With the money in hand, Tex and Rosina took off, with no plans to return.

"Tex was just getting his money back. The money that they had taken from him," Charlie told me. "That came out of his pocket. He wanted to get the money back, and instead of beating them up and killing them and taking the money, he promised to deal some drugs for them and took the money and ran." It's unclear where Tex went with his share of the money, though he did not stay with Rosina or go back to Spahn Ranch.

Late that same evening, the main phone at the ranch rang. It was answered by TJ Walleman, a twenty-six-year-old lanky ex-marine who had served in the Vietnam War and was living at the commune. TJ had a large, distinctive dark walnut-coloured beard and was bald except for a long, wild ring of hair that grew around the back of his head. When TJ answered the phone, Rosina was on the line desperately asking to speak to "Charles." Rosina knew Tex by his given name of Charles Watson as opposed to the nickname he used at the commune. Since everyone at the commune knew Charles Watson only as Tex, instead of getting *Watson* on the phone, TJ got *Manson*. On this fateful phone call, Rosina told Charlie that Crowe had found her, was holding her hostage, and would kill her if he didn't get his money back.

"This girl had Crowe fronted off," Charlie told me, meaning that Rosina's life was not actually in danger—Rosina had double-crossed Tex and lied to Bernard Crowe. "She told Crowe that *we* had stolen her money, but she was the one that stole his money," Charlie recalled. Charlie tried to reason with Crowe who put Rosina on the phone to plead for her life. At the time, Charlie didn't know that Rosina was not actually in danger—he believed what she was saying. "She said Bernard was going to kill her, so we went down to help her," Charlie told me.

According to TJ, who testified about the incident as part of the original Manson Family trial in September of 1970, "[Charlie] said that there was a guy coming over to do the ranch in, and he had a girl over there and he was going to do her in, if we didn't do something about it— somebody was living at the ranch and had stolen some money, and [Bernard Crowe] was going to do the whole ranch in for it."

Cappi was living at the ranch at the time and recalled the situation as a defining event for the commune. "We were up all night," Cappi recalled. "[Bernard Crowe and his people] were going to burn down buildings and kill all the girls, that's what Charlie was upset about." According to Cappi, Charlie felt backed into a corner. Spahn Ranch was essentially unguarded with little means of defence. Guns eventually made their way onto the ranch thanks to a resident biker gang, but this was shortly before that. One of the few weapons at the ranch was a communal .22 calibre longhorn revolver—the same gun that was later used by Tex during the Tate murders. With no other choice but to go and face Crowe, TJ put the revolver into his waistband and went with Charlie to Crowe's West Hollywood apartment. "That's why Charlie went to Bernard," Cappi told me, "to stop him before he killed somebody. Crowe just wanted his money."

In a bizarre exchange at Manson's original trial between TJ Walleman and Vincent Bugliosi, TJ testified that he and Manson got into a 1958 Ford with the .22 calibre revolver and drove to Franklin Avenue in Hollywood to rescue Rosina (who was not named at trial, only referred to as "the girl"). TJ further testified that once they arrived, he grabbed the revolver out of the car and gave it to Charlie before they walked toward Bernard Crowe's apartment. Vincent Bugliosi followed this account up by asking, "Did you ever see the revolver in a particular building out at the Spahn Ranch?"

"No," TJ replied.

"No further questions," Bugliosi told the court. The exchange was bizarre because Bugliosi was so fixated on tying the gun used at the Tate murders to Manson that he never asked about the fate of "the girl." When court let out on that day, reporters bombarded attorneys with questions, shocked and confused as to why no one seemed concerned about what happened inside the apartment. On the steps of the courthouse attorneys deflected questions, while TJ told a throng of reporters that prosectors were uninterested in the whole story. He explained, "They know I could never make Charlie out as a bad man…he isn't one."

In a calculating move, at Tex Watson's ensuing trial, the prosecution lobbied the court to make the full incident with Bernard Crowe admissible. They wanted to challenge Tex's depiction of himself as upstanding, clean-cut, and under Manson's control. The prosecution argued that the Bernard Crowe incident demonstrated Tex was acting of his own volition, telling the judge, "around the time of the murders, [Tex is] thinking clearly; he is acting deceptively."

When Manson and TJ arrived at the apartment on July 1, 1969, they had no idea where Tex was but felt something had to be done to rectify the situation. TJ stayed outside, while Charlie went in and confronted Crowe. According to Charlie he defended Tex, telling Crowe that Tex didn't steal his money, even though Charlie actually suspected otherwise. With Tex not there to defend himself, Rosina held firm on her lie, putting all the blame on Tex and Charlie. "She was telling Crowe that we took her money, and that we wouldn't pay her," Charlie recalled.

The confrontation continued to escalate, and Charlie drew the revolver, pointing it at Crowe. Crowe said to Charlie, "You better shoot me now. Do it! Do it!" In response to Crowe's dare, Charlie squeezed the trigger. Crowe was hit in the stomach and fell backwards, shocked that Charlie had actually shot him. The bullet cut straight through Crowe's stomach and lodged in his spine. With fluid pouring from the .22 calibre hole in his belly, Crowe screamed in pain, but he quickly realized that Charlie was still standing over him with the gun and played dead. After Crowe was shot, Rosina began screaming. She was so shocked that Charlie had seemingly killed Crowe, she gave up portraying herself as the victim. Charlie recalled seeing this transformation and realizing that she was playing both sides. "I ended up shooting him to help her," Charlie told me. "It wasn't [Crowe] that was doing it, it was her. She was faking on both of us."

Charlie immediately left the apartment, grabbed TJ, jumped in the car, and sped back toward the ranch. Crowe revealed to Rosina that he was in fact alive and made his way to the hospital. He survived the gunshot with no long-lasting repercussions.

When Charlie and TJ got back to the ranch they were in a panic, thinking Manson had just killed someone. They told the rest of the group that Tex had burned Bernard Crowe, who was a Black Panther drug dealer, and Charlie had cleaned up the mess by killing Crowe.

In the alternate theory, Charles Manson shooting Bernard Crowe left him with two problems. First, he had to be sure that no one in the commune would rat him out for the murder he believed he had committed. The group interacted with the police often, and any one of them could use the knowledge that Manson had killed Crowe as leverage, if they really had to. To try to lessen the likelihood of this, Charlie began to encourage commune members to commit violent crimes for the group, just like he had done. Charlie hinted at this idea to me many times saying, "If somebody's willing to put their life on the line for something, if they stand up for something, then they represent that."

Bobby recalled these conversations happening frequently. "[Charlie] wanted to get more people involved, like Leslie, who he saw as a loose cannon. In Charlie's mind, she was a weak link. He wanted to get her and others complicit so they couldn't snitch on him."

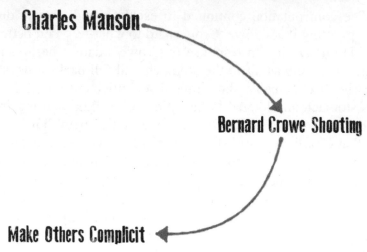

According to Bobby, this basic premise would be crystal clear for anyone who has spent time in prison. Charlie had learned his morality from behind bars since he was nine years old. People were either with him or against him, and if you were with him you better be willing to get into the fight to prove you wouldn't sell him out by snitching. "He wanted them to get their hands dirty," Bobby told me.

This idea made sense to me, but I knew I needed to ask Charlie about it directly. The next time he called I brought it up. We talked about the Bernard Crowe shooting and what position that left him in, prior to the Tate-LaBianca murders. "Bobby told me that everyone needed to get their hands dirty," I said.

"That's it!" Charlie replied enthusiastically. "Everybody needed to get things straightened around for themselves."

This was a breakthrough in establishing the true motivations for the murders. Charlie had been essentially telling me this in his own way, but, until then, I hadn't put it together.

"I play cards," Charlie said. "My whole family was different cards. In other words, everybody in my family was a card. My family was righteous, but they couldn't get away. Now, everyone in my family is dead, they're dead like me."

Manson's second problem was his belief that the Black Panthers would retaliate for the murder of Bernard Crowe. To this end, Charlie explained to me, "That's the difference between the underworld and being righteous with the underworld. In other words, you don't get

112

caught off base or you get tagged out. It's a simple game. They throw the ball; if you hit it you get to move. That's the underworld right there, man."

In a supplementary report from the Los Angeles Sheriff's Office dated May 5, 1970, a young woman named Ella Jo Bailey corroborated Manson's account. Ella Jo was a bright-eyed, curly-haired brunette who was an early member of the group and living at Spahn Ranch during this time. In her statement to the Los Angeles Sheriff's Office she claimed that in the first part of 1969, "Charles Manson talked about killing a Black Panther by shooting him over a narcotics transaction." Ella Jo continued to say that, "Negroes were seen around the Spahn Ranch area and Charles Manson started collecting guns and talking about killing." Barbara Hoyt recalled that time vividly, saying the group took a dark turn once it was believed that Charlie had killed Bernard Crowe. Barbara told me, "He was very worried about the Black Panthers attacking the ranch. It went from happy-go-lucky fun to intense and fearful." Barbara paused, her demeanour visibly changing. "It makes me nervous just to talk about it," she said.

Manson's fear of a Black Panther retaliation is the next step in the alternate theory, and it is the impetus for the next key event.

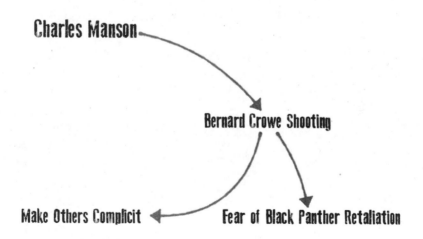

To protect the commune and himself from the Black Panthers, Manson enlisted a motorcycle club called the Straight Satans. In an interview with the LAPD from 1969, the then-president of the Straight Satans, a man named Al Springer, recalled meeting with Charlie and being offered a deal. According to Springer, Charlie said, "Move up here you can have all the girls you want, and all the girls, they are all yours." The Satans readily accepted and began living at Spahn Ranch along with the rest of the commune.

After Charlie recruited the Straight Satans, the commune was on high alert for the impending retaliation. It was then that Bobby Beausoleil committed the first Manson Family murder. The prosecution later claimed that Charles Manson ordered Bobby to rob and kill Gary Hinman because Charlie "needed money," but the specifics of this motive were never fully explained, only generally tied to Manson's preparation for a race war.

Bobby has long maintained that the truth is something else entirely. He told me emphatically, "Nobody sent me over to recruit Gary."

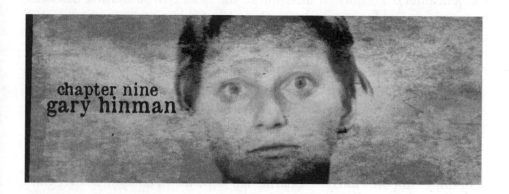

chapter nine
gary hinman

# Gary Hinman

*"Sadie and I were both in the kitchen. She said something about it. She said something to let me know we were going to kill him tonight."*
*- Mary Brunner, 1970, describing the decision to murder Gary Hinman.*

At the time of the Bernard Crowe shooting, Bobby was living in a studio apartment located in the basement of a house in Laurel Canyon, along with his pregnant seventeen-year-old girlfriend named Kitty. Bobby was a good-looking, self-confident kid who often wore a top hat and a cape. The sudden presence of the Straight Satans at Spahn Ranch was a welcome development for Bobby as he was in the process of rebuilding a motorcycle. "I had done a lot of things with cars and trucks. I was a hot-rodder from the time I was a little kid, but bikes were something new, to an extent," Bobby recalled. As a wannabe biker, Bobby valued the chance to get in with the Satans, and he spent more time at the ranch. "I was trying to find parts and learn about motorcycles from people who really knew about them," he told me.

Bobby tread carefully with the bikers, trying to make himself look a lot cooler than he actually was. The bikers would sit around the saloon trying to find shade. It was a futile attempt at escaping the Los Angeles heat wave of 1969 (given that they also had a tendency to wear black leather). To quench their thirst, the Satans would drink discount beer, which Bobby attempted to choke down just to fit in. "It was the cheapest shit they could buy," Bobby said laughing, "and they would drink it by the case."

Bobby knew why the Straight Satans had suddenly become a fixture of the ranch. It was obvious that Charlie was unravelling, suddenly full of paranoia and fear. Charlie constantly spoke about being attacked by the Black Panthers and the need to protect the group from whatever was coming. "He was so paranoid that there was going to be retaliation from Crowe's people," Bobby recalled. "That's really what sent things into this *tailspin*. Charlie had gone into a tailspin, so everyone else went down the drain with him."

Cappi echoed this sentiment. "He was worried about us getting killed. We had babies at the ranch, all these young people, and they were trying to kill us. It got very serious. I'm telling you. You don't know how scared you have to be, to be up all night, watching every car that comes down the road."

By mid-July, Charlie was convinced that an attack from the Black Panthers was imminent and asked Bobby to stay at the ranch full-time to fight off the attack. "I was a young kid and that sort of appealed to my ego," Bobby told me. "To be asked to be one of the fellas, you know. So, I brought Kitty out and we stayed at the ranch."

This brings us to the next event in the alternate theory. Two weeks before the Tate-LaBianca murders, Bobby overheard the Straight Satans looking to score drugs for an upcoming party. Wanting to prove himself, Bobby told them that he could get what they needed from his friend Gary Hinman. This event is called the Bobby Beausoleil drug deal.

Like Bobby, Gary was part of the scene in Topanga Canyon and became friendly with many people in the Manson group when they moved to Spahn Ranch. Gary was known to hang out with the girls and offer up his apartment if someone needed a place to crash. Both Bobby and Mary had lived with Gary for short periods of time. Bobby even continued to use Gary's address. When the police searched Gary's house after his murder, they found some of Bobby's mail lying around.

According to Bobby, Gary wasn't some sort of big-time narcotics trafficker, but he could get drugs when needed. "He used to sell pot from time to time," Bobby said. "He'd even given it to [people in the group] early on." Aside from weed, Bobby knew Gary had experience with mescaline, which Bobby offered to acquire for the Straight Satans. The

Satans readily agreed and asked Bobby if he could score them a thousand dollars' worth. Thinking this would endear him to the outlaw biker gang, Bobby told them he could get the drugs, no problem.

In a

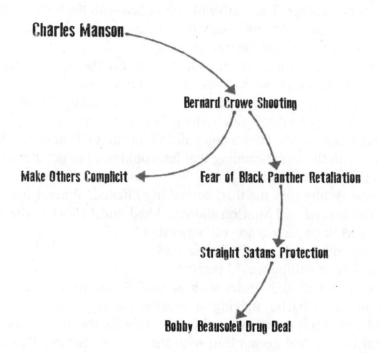

Charles Manson

Bernard Crowe Shooting

Make Others Complicit ← Fear of Black Panther Retaliation

Straight Satans Protection

Bobby Beausoleil Drug Deal

supplemental police report from the Hinman murder investigation, the investigators noted that "a homemade scale was observed in a kitchen cupboard containing a white powder on one pan. The pan and the powder were taken for examination." The powder tested negative for narcotics; however, mescaline is a naturally occurring hallucinogen and not one of the twelve drug classes (or panels) in the standard forensic drug test. Without knowing what test was used by investigators—it's not documented—it's entirely possible that the powder was mescaline, which would corroborate Bobby's account.

Bobby maintained that he had indeed gotten the mescaline from Gary, sold it to the Straight Satans for a thousand dollars, and thought that would be the end of things. He didn't realize he had actually gotten himself in way over his head. The next day the Satans rolled up to Spahn Ranch, told Bobby the mescaline had made them all sick, and demanded their money back. Being an incompetent drug dealer, Bobby had given all the money to Gary to prepare the drugs. This was an explanation that the Satans didn't accept. The confrontation ended with the Satans telling Bobby that he would get their money back or they would kill him.

Bobby agreed to get the money back.

Bobby told me that in retrospect it's clear the Satans realized early on that he was a stupid kid who looked up to them, and they used that to their advantage. "They were playing me for a sucker," Bobby said. "There wasn't any bad drugs or anything like that. They were trying to get the drugs for free." This insight didn't occur to Bobby in 1969, leaving him with the understanding that he would need to get the money back from Gary or be killed.

When Bobby told me this, something clicked. When I had first spoken to Bobby and told Manson about it, I had said, "Hey Charlie, I've been talking to Bobby a lot, do you remember him?"

"I remember him, yes," Charlie said.

"He's been calling me," I replied.

"Yeah he would, he rides with Satan." At the time, I wrote this comment off as Charlie making a bizarre metaphor that I didn't understand, but in this context it made sense. Charlie was referencing the trouble that Bobby had gotten into with the Straight Satans. Realizing this, I felt like I was on the right track.

The next time I spoke to Charlie, I was able to ask him about this more directly. "Bobby told me that he was in trouble with the Straight Satans. Is that true?"

"Yeah man," Charlie said. "He was in trouble with a motorcycle gang. We were all just wheeling and dealing in the underworld, man." According to Charlie, he knew what the Straight Satans were when he invited them to the ranch. They protected the ranch, but that didn't mean they were going to stop being an outlaw motorcycle gang, doing all the underworld shit they had always done. Charlie provided the girls, but if the Satans still wanted to be involved with guns, drugs, or raising hell, Charlie wasn't going to say anything. "That's what motorcycle gangs do," Charlie said. "In other words, the strongest survive." If they wanted to get drugs from Bobby or anyone else, that was their business.

On Friday July 25, 1969, Bobby planned to go over to Gary's house in the hopes of retrieving the money and returning it to the Straight Satans. As Bobby was leaving the ranch, Mary and Sadie asked to come along. "I took Mary because she had a relationship with Gary," Bobby told me, "and I don't remember why Susan Atkins came along."

At the time, Bobby thought there would be absolutely no issue going over to Gary's and explaining the situation. "I figured it was going to be no problem," Bobby recalled. "I'd get the money back and come back and give it to the Straight Satans and it would be done."

According to Mary's first statement to the Los Angeles Sheriff's Office, which was given four months after the incident, she, Sadie (Susan Atkins), and Bobby were driven over to Gary's house by Bruce Davis, another young man staying with the group. When they arrived around midnight, Mary and Sadie knocked on the door to Gary's apartment where they were greeted by Gary and let inside. Mary claimed that once in Gary's apartment, Bobby had told them to confirm that Gary was home alone, which he was, and then Sadie was to stand in the window and light a cigarette or match to signal to Bobby to come in, which she did.

When Bobby first joined them, he and Gary exchanged pleasantries, and they all talked for a while—until Bobby broached the subject of money. According to Mary's initial statement to investigators, "Bobby told Gary that we needed some money, and Gary said he didn't have any then jabber, jabber, and then Bobby took out the gun." Before leaving the ranch, Bobby had armed himself with a 9mm revolver, given to him by an empathetic member of the Straight Satans.

With the gun in hand, Bobby asked Gary for the money, knowing their relationship had been altered forever. According to Bobby, returning to the Straight Satans empty-handed was not an option for him, and the gun was how he intended to demonstrate this to Gary. At the same time, Bobby's threat of violence was empty. Bobby knew killing Gary would not achieve anything, especially after a search of the house had turned up nothing. Even if the money was hidden somewhere, there was no guarantee Bobby could find it, and at that moment retrieving the money was all that mattered. Bobby needed Gary to tell him where the money was, and Gary couldn't do that if he was dead.

With the confrontation escalating, Mary and Sadie got out of the way, only to see Bobby and Gary come to blows. Their fist fight was an awkward, impromptu wrestling match in Gary's kitchen. The two men slammed into the cabinets, punching and flailing, each trying to gain control over the 9mm revolver. Instead of shooting Gary, which Bobby clearly could have done, he resorted to using the gun as a blunt instrument, hitting Gary in the head. Bobby connected a few times with the butt and slammed Gary's head into the cabinets, causing Gary to bleed down the side of his face. The struggle continued and the gun went off, filling the small room with a deafening noise. The bullet lodged in a wooden cabinet, narrowly missing everyone. In response, Gary called an immediate truce to which Bobby obliged. Both men stopped to catch their breath and come to terms with what was happening.

Bobby still had the gun but didn't have the money. It's evident that at that point they still didn't intended to murder Gary, as they collectively went about tending to the superficial wounds he'd received during the fight. Bobby asked Mary to help Gary clean up and gave the gun to Sadie for safekeeping.

With cooler heads prevailing, someone placed a phone call to Spahn Ranch. According to Mary it was Bobby. In her statement to the Los Angeles Sheriff's Office, Mary said, "I was in the kitchen all along and Bobby came back in. He had gone to the living room to make a phone call." Bobby remembers things differently, telling me that he couldn't remember who called the ranch but was certain it wasn't him.

According to Charlie, he did speak to Bobby that day. In a 1994 interview with the BBC, Charlie recalled the phone call as follows, "Bobby said, 'Charlie help me.' I said, 'alright brother, hold on. Hang on man, you can make it. I'll help you all the way.'" One of the women at the ranch who was friendly with Bobby named Leslie Van Houten, who later became implicated in the murders, was interviewed by investigators in prison in 1977. At that time, she recalled, "[Bobby, Sadie, and Mary] were there for a lot of days and they would call up and they were real scared and everything, and Charles went over there to tell him to relax."

The key takeaway is that everyone involved agrees that a phone call was made to Spahn Ranch and the message got to Charlie. In a supplementary report from the Los Angeles Sheriff's Office, Ella Jo Bailey claimed that either Squeaky or Gypsy answered the phone, reporting that, "Hinman had somehow taken the gun away from the trio and fired two shots." Whether directly or indirectly, the message got to Charlie that members of the group—his group—were in trouble, and that Gary was in control of the confrontation. The situation echoed back to the night of July 1, when Charlie had to go to Bernard Crowe's house and take matters into his own hands.

Back at the apartment, Bobby was contemplating his next move. Gary still refused to give up the money, and Bobby couldn't leave without it. It was clear that no one would be backing down any time soon. Gary remained in the kitchen alone with Sadie who was still in possession of the gun. While Bobby and Mary were distracted, Gary saw an opportunity—he reasoned with Sadie to end the standoff. Sadie stepped back to consider his offer and Gary lunged for the gun. Once again two people were wrestling around the kitchen. This time Mary ran in, jumping into the fray to help Sadie. In response to the commotion, Bobby ran back into the kitchen and joined the fight. Despite being outnumbered three to one, Gary managed to escape, running to his front door, opening it, and screaming for someone to call the police. The three tackled him, and Gary was subdued before anyone heard his cries for help. Once on the ground Gary called a second truce, to which all obliged.

After two altercations, an exhausted Bobby had reached the end of this rope. He desperately wanted to leave but felt unable to do so until he had the money. Once again, Bobby made an attempt to reason with Gary, and to his complete surprise, Gary relented. Whether out of some sort of compassion for Bobby's situation or desperation to get Bobby and the girls to leave, Hinman offered to sign over two vehicles that were parked out front of his house—a red and white '58 Volkswagen bus and a mid-fifties white Fiat station wagon. According to Bobby, "Gary had these two old wrecks and I figured, between the two of them, they were worth maybe the grand that the Straight Satans were saying I owed them."

While Gary was signing over the papers, Charlie and Bruce Davis were pulling up to the house under the impression that Bobby, Sadie, and Mary were in trouble and needed help. According to statements made by Bruce Davis at a 2014 parole hearing, he was unaware of the specifics of the drug debt and was only told that the goal of the entire operation was to retrieve "some money" from Gary. Unbeknownst to Charlie and Bruce, the problem had come to a rough but acceptable resolution and the three were finally leaving. When Charlie arrived, he went up to the house in a rage, armed with a vintage confederate sword that he was known to carry around the ranch. While Charlie rushed toward the front door, Bruce stood back, armed with a handgun should the situation escalate beyond Charlie's control.

According to Bobby, "[Charlie] he didn't bust in, Gary opened the door and said, 'Hi Charlie,' and the first thing Charlie did was slash Gary across the face." The slash that Charlie inflicted was a five-inch gash cutting through Gary's left cheek, leaving his ear hanging, nearly severed.

Speaking to Bobby, he recalled this turn of events vividly. It was a moment that decided the course of his life—one that he had revisited for decades. "Charlie had come over to Gary's house thinking that his girls were in trouble. He slashed Gary's face thinking that Gary had the gun and was in control of the situation, but he wasn't. Charlie went there to try and save the day, just like what he had done with Bernard Crowe, when he went to clean up the problem that Tex Watson had created. In Charlie's mind, I was completely incompetent, just a kid, and he had to go in and fix things." But Bobby had already fixed things, at least without anyone being killed, and he was on his way out. Charlie's actions changed everything.

Mary Brunner later testified to the aftermath of this event. "Charlie just stood there looking. He looked like he wasn't sure what had just happened. And, Sadie was all freaked out (because Sadie always had a heavy thing for Charlie). So, I said to Bruce and Charlie, 'Just go. Just go, and I will do everything, I can take care of this situation.'"[7]

Bruce and Charlie left as quickly as they had arrived, which left Bobby, Sadie, and Mary to deal with a severely injured Gary. The cut was deep and painful, and Gary's face became covered in the blood pouring from his ear into his mouth.

Panic set in.

Gary demanded to be taken to the hospital, which didn't seem like an option to the three people who had essentially held him captive and were now party to his severe injury. Hospitals would mean questions, which would lead to police.

The girls managed to calm Gary down and promised to tend to his wounds. Mary was able to construct a makeshift bandage that seemed to stop the bleeding. Bobby still had the gun, which ensured that Gary stayed in the house while they contemplated their next move. The girls

---

[7] State of California v Manson, 60, Cal Supp. 10,159 (1971, October 15).

looked to Bobby for answers and he had none. At twenty-one years of age, his life threatened by a biker gang, and the situation continuing to escalate, Bobby was well beyond his ability to reason sensibly and desperate to regain some semblance of control.

Hours had passed since the three had arrived at Gary's house, and, as the sun broke over Topanga Canyon, they collectively decided they needed to sleep. They convinced an exhausted Gary to sleep on the floor in the corner of the living room, while Bobby settled into an armchair with a good view of the room. Mary and Sadie set up camp nearby, and the three took turns staying awake to watch Gary.

It's worth noting that they still had the means to kill Gary at any point but chose not to. In fact, by the next morning, Bobby, Mary, and Sadie still held out hope that they could leave Gary amicably. They reasoned amongst themselves that if they could just stay long enough for Gary to calm down and for his wound to clot, they could all agree that the injury was less severe than originally believed, and something could be worked out.

Bobby, Sadie, and Mary spent Saturday with Gary in his apartment periodically checking his wounds, which were not getting any better. By Sunday morning it was clear that the five-inch-long, one-inch-deep cut was getting worse, prompting them to take action. Once again, killing Gary was not in the cards at this point. The actions the three took next clearly indicate that they earnestly wanted Gary to recover so they could leave.

Sadie went to the grocery store for supplies. She bought food, bandages, and ice. When she returned, Mary created a makeshift suture kit using a sewing needle and dental floss. Before she began to sew up Gary's cut, she cleaned the wound with tap water and was happy to see that the bleeding had subsided. Mary began her bizarre attempt at stitching Gary's face with dental floss, but halfway through she loosened a large clot, which caused blood to gush from his face with more intensity than before. This stopped the operation, and Mary used the fresh bandages to cover up the now seeping wound as best she could.

As they waited for Gary's wound to heal throughout Sunday, Gary's social life continued without him. Gary was supposed to play bagpipes in a Buddhist parade, and when he was a no-show, friends became concerned. One of them called Gary's apartment looking for him, but Sadie answered the phone feigning a bad English accent and said Gary had gone to Colorado to take care of his parents who had been in a car accident. The same friend called back later, and this time Mary took a message, assuring him that Gary would call back. At one point when someone came to the door, Sadie was able to quickly get rid of the person with the excuse that Gary wasn't home.

By Sunday evening, the group had been in the apartment for about a day and a half. Gary had grown more desolate, and their attempts to treat his wounds had only made things worse. In Bobby's mind, even if he could still use Gary's cars as some sort of repayment to the Straight Satans, Gary would surely go to the police and Bobby would go to jail. "I didn't know how to get out of it," Bobby told me sombrely. A sleep-deprived Bobby resolved that he was out of options, deciding there was only one thing left to do—Gary had to die. "I didn't know how to get away without getting arrested. Unless I killed him," Bobby told me, his voice wavering.

"This was not something that was gleeful," Bobby remembered. "Charlie had insinuated himself in the situation between me and Gary and the Straight Satans and then left me with this problem. I wasn't there to do anyone any harm, but my desperation to get out of it—that was essentially the motive for killing Gary. The reason I killed him was to try to extricate myself from this problem that had been created by Charlie having slashed him across the face."

The plan was this: first they would kill Gary, preventing him from going to the police; next, they would stage the crime scene to make it look like someone else had done it. The most obvious choice was the Black Panthers. The Spahn Ranch commune was still under the belief that Charlie had killed Bernard Crowe, so the Black Panthers remained their biggest fear and their chief enemy. According to Bobby, "It was in everyone's mind. Everybody believed that Charlie had killed a Black Panther. Those guys were the enemy then. They were symbolic of the fear of retaliation."

In Bobby's mind, Gary's death at the hands of the Black Panthers would not be completely unbelievable. "Gary was a political science major, so he was socializing with a lot of people at UCLA who would have been considered radical at that time. Not that he was a radical himself or anything like that," Bobby told me. After Gary was dead, Bobby planned to give the two cars to the Straight Satans to satisfy his debt, then get out of town until the heat died down.

On Sunday evening, Mary prepared dinner and they all ate. After they finished, Mary did the dishes while Sadie and Bobby went into the living room to deal with Gary. Gary's death was not frantic; it was almost surgical. Bobby stabbed him twice—two plunging stab wounds to the heart. As Gary's punctured heart pumped blood into his chest cavity, he chanted a personal mantra and lay slowly dying in his living room. Bobby covered him with a blanket and paced around the apartment. The girls started to carefully collect all their garbage, blankets, towels, and anything else that could tie them to the crime. They used rags to wipe down all the surfaces. Gary began choking and breathing loudly. Bobby called to Sadie and Mary to hold a pillow over Gary's face to muffle the sounds, ultimately suffocating him. Mary took a turn with the pillow and then continued to clean, while Sadie held the pillow over Gary's face as he took his final breath.

The chain of events is one that Bobby still reflects on to this day. "It was foolish," Bobby recalled. "I was out of my depth, man. There was no way that I could see to get out of there without going to prison or worse." Bobby paused, talking to me from a communal phone in the California prison where he has been since 1969. After a moment, he said plainly, "That was not a good enough reason. I should have taken him to the hospital. I would have done some time, but nothing like this."

After Gary was dead, it was time to stage the crime scene. Bobby took Gary's blanket and grabbed the pillow off his face. The pillow and blanket were still fresh with Gary's blood. He propped the pillow against the wall and, above the pillow, used the blanket to write "POLITICAL PIGGY" in Gary's blood. Bobby dipped his hand in blood and used it to draw a Black Panther paw print beside the message. I asked Bobby about this moment. I wanted to understand his decision to turn the crime scene into a real-life horror movie by decorating the walls in blood. Bobby was careful with his words. "I don't remember it to be honest with you. I don't remember a lot of what happened immediately after I killed Gary. That really devastated me," Bobby said. "My memories of what happened afterwards have never been clear. I'm not saying that it wasn't me. I remember everything up to the point of stabbing Gary. I was emotionally unable to really connect in a rational way with what was happening." With that caveat, Bobby was clear about the intent to frame the Black Panthers for Gary's death. "It was in everyone's mind," said Bobby. "There was a concerted effort to throw off the police and make it look like someone else had done it."

From this perspective, the Gary Hinman murder was directly related to the Bernard Crowe shooting. Bobby staged the crime scene in an attempt to frame the Black Panthers because the entire commune feared retaliation. At the same time, Manson's aim to make the others complicit had been unexpectedly furthered. Another violent crime they were all in together prevented members of the group from telling the

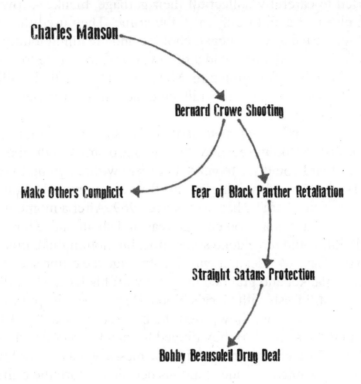

police about what Manson had done.

The decision to draw the Black Panther paw print would come to haunt Bobby. Despite carefully wiping down the fingerprints in the apartment, Bobby's palm print was preserved in the message on the wall. This was later identified by the forensics team of the Los Angeles Sheriff's Department, about two weeks after the murder.

Four days after Gary was murdered, two of his friends came to his house after they were unable to get ahold of him for a week. When they arrived at his apartment, they noticed his cars were missing and

126

knocked on his front door. At that point, they were overwhelmed by the smell of a decaying body and called the Sheriff's Department. When investigators went inside the apartment, they saw the aftermath of Gary's murder, issuing an All Points Bulletin for his cars.

In the meantime, Bobby had returned to the ranch and was planning to leave town. According to Bobby, he was in shock and said little to anyone. When I asked him what, if anything, he told Charlie, he said they barely spoke, but he did remember one brief exchange. "I remember this, because it really hit me hard. Charlie said, 'How does it feel to kill your brother?'" When Bobby told me this it triggered a memory of something Charlie had said, when I first mentioned Bobby to him. In reference to the murders, Charlie had said, "Bobby was the brother in that episode, he was staying with us, we were driving his truck." It light of Bobby's account, I was able to unlock another of Charlie's riddles. Bobby *was* the brother. Charlie meant Bobby was not just Charlie's brother; Bobby was Gary's brother, too. Bobby had killed his friend to save himself. Charlie and the group were driving Bobby's truck, because Bobby had given them the '58 Volkswagen bus that he took from Gary so they could give it to the Straight Satans. Bobby took the Fiat and skipped town.

On August 6, 1969, ten days after Gary's murder, Bobby was headed north and had made it as far as San Luis Obispo, about 175 miles from Spahn Ranch. At 10:50 a.m., a police officer was on a routine patrol and saw Gary's Fiat station wagon parked by the side of the road. When he approached the car, Bobby sat up in a sleeping bag, telling the officer that the car had broken down overnight and he'd become stranded. Bobby identified himself as "Jason Lee Daniels" and explained that he had left his ID at home. The suspicious officer called in the licence plate, which quickly came back as being wanted in connection with an unsolved murder. Bobby was taken into custody and identified as Bobby Beausoleil.

Bobby told investigators that the week before, he and two women had hitchhiked to Gary's apartment (Bobby declined to name the women in his initial statement). When they arrived, they let themselves in and found a distraught Gary in the bathroom bleeding heavily, having suffered a deep cut to the side of his face. According to Bobby's statement, Gary had told them that two black men jumped him over a political disagreement. Bobby stated that he'd told Gary to lie down and covered him with a blanket while attempting to sew the wound shut with a needle and dental floss. After that, Bobby claimed that he and the two women stayed overnight with Gary out of concern. Bobby said they had left Gary the next day, as Gary told them he was leaving on a trip to Colorado. Police had already discovered that Gary had purchased tickets to Japan for the following week and had told no one of any plans to go to Colorado. Bobby was unable to explain the descrepancy and claimed that Gary had given him his car for an unknown reason.

After speaking with Bobby for twenty minutes, the Sheriff's Department charged him with first-degree murder.

Bobby's arrest hit everyone at the ranch hard. According to Barbara Hoyt everyone was talking about it. Barbara recalled, "I heard he got arrested for murder, I thought that the police had just made it up. I didn't believe it."

Bobby's arrest in San Luis Obispo on Wednesday, August 6 is a key moment because it set forth a series of events that culminated in the Tate-LaBianca murders only a few days later. It took the authorities most of the day on Wednesday to take Bobby into custody, find out who he was, charge him with murder, and have Gary's car towed. That evening, authorities searched the car and briefly interrogated Bobby.

On Thursday, August 7, Bobby was transported back to Los Angeles for his initial court appearance. On Friday, August 8, Bobby was arraigned in the morning. His bail was denied, with a preliminary hearing set for a week later on Friday, August 14.

It's not a coincidence that the day Bobby Beausoleil was arraigned is the same day the group committed additional murders. Sharon Tate and those who were at her home were killed less than twenty-four hours after Bobby's first court appearance.

In the alternate theory, on August 8, the group planned to kill someone and stage the crime scene to make it appear as if Gary Hinman's killer was still on the loose. They reasoned this would compel the police to let Bobby go. When I confronted Charlie with this rationale, he admitted to me that it had been their thinking. "[Bobby] was in prison. He was in the LA County Jail when it happened," Charlie said, referring to the murders. "See we were all in a brotherhood. We were all in one family, and we were helping our brother. It happened to be Beausoleil."

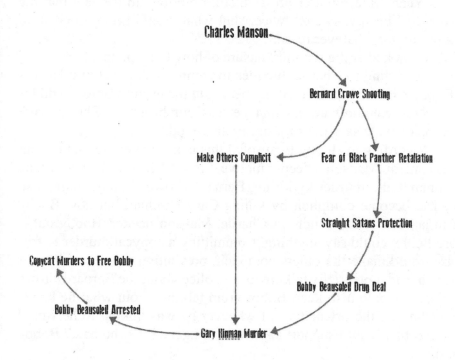

According to Bobby, Charlie admitted the same thing to him while they were both in the county jail after Charlie was also arrested. "He told other people he was trying to send a message to me. To make the police think that they had the wrong person," Bobby told me.

In retrospect, it seems like this motive was hiding in plain sight. It was well-known to the other members of the group. In a 1970 interview with TJ Walleman during the trial, he had the following exchange with a local TV news reporter. The reporter asked, "Why do you think these killings took place in the first place?"

TJ replied, "Oh, you mean to get Bobby out?"

"No, no, I mean why would they go in and kill a whole slew of people over two nights, why did that take place. No one seems to be able to answer that question," the reporter continued to ask, ignoring the fact that TJ had answered the question.

"The girls said they did it for the reason of copycat killings to get Bobby out," TJ said plainly.

"Yeah," the reporter pressed, still oblivious to the fact that the question had been answered twice, "but what would bring a person to kill a person for whatever reason?"

TJ looked at the reporter, unsure of how to respond.

According to Charlie, the idea to commit a copycat murder was not Bobby's idea; it was something people in the group wanted to do for Bobby. "He wouldn't accept that he was our brother," Charlie said. "Everybody made sacrifices for our brotherhood."

According to Bobby Beausoleil this is not the entire picture, but it does reaffirm Manson's deeper motive. From Charlie's perspective, he had committed a murder by killing Bernard Crowe. Bobby, Sadie, and Mary had become complicit by killing Gary Hinman, but now Bobby was in jail and could snitch on Charlie. Manson needed Bobby out— before Bobby could say anything. Committing a copycat murder to free Bobby would make the others complicit, preventing more members of the group from potentially talking to the police about the Bernard Crowe shooting. It would also keep Bobby from talking about what he knew. "Depending on the orientation of whoever he was talking to he would say things that would support some sort of agenda that he had," Bobby told me.

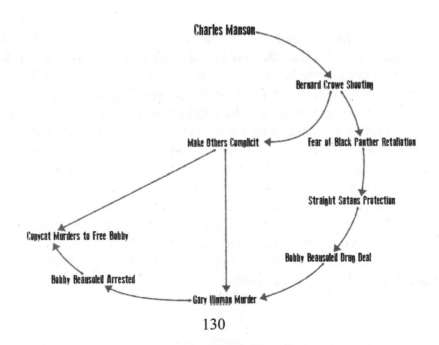

Manson's agenda comes full circle when you consider that he still harboured a grudge against Terry Melcher for the song Manson had contributed to The Beach Boys' album. "He played on that," Bobby said, "then eventually he called in the favour, which was to go to Terry elcher's house and kill Terry Melcher and whoever else might be there."

In Susan Atkins' 1969 recorded interview with her attorney she said, "We know Terry very well. The reason Charlie picked that house was to instill fear into Terry Melcher, because Terry had given his word on a few things and never came through with them. So, Charlie wanted to put some fear into him, let him know that what Charlie said was the way it is." It's worth noting that in this interview, which was Susan Atkins' earliest full account of the murders, there is no mention of The Beatles or an impending race war.

According to the alternate theory, the image below explains why four members of the commune ventured out to Terry Melcher's house two days after Bobby Beausoleil's arrest—on August 8, 1969.

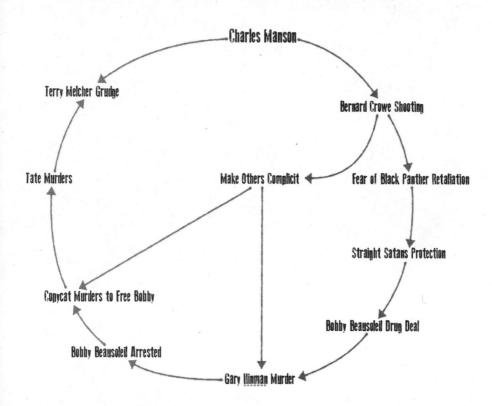

# August 8, 1969

*"I heard about the Gary Hinman murder. I couldn't believe it
happened you know. I just couldn't believe it, and here I was four or
five days later doing the same thing."*
*- Charles "Tex" Watson, 2016, Parole Hearing*

On the afternoon of August 8, two more members of the
commune went to jail—Mary Brunner, the mother of Charlie's child, and
Sandra (Sandy) Good. They were arrested together at a Sears in San
Fernando for allegedly using stolen credit cards. The group now had
three people in the LA County Jail, and any one of those people could
trade what they knew about Bernard Crowe and/or Gary Hinman to help
themselves. According to Charlie, those in jail and those still at the ranch
were all a liability, with the exception of Mary. "There's no women that
won't rat on people; you won't find too many of them. Mary's one that
won't rat on you," Charlie told me.

This still left some urgency in getting Sandy—and most
importantly Bobby—out of prison. This would require bail money, and
in Bobby's case, evidence of his innocence. On the night of August 8,
1969, a decision was made to take action. Barbara Hoyt recalled seeing
Charlie speaking with Tex. "I remember it was after dinner in the back
house, and Charlie and Tex were talking in the corner. It was like there
was a black cloud all around them. It was just like evil around them."
Barbara shivered recalling the scene. She paused, lost in her thoughts.

Though not involved in the murders, the sights and sounds of August 8 stuck with her throughout her life.

By that evening, Bobby had been in the county jail for two days, so he was not privy to what was said between Charlie and Tex. Bobby explained, "I was in jail when the murders happened, but I was there after the Bernard Crowe shooting and heard [Charlie] say to Tex on a number of occasions, 'You owe me.'" Bobby recalled that Tex and Charlie's relationship was one of exploitation. "Charlie saw something in Tex," Bobby said. "He saw that Tex was foolish; he saw that Tex could be manipulated." According to Bobby, "Charlie really worked on [Tex] to get him to be his minion in a way, to get him to submit. The first thing Tex did when he came to prison was to give up Charlie and replace him with Jesus. He had this messianic need, and Charlie played into that."

Bobby and I spoke about numerous interactions he witnessed between Charlie and Tex, interactions that continually demonstrated Charlie pushing Tex to see how far he would go. Bobby said, "Charlie knew that Tex was a weak link. He was really the only guy who would have gone out and killed for Charlie. *The only one.*"

I asked Charlie about Tex, but at first his answer was cryptic. Charlie said, "Tex is perfect. A soldier who's in service is righteous and real. There's no in-between." Charlie ended this statement by saying, "Semper Fi!" the motto of the US Marine Corps, which means "always faithful."

*Is Charlie saying that Tex was his soldier?* I thought. *Always faithful to what? Is Charlie just fucking with me?*

Charlie always had an odd affinity for the military. He called everyone "soldier" (including me) and dropped in militaristic references from time to time. I always thought this was strange considering Charlie was staunchly critical of the government, and the major principle of his era was opposition to the Vietnam War. With that in mind, the concept of loyalty was still of the utmost importance to Charlie. In prison, he'd learned that you don't break your word, you don't snitch, and you don't talk out of school. I suppose loyalty and respect for the chain of command are aspects of the military that resonated with Manson. As far as Charlie was concerned, the conversation he had with Tex on the evening of August 8 would stay between them.

Tex did not share Charlie's principles. Three years later, in 1971, Tex testified on his own behalf that Charlie gave him explicit instructions to go to the house on Cielo Drive and kill everyone inside. As recalled by Tex on the witness stand, Charlie said, "Make sure everybody is dead, as gruesome as you can." Tex went on to say that he believed Charlie had mentioned something about a movie star being at the house. This rather important detail was one Tex only seemed to remember once he was on the witness stand facing the death penalty—with a defence consisting of, Charlie made me do it.

Tex's account in his 1978 book *Will You Die For Me* is quite different. He corroborates that Charlie brought up the Bernard Crowe shooting and the idea that Tex owed him as a result—something he did not mention at his own trial. As opposed to the general instructions Tex recalled in 1971, in 1978 he quoted Charlie as giving very explicit instructions to murder and rob all the occupants of Terry Melcher's house. Tex also remembered Charlie telling him that the reason for committing a copycat murder was to get Bobby out of prison.

At a 2016 parole hearing, Tex further clarified this interaction saying, "I was in the back ranch house kind of in the back there, and I was actually with Leslie Van Houten at that time and other people were around and laying around and stuff. And Manson came and got me and walked me up to the main ranch and said that, you know, 'you owe me,' you know, for taking care of a drug deal that had went wrong with my ex-girlfriend Rosina in Hollywood there…[Manson said] 'I cleaned that up for you and therefore, you got to take care of this for me.'" In contradiction to many of his own statements about Manson's explicit instructions on the night of August 8, 1969, at the same 2016 parole hearing, Tex claimed that Manson didn't tell him to kill anyone. Tex told the parole board that, "[Manson] he told me that he had already instructed the girls what to do. I'd been taking methamphetamine for about—or speed I think we called it back then—for about thirty days, and I knew I couldn't do what he was asking me to do unless I took some of that. So, Susan Atkins and I went and started some methamphetamine and got in the car."

It should be noted that during his trial, Tex frequently minimized his involvement in the murders. He testified that Linda Kasabian, another commune member, drove them to the house on Cielo Drive and gave instructions while he slept in the backseat. He was unable to explain how she found the house, since Tex was the only one in the car who had been there on previous occasions. He also claimed that one of the girls was the leader of the murder party—though he couldn't recall which one—and that he was a secondary and reluctant participant in the stabbings. This account not only contradicted all the other witnesses, but also Tex's own account of the murders, which he'd previously given to court-ordered psychiatrists prior to trial. Tex also testified in great detail about his feelings of being under the spell of Charlie's active mind control while killing people, but then claimed that he couldn't remember many of the gruesome details because he was so high.

I pushed Charlie to tell me more about what he said to Tex that night, without success. The closest I came was Charlie explaining that everybody—including Tex—is for themselves.

"You are for you, right?" Charlie asked me.

"Yeah," I replied.

"You are for you, and I am for me. I'm for Charlie," he said definitively.

Bobby recalled conversations with Charlie from shortly after the murders—both Bobby and Charlie were in the custody of the LA County Sheriff's Department being transferred back and forth from jail to the courthouse. Bobby told me, "I met up with Charlie a couple of times in the holding tank while we were going to court on the same days, so I had these conversations with him, and his intentions were clear." Bobby's account of these conversations is extremely significant; unlike a parole hearing or interview years or decades after the fact, what Charlie said to Bobby in the holding tanks was Charlie's unvarnished take, within months of the murders. "His intention in sending Tex Watson to the house on Cielo Drive was twofold," Bobby said. Charlie's first intention was "to make Tex get his hands dirty— make him complicit because he saw Tex as a weak link. He knew that he could not depend on Tex not to rat on him for the Bernard Crowe thing," Bobby explained. Charlie's second intention was to deal with Terry Melcher. "Terry Melcher had broken his word and that stuck in Charlie's craw," Bobby said. "And so he sent Tex to kill Terry. In my mind—and having spoken with [Charlie] subsequently—he didn't know that Terry had actually moved out of that house." Bobby was clear, "this is what [Charlie] told me."

According to Bobby, he subsequently served time with others convicted and labelled as members of the Manson Family—including Tex himself—who told him the same thing. "Killing a house full of people is not what Charlie thought was going to happen. Not that he wasn't insane and somewhat homicidal in his attitudes about life, but he thought it was going to be Terry and maybe a friend who was with him," Bobby told me.

I continued to take this back to Charlie on several occasions. He was never enthusiastic about discussing the topic of whether or not he ordered the murders. Charlie replied curtly, "I never ordered nobody to do anything other than what the fuck they wanted to do."

In a previous conversation with Michael Channels, which Michael recorded and played for me, Charlie recalled the event by saying, "I gave my life to what I thought was a brother. Every time I do that, man, I always end up on the short end of everything because I'm stupid. I can't do school books stuff. I'm a stupid hillbilly is what it boils down to."

In terms of the alternate theory, we can establish that on August 8, 1969, Charlie conspired with Tex, either directly or indirectly, to leave Spahn Ranch and commit a violent act that would make Tex complicit—and help liberate Bobby and the others. We can also establish that Tex went to 10050 Cielo Drive because that was the residence thought to be owned by Terry Melcher, against whom Charlie had a grudge.

When Tex left Spahn Ranch he was accompanied by three of the girls who were all barefoot, dressed in black, and armed with buck knives.

The first female member of the murder party was Patricia "Katie" Krenwinkel, who was one of Charlie's earliest group members and

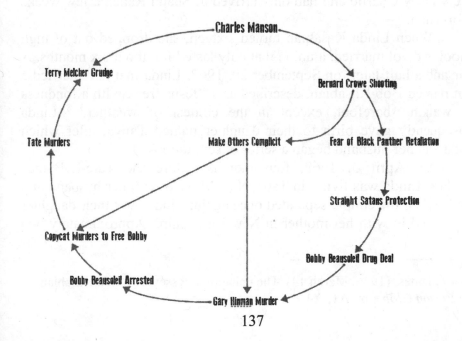

137

known to be incredibly loyal to him. There's no question that Katie's devotion to Charlie and the group made her a practical choice.

The second female member was Susan "Sadie" Atkins, who was not only present when Gary Hinman was murdered, but was also known to be one of the most erratic members of the commune. Bobby remembered Sadie as "extremely unstable." According to Bobby, Charlie often spoke about Susan being an unpredictable, wild force that needed to be tamed. "[Charlie] didn't trust her, so he involved her in everything, trying to get her where she was basically trapped," said Bobby.

Leslie Van Houten echoed this sentiment when testifying on her own behalf in 1977, saying, "Sadie was more or less the rougher of us girls—we were all almost fascinated by the thought of killing people just because, you know, we'd been taught to stay away from it and nobody knows about death—[Sadie] was almost infatuated by it. She kept the sharpening knives, getting them real sharp."

The final member of the murder party is perhaps the most significant. Along with Tex, Katie, and Sadie, a young woman named Linda Kasabian was picked. Linda was unique among the members of the murder party, a petite, plain-looking young woman not known for violence, whose loyalty to the group was questionable. Unlike Katie and Sadie, who at that time had been with Charlie for over a year, Linda barely knew Charlie and had only arrived at Spahn Ranch a few weeks beforehand.

When Linda Kasabian turned sixteen, she dropped out of high school and got married, a union that only lasted for about six months. A year and a half later, on September 20, 1967, Linda met and married a man named Bob Kasabian, described as a "Jesus freak with a fondness for walking barefoot, except in the coldest of weather." [8] Linda subsequently gave birth to their daughter named Tanya, after which Linda and her husband began a series of separations.

By April of 1969, four months before the Tate-LaBianca murders, Linda was living in Taos, New Mexico with her husband and child. When the couple separated once again, Linda took their daughter and moved in with her mother in New Hampshire. Approximately two

---

[8] Stack, James, (1976, March 14). The unhappy odyssey of Linda Kasabian. *The Boston Globe,* pp A1, A4.

months later, Bob called Linda, telling her that he had relocated to Los Angeles. He promised that if Linda and Tanya came out west, he would take them on a trip to South America, which he had planned with friends. Linda agreed and took their daughter to California. They landed in Los Angeles on June 27, 1969 and moved into a trailer with Bob and three friends.

After six days, it was apparent that Linda's west coast excursion was not going as planned. Bob told Linda that he no longer wanted her to come to South America. Linda did not want to return to her mother's house, so she began looking for a place that would take both her and her daughter. Having few friends in Los Angeles, Linda confided in a woman she'd recently met named Gypsy, who offered to bring her to Spahn Ranch.

Linda spent an afternoon meeting the people living at Spahn Ranch—with the exception of Charlie. After sunset, Linda was weighing her options when Tex walked over and put his arm around her—minutes later they were in one of the ranch houses having sex. The next morning Gypsy and Mary took Linda back to her husband's trailer to collect her daughter and her belongings. While inside the trailer, Linda stole all the money her husband and his friends had saved for their trip to South America—approximately five thousand dollars. The girls made a quick escape back to the ranch, where Linda met Charlie Manson for the first time. Linda had sex with Charlie that evening and stayed at Spahn Ranch thereafter.

Linda became a part of the commune in the midst of the chaos. She arrived less than three weeks before Gary Hinman's murder and a month before the Tate-LaBianca murders. I asked Charlie about Linda, and he said that he hardly even knew who Linda was and couldn't remember saying more than a few words to her. This is what makes Linda such an odd choice for the "mission" on August 8. Katie and Sadie were close with Charlie, having been with the group since the beginning, and the reason Tex was involved has been well-established. But why, of all the people at the ranch, would Charlie pick Linda—the twenty-year-old single mother who had just arrived?

According to the prosecution, Linda was chosen because she was one of the only ones with a valid driver's licence, and the group needed a getaway driver. At trial Linda testified, "Charlie specified later on that only the people with a driver's licence should drive the car."[9] Linda also clarified that she and Mary Brunner were the only members of the group with a valid driver's licence.

This rationale doesn't make a lot of sense considering the fact that Bobby drove Gary Hinman's vehicles without a driver's licence, Tex drove on the night in question without a driver's licence, and Charlie drove the next night to the LaBianca house without a driver's licence. If the prosecution's reasoning is true, why the group suddenly became concerned about valid documentation—on a night they intended to murder people and write on the walls in their blood—remains unexplained.

On top of this, it's not clear that Linda even had a valid driver's licence—she'd been arrested in New Hampshire three months earlier and pled guilty to operating a vehicle without a licence. Despite all this, someone picked Linda to go along that night.

In my mind, it seems most likely that Tex picked Linda, which would suggest that Tex was at least working in collaboration with Charlie, rather than being his helpless subordinate. This is consistent with the instructions that were given to the girls. In Sadie's grand jury testimony, she said, "I never recall any actual instructions from Charlie other than getting a change of clothing and a knife and was told to do exactly what Tex told me to do."

In Linda's testimony, she echoed this statement saying, "Charlie told me to go with Tex and to do what [Tex] told me to do." Sadie went on to testify that once in the car, Tex informed them they were going to the house on Cielo Drive. As Sadie recalled, "The only reason we were going there is because Tex knew the outline of the house."

At Tex's trial, Terry Melcher himself testified that after he met Manson at Dennis Wilson's house, he only saw him on two other occasions—both at Spahn Ranch. On the other hand, Melcher re-called that after he met Tex at Dennis Wilson's they became friends. Melcher even described bringing Tex to social gatherings on numerous occasions. When Terry Melcher was asked specifically about his relationship with Tex during the time period in which Terry was living at Cielo Drive, he recalled bringing Tex to the house "approximately six times."

---

This is key information because even though Manson harboured a grudge toward Terry Melcher, he was always careful not to tell people what to do. I would often ask him what he thought I should do about one thing or another, in terms of the documentary, to which he would reply, "You can do what you want to do, when you make up your mind and you decide that that's what you're going to do." On August 8, 1969, this was Charlie's trick. All the people in the car driving toward Sharon Tate's house were doing so not because Charlie had *ordered* them to do it, but because he had gotten them to *choose* to do what he wanted. They were willing participants who didn't truly know what they had signed up for. As Bobby told me, "What they volunteered to do was something they didn't understand, which was [Charlie's] need to protect himself. He manipulated them."

In a moment of self-reflection Charlie told me plainly, "nobody's anybody to me." I don't think he meant that he was a psychopath devoid of feeling. I believe he meant that he was aware he was inherently only concerned with his own survival, a view that he believed was shared by all people. "Everybody wants everybody else dead. Nobody likes anybody," he said. If Charlie's friends needed to kill a person, or multiple people, to solve a problem, it was nothing to him—that's just how the underworld worked.

When they pulled up to Cielo Drive, Tex drove past the gated entrance and parked on a hill next to a telephone pole. Tex grabbed a pair of bolt cutters that he'd found at Spahn Ranch and scurried up the pole, cutting two wires that he thought would prevent his intended victims from calling for help. After making his way back to the car, he drove the group down the hill and parked on a side street. They left the car and walked back up toward the gate. The gate was tall and electrically controlled by a button only accessible on the inside. The height of the gate was such that they couldn't climb over, but it was located next to a dirt hillside and a fence covered in barbed wire. Tex used a large coiled rope and placed it onto the barbed wire so the girls could climb over. Tex climbed over next and took the rope with him.

Once over the fence, Tex, Sadie, Linda, and Katie ran right into Steven Parent, the nineteen-year-old visitor who had briefly stopped by Cielo Drive to try and sell the groundskeeper a clock radio. Steven truly was in the wrong place at the wrong time. It's clear that Tex was the one who shot Steven four times. By all accounts, Tex was the only person that night who wielded the .22 calibre long-barrelled pistol, which Charlie had also used to shoot Bernard Crowe.

It's unclear who slashed Steven's wrist. Steven put his left hand up and received a single, deep knife slash that began between his middle and ring fingers, going down toward his thumb, and continuing through the band of his wristwatch. If Tex was the one who slashed Steven, then he had to be carrying a gun in one hand and a knife in the other.

In a brief video from Tex's 1984 parole hearing, he leaves the hearing carrying a manila folder in his left hand. When he gets to the door, he pauses to switch the folder into his right hand so he can reach across his body to pull open the door. This action is less practical and more difficult, unless Tex is more comfortable using his left hand for these kinds of body mechanics.

If Tex was holding the gun with this left hand, he would have had to slash Steven with a very awkward motion, swinging his right arm through the driver's side window. This motion would have ended with Tex standing with his arms crossed. If Tex held the gun in his non-dominant hand, he would have had an easier stabbing motion but would have had to awkwardly shoot Steven with his right hand—the same hand he wouldn't use to open a door at his parole hearing. This suggests that though Tex shot Steven, one of the girls stabbed him.

All three girls were armed with knives, but we can rule out Sadie or Katie as the one who stabbed Steven. Sadie's clearest accounts of the murder of Steven Parent are from the transcript of her conversation with her lawyer, which leaked to the media in 1970, and from her testimony to the grand jury in 1969. In both, she consistently says that she was in the bushes when Steven was killed, because when they climbed over the fence she got caught up and fell. During her grand jury testimony Susan said, "[I] held the knife between my teeth and climbed over and got my pants caught on part of the fence and had to kind of boost myself up and lift from where I was caught off of the fence, and fell into the bushes on the other side of the fence." Katie was the one who helped Sadie recover after she fell. Because of this, both Katie and Sadie were not walking up the driveway when Steven pulled up, so they didn't witness the entire exchange. This also seems to be corroborated by the fact that in all Sadie's statements, she didn't seem to be aware that Steven Parent was also stabbed—only ever referring to him as being shot.

The only one who claims to have actually witnessed Steven's death is Linda. At Tex's trial, Linda said she was standing on the driver's side of the car "just a couple feet away." This would make her the only person aside from Tex who could have stabbed Steven. By Linda's account, she was the one who reached into the car and turned off the ignition after Steven's murder.

When they walked up to the house, Tex used a knife to slit the screen of an open window. He climbed inside and let the others in through the main door. In a 1976 prison interview, Sadie recalled going into the house before the slaughter, "I remember when we first went in, one of the people said, 'who are you?' Tex said, 'I'm the devil and I'm here to do the devil's business.'"

I have always found this quote chilling. I also find it telling that Tex referred to himself in the first person, saying he was the "the devil," and the impending slaughter was his choice, "the devil's business." This suggests that Tex believed he was acting of his own free will. If he was under Manson's control, he could just have said, "I'm here to do the devil's business," or "I've been sent here to do the devil's business." Instead, Tex clearly said, "I'm the devil" as if to say, "I'm in control."

Sadie had a similar insight in her 1976 prison interview, saying, "I don't think Charles Manson's mind was in control of Tex's mind that night. Charlie's human too and his mental powers are just as limited, maybe not as limited as other humans, but there was an evil force in control of Tex that night."

Tex's chilling line of dialogue also reminded me of something Manson had told me about the murders of August 8. "Episodes like that happen every day in the underworld," Charlie had said. "There is always someone getting shot and killed for doing something, or lying about something, or playing some sort of stupid game with the devil." When Manson first said this, I assumed he meant a "game with the devil," in a metaphorical sense, as if to say someone was "playing with fire," or something to that effect. But—in light of reflecting on Tex's words—I wondered if Manson was referring to Tex specifically.

I asked Manson about this, and, even though Charlie was reluctant to open up more about the night of August 8, he did confirm my suspicions. "People think the devil doesn't exist," Charlie said. "The devil exists."

# Sharon Tate

*"I can remember seeing people scattering in different places, and running in different places, and I was left sitting with Sharon Tate. And, she was talking to me, and I remember that—I felt nothing, I felt absolutely nothing for her as she begged for her life, and for the life of her baby."*
*- Susan "Sadie" Atkins, 1976*

      Charles Manson and Sharon Tate have become synonymous with one another. Surprisingly, this was something that Charlie had given a lot of thought to. "The only reason [the murders] got all that publicity is because there was a movie star involved," Charlie told me, bitterly aware of this fact. Make no mistake, Sharon Tate is the reason that Charles Manson became infamous. The panic and outrage over her bizarre and horrific murder captured the nation's interest, putting immense pressure on the LAPD to make an arrest. When the wild-eyed hippie guru named Charles Manson was revealed to be the architect of her demise, he was catapulted into a level of infamy few ever achieve. Manson became the most infamous killer in America, his name engraved in the English language as a shorthand for evil. A man so devious he could convince others to slaughter a pregnant movie star for him.

      It's important to note that Sharon Tate wasn't just an ordinary movie star; she was an alluring, sought-after sex symbol who had been introduced to Hollywood with premeditated fanfare. At only twenty-six years old, Tate was in the midst of a meteoric rise to fame when she died. She has since been remembered with her gorgeous dark eyes, platinum blonde hair, and signature pouty lips.

Long before she was a Hollywood mainstay, Sharon was a Texas-born army brat who moved around the country with her mother and her two sisters following her father's assignments. Sharon's father, Paul Tate, was a US Army intelligence officer who retired as a Lieutenant Colonel, after twenty-three years of service. In 1963, Paul Tate was stationed in Vietnam, and Sharon was trying to grab a foothold as an actress in Hollywood. After numerous unsuccessful auditions and a few small parts, she booked what would be a defining interview with an LA producer named Marty Ransohoff.

In 1952, Marty Ransohoff had cobbled together two hundred dollars to start up a production company called Filmways, Inc. They began by making TV commercials before transitioning into major television productions, churning out some iconic titles like *The Addams Family*, *Mister Ed*, *The Beverly Hillbillies*, and *Green Acres*, before breaking into feature films. By the time Ransohoff met Sharon Tate, he was one of the few major independent producers at a time when Hollywood was dominated by studios.

When nineteen-year-old Sharon Tate walked into Filmways, Inc., she was wearing an orange patchwork dress and looked nothing like the blonde bombshell she would later be remembered as. Despite her simpler appearance, Marty was immediately taken by her potential and signed Sharon to a seven-year contract. Ransohoff was not naive when it came to talent—he notably helped launch the careers of Steve McQueen and Julie Andrews. There's no question he saw something special in Sharon Tate. Before she had even set foot on a Hollywood set, Marty made the bold decision to secretly groom her for stardom—then launch her with a massive publicity campaign. Tate was sent to New York to study acting, with strict instructions to keep her deal quiet and turn down all acting jobs and auditions. For thirty months she took classes in singing, dancing, and make-up, all while toning her body and crafting the look she became famous for. To gain experience, Tate was brought in under fake names for bit parts in several of Ransohoff's TV shows, wearing a black wig to hide her true identity. When she was finally deemed ready, Ransohoff spent half a million dollars to produce a series of films featuring Sharon Tate, all to be launched at the same time.

While being transformed from a natural Texas beauty into a Hollywood starlet, Tate worked with a hairdresser named Jay Sebring. Like Tate, Sebring was a California import. He had grown up in Detroit, and after high school he had enlisted in the navy and found his calling working in the on-base barbershop. After serving his four years, he settled in Los Angeles where he opened a tiny one-chair salon on Fairfax. At the time, he was so strapped for cash he would sleep in the back of the store. Sebring was initially known by his birth name Tom John Kummer or "TJ" for short. Over the next several years, TJ changed his named to Jay Sebring, managed to endear himself to an array of Beverly Hills royalty, and grew his one-chair shop into a small empire with storefronts in New York, San Francisco, and New Mexico. When Jay Sebring met Sharon Tate, they dated for a short period of time, ultimately ending their romantic relationship but remaining close friends.

Sharon Tate's first movie was filmed in London—an occult horror film called *Thirteen*. It's the story of a cursed wine vineyard that requires a blood sacrifice at the behest of Sharon Tate's character, an evil witch. After filming, Sharon was brought back to Hollywood to film *Don't Make Waves*, in which she played a bikini-clad sexy surfer opposite Tony Curtis, then off to Italy to film *The Fearless Vampire Killers,* or *Pardon Me, But Your Teeth are in My Neck*, a horror comedy in which Tate appeared as a sexy redhead.

Marty Ransohoff's grand plans for Sharon Tate didn't work out. The films were all terrific failures, both critically and financially. Of the three, *Vampire Killers* was perhaps the worst. It ran way over budget, and both Ransohoff and Sharon Tate clashed with the director. Rumours of this discord leaked to the media, and after watching a cut of the film, Ransohoff thought it was so bad that he cut twenty minutes. This decision sent the director into a tailspin, and he demanded that his name be removed from the film—an impossibility since he wrote, directed, and starred in the movie. The director's name was Roman Polanski.

Polanksi and Sharon Tate got off to a bad start; he didn't want to cast her in his movie, and she found him overbearing. At Ransohoff's insistence they collaborated on *Vampire Killers*, and despite the movie being a complete failure, Tate and Polanski fell in love and were married not long after the film's US release. Sharon officially changed her name to Sharon Marie Polanski, but she maintained Sharon Tate as a stage name.

At the same time, Ransohoff worked out a deal lending Sharon Tate to Twentieth Century Fox for an adaptation of the hit book *Valley of the Dolls*. Sharon's casting in the movie was itself newsworthy. Speculation as to who would star in the movie had been rampant, especially after Judy Garland was hired and fired, allegedly for showing up to set drunk. Tate played a despondent actress who succumbs to moral failures and drugs before committing suicide. *Valley of the Dolls* was such an unexpected box office hit that studio insiders began to call it *Valley of the Dollars*. Sharon Tate did numerous interviews for the movie, and newspapers latched on to her narrative and secret training, describing her as Ransohoff's "secret sex missile."

By the summer of 1969, Tate had grown tired of being called a "Hollywood sexpot." She pledged to focus on more dramatic roles. Roman Polanski had gone to London to work on the science fiction thriller *Day of the Dolphin*, which he was directing and writing. In his absence, Tate had invited her friends Jay Sebring, Abigail Folger, and Wojciech Frykowski to stay with her at the house she and Roman had rented on 10050 Cielo Drive.

On the afternoon of August 8, Abigail Folger bought a bicycle, which was delivered to her at Cielo Drive around 7:00 p.m. Jay Sebring, Sharon Tate, and Wojciech were all there. The four stayed at Cielo Drive before driving to the Beverly Hills restaurant El Coyote Café, the interior of which remains unchanged to this day. The restaurant has since become a macabre tourist attraction for those who wish to replicate the last supper of Sharon Tate. If you care to dine there on August 8, you'll find a large group of Manson enthusiasts in the back corner.

After dinner, Sharon Tate and her three friends returned to Cielo Drive for the evening, not realizing they would never leave. Their bodies were discovered the next morning by the housekeeper who called the police. The murder of Sharon Tate and her friends was ghastly and tragic. Sharon Tate was the reason these brutal crimes made national news and why August 8, 1969 will live in infamy. Sharon Tate was a beautiful movie star married to a sought-after film director. Not only was she gorgeous, wealthy, and vibrant, but Sharon Tate was also nearly nine months pregnant. The twisted irony of the Manson Family crimes is that when they went to Cielo Drive, they had no idea they would find a famous movie star living inside, let alone one who was about to give birth.

Years after the murders, Barbara Hoyt befriended Debra Tate, one of Sharon's sisters who became an outspoken advocate against the Manson Family. The murders of August 8 affected Barbara greatly. It was difficult for her to speak about it without almost bursting into tears. "They died so horribly," Barbara told me. "I don't know if people really think about how much they suffered. You know, I think about Sharon Tate and she must have been *insane* with fear by the time they got to her."

Sadie was the last person left inside the house after the murders and the sole person who was present for both the Tate murders and the murder of Gary Hinman. In her 1968 interview with her attorney, Sadie even recalled hearing Sharon Tate's death rattle, commenting that it was the same sound that Gary Hinman had made.

Sadie and Mary were in Gary's house when Bobby staged the crime scene to make it look like the Black Panthers had killed Hinman. According to a transcript of Mary Brunner's statement to Sergeant Paul Whiteley of the Los Angeles Sheriff's Office on December 4, 1969, after the Manson Family had been discovered, the following exchange took place:

Mary: [Bobby] wrote "pig" on the wall and then made a paw print.

Sergeant Paul Whiteley: What kind of paw print?

Mary: A cat's paw print.

Sergeant Paul Whiteley: That was supposed to represent?

Mary: The Panther, the Panthers.

Sergeant Paul Whiteley: When you say "Panthers" you are speaking of the Black Panthers?

Mary: Yes.

According to trial testimony, Sadie recounted the following about Sharon Tate's final moments. Sadie said she stood over Sharon's body as she died and licked the blood off her hands because she wanted "to taste death and yet give life." Sadie enthusiastically described the scene calling it a "trip" and saying, "the blood was beautiful, warm, and sticky." Sadie knelt down beside Sharon's body and dipped a towel in her blood, walking over to the large white door to scrawl the word "PIG" in large block letters. Recall that Bobby writing on the wall in blood at the Hinman house was a week before Sadie wrote on a door in blood at

149

the Tate house. It seems fairly apparent that Sadie's intention was to stage the crime scene to make it look like the person who had killed Gary Hinman was still on the loose.

Despite this, Manson Family prosecutors claimed that the events of that summer were not connected in that manner. They maintained that Charles Manson led a religious cult and was trying to start a race war called Helter Skelter, inspired by The Beatles. In prosecutor Vincent Bugliosi's own words from the trial, "Helter Skelter was Charlie's religion, a religion that he lived by. To Manson, Helter Skelter was the black man rising, up against the white man and then the black-white war."

I know that not everything Manson said and did made a lot of sense. He said strange things and did strange things, but this logic always mystified me. If we are to believe the prosecution, then we must believe that Manson's evil plan was to commit murders to frame black people by writing obscure references to The Beatles on the walls of his victims. This is something I have never understood. Manson couldn't explain it to me because according to him it was all bullshit. Sadie—who actually wrote "pig" on the wall—couldn't explain this logic either because until her death she also maintained it was bullshit, even writing a book called *The Myth of Helter Skelter*.

When I met co-prosecutor Stephen Kay, I decided that I would ask him to explain. I wanted to at least understand how the prosecution arrived at these conclusions. I asked Stephen, "Did you ever determine why they didn't write racial things on the walls? I mean, why were the writings so abstract?"

Stephen said, "Oh it wasn't abstract at all for them." Stephen reasoned that the Manson Family was under the impression that black people would understand the references just as they themselves had come to understand them. "[Black people] would know that, of course, because The Beatles were sending [the Manson Family] subliminal messages through their music in *The White Album*," Stephen explained.

I felt like this was circular—and very confusing—reasoning. I decided to press Stephen further.

I asked, "But why wouldn't they just write, 'Kill White People' or something very obvious? At Gary Hinman's apartment they drew a Black Panther logo, so why not continue to be as obvious?"

Stephen replied, "Probably because they didn't think about it. They were so engrossed with The Beatles' *White Álbum* that it all made sense to them. They thought, 'of course people will connect blacks [to the murders] because of The Beatles' *White Album*.'" Stephen seemed to be having difficulty explaining what this meant. He continued, "They thought that some black person would figure it out and tell somebody."

"It just seems like a lot of dots to connect," I said.

Stephen replied, "Well, remember these weren't ordinary people."

For the purposes of the alternate theory, set aside the prosecution's conclusions and consider that the reason Sadie wrote "PIG" on the wall at Sharon Tate's was with the aim of connecting that murder scene to the Gary Hinman murder scene. Both instances were motivated by pointing the police in the wrong direction.

Immediately after the Tate murders, Tex, Sadie, Katie, and Linda all made their way back to the car. They sped along Benedict Canyon Drive, frantically trying to change their clothes in a moving car. They drove about a mile and a half up the road onto Portola Drive, where they saw a house with a garden hose attached to the side. They pulled over and got out of the car, using the frigid water from the hose, to scrub the blood off their hands, feet, and faces. Tex was most notably covered in blood. The hose was attached to the home of a West Los Angeles resident named Rudy Weber, who was woken up by the sound of running water. Thinking there was some sort of plumbing emergency, Weber began searching his home with a flashlight when he heard voices from beside his house. Weber ran out and yelled, "what do you think you're doing?"

Tex replied, "We were just walking around and wanted a drink of water." Tex and the girls began walking down the street toward their car. By this point, Rudy's wife had joined him, shouting from the doorway. A brazen Rudy Weber followed the group, unaware that he was in pursuit of the Manson Family, who had just used his garden hose to wash blood off their hands. Tex and the girls got into the car quickly, with Weber and his wife yelling after them. Once in the car, Tex turned on the engine, but Rudy had caught up and reached into the driver's side window to try to turn it off. In a panic Tex swatted his hands away and sped off. Weber took note of the licence plate: GYY-435. At trial Weber testified that the next morning he called the police and gave them the licence plate number. Despite the shocking murder that had been committed down the street, the LAPD did not follow-up with him.

Tex, Sadie, Katie, and Linda all returned to the ranch and presumably told Charlie what had taken place, which somehow led to a second night of carnage. I found this next step perplexing because it seemed unclear what they were trying to accomplish that had not already been accomplished. In the alternate theory, Charlie shot Bernard Crowe, which led to paranoia that the Black Panthers would retaliate, which led to the recruitment of the Straight Satans motorcycle gang for protection. The presence of the motorcycle gang led to the Bobby Beausoleil drug deal, the murder of Gary Hinman, and Bobby's subsequent arrest. At the same time, Charlie wanted revenge against Terry Melcher and sought to make members of the group complicit through criminal acts. All this culminated in the murder of Sharon Tate and her friends.

*If this is true, then why go out again the next night?*

According to Bobby, "The second night at the LaBiancas was to cover up for what Charlie had inadvertently done the first night, which was to kill a house full of people. He didn't realize it was going to be this big thing that had unfolded up there at the house on Cielo. He didn't know that Terry Melcher had rented the place out, so it basically turned into a fiasco." On the surface that made sense to me, but I felt there had to be more.

I put the question to Charlie who responded with, "How would I know. I didn't kill those people."

"Then who did kill those people?" I asked.

"The people that told you they killed 'em. They said on the witness stand, 'yeah I killed 'em,'" Charlie said, yelling at me.

152

The alternative theory as illustrated starts to connect all the dots in a logical way based on the mindset of Charles Manson and all those involved in other crimes with the group.

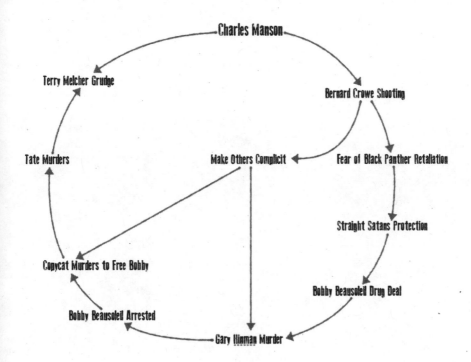

# Death to Pigs

*"The next night—well, I was feeling bad, to tell you the truth, because Katie was my best friend. And to think that she was strong enough—to be able to go kill, I wanted to, too. Because I wanted to be just like Katie.*
        *- Leslie Van Houten, 1977*

The murders of Friday, August 8, took place sometime around midnight. When Tex, Sadie, Katie, and Linda returned to Spahn Ranch, it was early in the morning of Saturday, August 9. They slept through most of the day and didn't leave the ranch again until the following evening, which was Sunday, August 10. Even though the entire affair actually took place over three days, the Sunday night murders are commonly referred to as "the second night" or "the next night."

On the second night, a different mix of people ventured out from Spahn Ranch, piling into the same car that had been driven to the Tate house. The group included the Tate killers—Tex, Linda, Katie, and Sadie—but also included Charlie, another man named Clem, and a young woman named Leslie Van Houten.

"Clem," whose real name was Steve Grogan, was an eighteen-year-old high school dropout who had lived at Spahn Ranch off and on from the time he was fifteen. Prior to Charlie and group's arrival, Clem had done odd jobs around the ranch in exchange for clothes, food, and a place to sleep. He could often be found in an old shack near the back of the property that had no electricity or water. When the Manson commune made Spahn Ranch their home, Clem gradually endeared himself and began to live at the ranch full-time.

Like many of the other women, Leslie Van Houten was a lost soul searching for acceptance when she fell in with the group in 1968. I reached out to Leslie in prison, but she declined to be interviewed because of her ongoing appeals for parole. As of this writing, Leslie has been paroled three times and yet remains in prison. Like many others who have been labelled as members of the Manson Family, Leslie's parole has been continually overturned by the governor of California, despite numerous recommendations by the parole board to release her. I was able to meet Leslie's lawyer, Rich Pfeiffer, at his home in Southern California, who offered to speak on her behalf. According to Rich, "The problem people have with understanding Leslie's story is wrapping their minds around how can you go from a homecoming queen to being a Manson follower?"

Leslie Van Houten grew up in a middle-class Southern California neighbourhood and had an all-American childhood. She was pretty, likeable, and popular in school. Everything changed when Leslie was fourteen, and her parents filed for divorce. "Back then it was very different than it is now. It was a big social stigma," Rich told me.

Leslie handled the divorce terribly. She began using drugs, and when she was seventeen, she ran away to San Francisco with her boyfriend. When Leslie returned home, she was broke, alone, and pregnant. With few options available, her mother consulted a local psychologist who arranged a backroom abortion, to which Leslie reluctantly agreed. After the procedure, Leslie and her mother were given the lifeless fetus in a coffee can, which they buried in their backyard. Leslie continued to live at home for the next few years, eating breakfast with the knowledge that her unborn child was laid to rest a few feet away. Leslie returned to high school and sank into a pit of drugs and alcohol. Somehow, she still managed to graduate.

After graduation, she briefly attended a business college, becoming a trained secretary, before leaving home once again to travel around California. It was then that Leslie met Bobby in San Francisco. Bobby was travelling around in a truck with his then-girlfriend named Gayle. Despite this, he and Leslie began a relationship. In the spirit of the sixties, Leslie and Bobby kept things casual, enabling them both to practise "free love." I asked Bobby about meeting Leslie, which he recalled warmly. "Leslie was living with me and Gayle, and we were travelling in a truck, and we saw the entire state. We were having a great time," Bobby said.

It's often been reported that Leslie met Bobby when he was travelling with Gypsy, who recruited Leslie, telling her infectious stories of Charlie and bringing Leslie back to the ranch. Gypsy's birth name was Catherine Share. According to all involved—that I've spoken with—the story of Gypsy recruiting Leslie isn't true. Instead, after a few weeks together, Bobby, Gayle, and Leslie ended up in Los Angeles and visited Spahn Ranch, where Leslie met Manson for the first time. Leslie wasn't won over by Manson's enigmatic charisma; instead, after meeting Charlie, she actually wanted to stay with Bobby and Gayle, who were planning to continue on to Santa Barbara. Before they could leave, Charlie pulled Bobby aside and told him that he needed a favour.

Charlie told Bobby that several of the girls had driven a rundown school bus to San Jose, and the bus had broken down. Bobby was known to be proficient with cars at the time—he was also driving a military-style Dodge Power Wagon complete with four-wheel drive and a winch. "Towing a bus would've been no problem," Bobby recalled.

Bobby, Leslie, and Gayle made the nearly six-hour drive to San Jose. When they arrived, Bobby realized that the bus had suffered a broken axel. "While I was looking for a garage that I could tow the bus to, the girls in the bus were working on Leslie, and they pulled her in," Bobby told me, explaining the real reason that Leslie joined the commune. "I was pissed off about that because I think Charlie put them up to it." This event was prior to the Bernard Crowe drug deal, the Straight Satans' protection, and Bobby subsequently agreeing to stay at the ranch. Prior to this time, Charlie had often asked him to join the growing commune at Spahn Ranch, but Bobby had always refused. "Charlie thought if he could pull in Leslie or Gayle or both of them, then I would come along with them," Bobby said. "If anything, it had the opposite effect. It pissed me off, and I didn't see Charlie for months after that." Leslie, however, stayed through the winter of 1968 and into the summer of 1969, earning the nickname "Lulu" and becoming close with many of the other women, including Cappi and Katie.

On the morning of August 9, Katie had told Leslie about the savagery that had gone on at Sharon Tate's house the night before. When the group ventured out on August 10, Leslie was an ideal choice to join them for two reasons: First, she was close with Bobby and would be invested in the bizarre plot to cast doubt on his guilt. Second, she had always been one of the more independent women in the group, making her potentially more inclined to snitch on Charlie and an ideal candidate to make complicit through violence.

Charlie never spoke to me about Leslie Van Houten; however, in a recovered audio cassette recording made by the Los Angeles District Attorney in 1977, a prison psychiatrist interviewed Charlie. The psychiatrist asked Charlie how Leslie had come to be with the group, and Charlie matter-of-factly explained, "People had Leslie Van Houten long before I had her. Her mother had her, her dad had her, her parents had her, her school had her, the TV had her, the movies had her." Charlie later continued, "You come up and ask me if I had influence over her. Man, I seen the broad a few times. Certainly, I had influence over her, I have influence over everybody I meet." After some back and forth for specifics, Charlie told the investigators, "I never paid that much attention to her."

That same year, Leslie gave a candid, recorded interview to her lawyer, recounting what happened on August 10, 1969. As Leslie recalled, "We were all sitting in the kitchen and Charlie pulled me out to the side."

"Are you crazy?" Charlie asked.

"Well yeah," Leslie replied.

Charlie continued, "Are you crazy enough to go out and be able to kill someone?"

Leslie thought for a moment and answered with a simple, "Yeah."

"OK," Charlie said. "Go get two changes of clothes and get in the car."

I asked Cappi if she remembered that evening and she did, recalling that she saw Charlie and the others getting into a car for an unknown mission. Cappi explained that on that particular night she was distraught because Katie and Leslie were going and had not included her in their plans.

"Where did you think they were going?" I asked Cappi.

"I had no idea where they were going but Katie and Lulu were the closest people in the universe to me," Cappi said. "[Lulu] was my other me, and Katie was like our big sister, and they were in the car and they were going somewhere without me, so I tried to get in the car, and they wouldn't let me. I didn't know why." In light of what later happened, Cappi looked back on the moment soberly, realizing that she was left out by the two people closest to her to ensure she would not become complicit. "They were protecting me," she said gratefully.

It's amazing to think that on August 10, 1969, the group was in the midst of one of the most infamous crimes in American history; yet in retrospect most of them didn't seem to know what the hell was going on. For Manson's part, he told me cryptically, "What's real has different levels. You could go on certain levels of reality that other people don't really understand at all. So, they call it insanity."

Cappi confirmed—as have many other commune members from that time—that many people had no idea what was happening. Perhaps this is why it was Charlie who drove on the second night. He drove the group to Los Feliz and parked near an intersection on Waverly Drive. To the west was the home of an affluent couple named Leno and Rosemary LaBianca, who owned a chain of grocery stores. In filming the documentary, we spent time exploring the LaBianca residence, which is a large, white house on a generous lot. When you see it first-hand, what's striking is how isolated it feels—you can't see the house until you drive right up to it. Even though it's in the middle of a populated suburb in a busy city, it's very secluded—with one exception. The LaBianca house is on what's almost a shared lot with the next-door neighbour to the east—as if someone bought an acre and built two houses on it. The houses are not easily accessible from the street, but if you stand at one house you can easily walk to the other.

In 1969, the house next to the LaBiancas' was a rental property that was once home to a man named Harold True. Harold True was good friends with Phil Kaufman. Prior to meeting Charlie in Terminal Island Prison, Phil had been arrested for marijuana possession and decided to leave the United States while the heat died down. Phil told me, "When I skipped the country at the time of my marijuana bust, Harold True gave me his passport. He had never had a passport, so I was able to get one in Harold's name—and then later, when I got out of prison and I went to see Charlie, I took Harold along. Harold was a big old lumpy guy and he thought he might get laid."

In a 1970 interview with Los Angeles prosecutors, Harold recalled first meeting the group—he'd been living next to the LaBianca house at the time. Harold said, "[The Manson group] called and asked if they could spend the night in [my] house." According to Harold, Manson and several other members of the group subsequently spent a lot of time at his house. Harold said, "It was a big house, a lot of people stayed there." When asked how the Manson Family found the house, Harold told investigators, "It was really a party house. It was a big house and nice, so we had these little maps printed up and we'd say, 'we're having a party, here it is.'"

Bobby remembered Charlie telling him and others about Harold's house and that Charlie had specifically mentioned the neighbours. According to Bobby, "They were camping out with the bus living at Harold True's place, and the neighbours called the cops. They had to *leave* because the neighbours called the cops. And the neighbours were the LaBiancas."

It should be noted that Leno and Rosemary LaBianca didn't move into the house on Waverly Drive until after Harold True had moved out. According to Harold's statements to investigators, he believed that he had moved out in September of 1968, when he moved his belongings to his grandmother's house. According to investigation notes, Leno and Rosemary LaBianca moved in around November of 1968, about two months later; however, the LaBiancas purchased the house from Leno's mother, so the family did overlap with Harold True. It's reasonable to assume that Leno's elderly mother might have asked her son to call the police if the neighbours were having a wild party, as opposed to calling herself. According to Bobby, this demonstrates one of Charlie's key motivations. "Charlie picked people he had grudges against. He didn't just pick people at random. That's critical because it's not what Bugliosi was saying—that Charlie was just sending people out to kill, willy nilly."

This adds to the alternate theory that on the second night, Manson continued manipulating the others. It wasn't because he would rule the world after a race war; instead, it was a series of interconnected events. It began with the Bernard Crowe shooting, which led to the Gary Hinman murder and Bobby Beausoleil's arrest. This culminated in the Sharon

Tate and LaBianca murders. A significant number of commune members became complicit and Manson's outstanding grudges were satisfied.

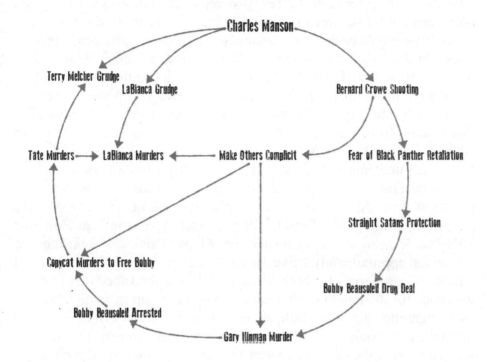

As my alternate theory continued to solidify, and I spoke more to Bobby and others, I would report back to Charlie to get his reaction. In one such conversation, Charlie said, "You've got to realize that everyone's got their own perspective towards everything. There's only one me, and that me lives inside of you. You've got to look out for yourself first. You're making your documentary according to your perspective, and you're getting information from people who are doing the same."

"That's why I'm talking to you, Charlie. I want to get to the truth," I said.

"There you go. That way your documentary will ring true and will ring through," Charlie replied.

I knew Charlie would never give me a ringing endorsement, but I felt I was getting as close as one could get.

On the night of August 10, once the group had parked out front of the LaBianca house, Charlie and Tex got out of the car telling the others to wait. According to Tex Watson's account, summarized from numerous public statements, he and Manson went up to the house and broke in through a back door. Manson woke up Leno LaBianca, who was asleep in the living room, and tied him up with a leather thong. They retrieved Rosemary LaBianca from the bedroom and tied her up, before threatening the couple together. Manson disputed Tex Watson's version of events to me, saying, "What has he told you about me? Everything that's going to help him, right? You are for you. I am for me. I'm for Charlie. I didn't kill nobody."

It's undisputed that Manson drove to the LaBianca house, walked up Harold True's driveway, and went into the LaBianca house for some period of time. All the witnesses—including Charlie—have given this account in some public forum over the years. In Leslie Van Houten's 2016 parole hearing, she estimated that Manson and Tex went into the house for approximately "five to ten minutes." In Linda Kasabian's testimony at the trials for both Manson and Tex, she stated that Manson was gone for the length of time that it took the group to smoke, "A Pall Mall cigarette, not the whole thing but three-quarters of it, where a normal filter would be." This corroborates Leslie's claim that Charlie was away from the car for between five and ten minutes. Depending on the exact route Charlie took, it would be about 300 feet to walk from the car, to the base of Harold True's driveway, to Harold True's house, to somewhere near the front of True's house. Charlie then would have taken a left turn, cut across the lawn, and gone around the LaBiancas' garage to get to their house. After going into the house, it would be approximately 175 feet back to the car.

Unless Charlie was in an Olympic-calibre sprint for the duration, it's hard to see how he had time to go up to Harold True's, cross over to the LaBiancas', go into the house and tie them up, and get back to the car within fifteen minutes, let alone ten. So, what do we know for sure? We know Manson went up to the LaBiancas' for some period of time because multiple people saw him do it. We also know that he actually went into the LaBianca house because when he came back to the car, he'd brought with him a specific item.

Those in the car claim that when Manson was in the house, he took Rosemary LaBianca's wallet. This makes sense because—by all accounts—he was the only one to go up to the house and come back to the car. In Sadie's testimony to the grand jury she said, "Charlie also had a wallet which he supposedly got from the house. He said it was the woman's identification." The wallet was brown leather and feminine with a fleur-de-lis in the bottom left-hand corner. The wallet contained the personal identification and credit cards of Rosemary LaBianca, which police later found twenty miles away in a gas station bathroom located in the community of Sylmar.

According to the prosecution, the wallet is significant because Manson's plan was to plant the wallet in a black neighbourhood, reasoning that a black person would use the credit cards and become connected to the murders—thus fueling the race war. In her testimony for the prosecution, Linda Kasabian explained, "[Charlie] said he wanted a black person to pick [the wallet] up and use the credit cards so that people, the establishment, would think it was some sort of organized group that killed these people." Linda claimed that Charlie told her to put the wallet in the bathroom as part of his plot.

While making the documentary, I took it upon myself to ask a basic question, *Was Sylmar actually a black neighbourhood?* I tracked down a publication from the US Department of Commerce entitled *Social and Health, Indicators System, Los Angeles* published in 1973. The report contains the complete demographics for many Los Angeles neighbourhoods—including Sylmar. According to the report, in 1970 the Sylmar community had a black population of 1%. This brings into question Charlie's motive, or at least his knowledge of the community. The question becomes, *If Charlie was trying to hide the wallet in a place a "black person" would find it, why would he hide it in Sylmar?*

I put this question to Manson Family prosecutor Stephen Kay, who admitted that in 1969 the prosecution knew Sylmar was *not* a black neighbourhood; however, they reasoned that Manson "got his jurisdiction wrong. He thought that the wallet was getting planted in Pacoima, which was predominantly black at the time, but it was accidentally planted in Sylmar, which was right next to Pacoima." Stephen was clear on what the prosecution's theory was at the time. "The wallet got planted in the wrong city. I mean there's no point in planting it in a white area and having a white person use the credit cards. That defeats the whole purpose of blaming the murders on black people," Stephen told me.

I readily agreed with his second point—putting the wallet in Sylmar defeats the purpose of murdering people to starting a race war;

however, I believe it's a massive leap to think that Manson couldn't tell the difference between Pacoima and Sylmar, especially considering Sylmar is only about eleven miles from Spahn Ranch. Incidentally, Pacoima wasn't predominantly black in 1969. According to census data it was 23% black—meaning that according to the prosecution's theory, Manson mistook one white neighbourhood for a different white neighbourhood, thinking both were black neighbourhoods. *It doesn't make any sense.*

If framing black people was not Manson's motive, then what was he trying to achieve in the few minutes he was in the LaBianca house? And what was the real reason for taking Rosemary LaBianca's wallet?

The answer could be—*money.*

The LAPD investigation notes reveal that Leno LaBianca was a chronic gambler, with outstanding personal loans. A 1969 homicide investigation progress report from the LAPD Robbery Homicide Division states: "Subsequent investigation into the business dealings of Mr. LaBianca revealed he had been misappropriating money from his own company's treasury. The bookkeeping records of the Gateway Markets show a deficit of approximately $200,000 since 1964." What this means is that it's likely there was cash in the LaBianca house, and if it went missing on the night of the murders, police would have no way of knowing.

In Tex Watson's 1978 autobiography, he claimed that Leno LaBianca offered to take Charlie to his store to get money, but Charlie declined and instead took the little money that LaBianca had in the house. At the time, Leno was embezzling money from his store, so it stands to reason that he had a fair amount of money in his house—not the small amount Tex claimed. In furtherance of the alternate theory, I propose that there was in fact a lot of money accessible to Charlie in the LaBianca house, and Charlie took that money and left. Since no one disputes that Manson and Tex Watson went up to the house, and, after a few minutes, Manson returned with Rosemary's wallet, in the alternate theory, Charlie retrieved the money he had come for, got into the car, and drove away.

We know Katie and Leslie went into the house as Manson drove away with the others. Tex, Katie, and Leslie have all given accounts at numerous parole hearings as to what happened next.

Tex untied Rosemary LaBianca and demanded more money. Leno listened to his wife's pleas for mercy but remained restrained—his hands were still bound behind his back when his body was found the next day. Rosemary frantically searched the house and found a small box of collectable coins that she offered to Tex and the girls as payment to leave peacefully. Leslie took the coins, putting them aside, while Katie went into the kitchen to search for knives. Leslie took Rosemary back into the master bedroom, and with no supplies to restrain the panic-stricken Rosemary, Leslie claims she improvised. She took a pillowcase off the bed and covered Rosemary's head, then used the cord from her bedside lamp to secure it, wrapping it around Rosemary's neck several times. The odd part of Leslie's claim is that when Leno LaBianca was found, his head was *also* covered with a pillowcase, and he was *also* throttled by a lamp cord. According to Leslie, she did not see Leno being murdered. If this is true, then we are to believe that Leslie improvised the lamp cord and the pillowcase with Rosemary, while at the same time, by sheer coincidence, Tex was doing the exact same thing to his victim in the other room. I point this out only to note that the Manson Family murderers have a tendency to minimize their actions and their free will, when the evidence in fact suggests that they were constantly working together—as opposed to following orders.

Based on the autopsy reports, we can say that Leno was killed first. Blood spatter shows that Leno was killed lying flat on his back, while Rosemary's stab wounds indicated she fought back—reacting to the screams of her husband. This is corroborated by the trial testimony from Leslie Van Houten. "The woman heard her husband. She must have because all of a sudden she jumped up, and it surprised me—she kept going, 'What's happening to Leno?' And, we kept telling her, 'He's alright, he's alright.' And then Katie tried to stab her."

Katie lunged holding a knife she'd found in the kitchen. With Rosemary struggling, Katie stabbed Rosemary. Instead of a clean stab through flesh, the knife came to a jarring stop when it hit Rosemary's collarbone. The force of Katie's stab curved the blade, causing Katie to recoil from the flash of pain in her hand. Rosemary's screams intensified, and she grabbed the lamp and attacked Leslie.

Tex was still stabbing Leno in the living room when he heard the lamp crash on the floor still hanging from Rosemary's neck. With all her strength, Rosemary managed to blindly grab hold of Leslie and the two fell onto the bed, with Rosemary literally fighting for her life. "We called

Tex in," Leslie recalled. "We said, 'Tex, we can't kill her.' She was dead within a minute it seemed."[10]

Tex interjected stabbing wildly, until Rosemary ceased struggling. As Tex stood up, he handed Leslie his knife. At that point Leslie crouched over Rosemary, who was bleeding to death on the floor but still alive. As Leslie later recalled to investigators, "I lost control, I went completely nuts at that moment." Leslie went on to say, "When I thought of stabbing—it's a real feeling. It's not even like cutting a piece of meat. It's much tougher. I had to use both hands, and all my strength behind it to get it in. And, so once I started, the feeling was so weird. I just kept doing it. I did it about ten times, I think."

After the LaBiancas were dead, Tex, Katie, and Leslie did something I always found to be one of the most chilling sequences of the entire crime spree. First consider that there was blood everywhere. The LaBiancas had been savagely stabbed, and Leno was stabbed in the jugular. Tex, Katie, and Leslie were covered in blood; Tex must have had blood dripping from his arms. Next consider that the LaBiancas screamed at the top of their lungs while they were being stabbed to death. In the aftermath, the three murderers didn't run from the scene in fear of the police. Leslie relaxed in the house surrounded by the gruesome sight of a couple she and her friends had just slaughtered, and Tex and Katie took a hot shower. "I remember seeing her (Rosemary LaBianca) laying flat in front of her closet and it was really bloody on her stomach. I remember the man (Leno LaBianca) laying on the sofa gurgling, a deep bloody gurgle," Leslie recalled.[11]

When they were finished cleaning up, they all went into the kitchen to get the tools to further desecrate the corpses of their victims. Katie crouched carefully over the body of Leno LaBianca in the living room and lifted his shirt. She carefully carved the word "WAR" into his abdomen. When she was finished, she shoved a tinged carving fork, which she'd found in the kitchen, into his abdomen seven times, then took the knife, driving it through his neck all the way to the handle, leaving it to be found by the coroner the next day.

---

[10] State of California v Van Houten, 28, Cal Supp. 4,044-45 (1977, May 18).

[11] Van Houten, Leslie. (1977). Audio recorded interview provided by The District Attorney of Los Angeles County.

As they lingered in the house, they drank chocolate milk, ate cheese from the fridge, and then calmly changed their clothes. Tex struggled to put on his pants, breaking the zipper, so Leslie volunteered the pants she had brought. Tex thanked Leslie and put them on, and Leslie changed into a pair of Rosemary LaBianca's shorts. Leslie walked around the house carefully and wiped down all the surfaces to ensure no fingerprints were left.

The three finally finished their work by writing on the walls in blood for the third time. Katie, who was present at the Tate murders, used Leno LaBianca's blood to write "Rise" on the inside of the front door. On the living room wall overlooking Leno's body, she used his blood to write "Death To Pigs," and on the refrigerator door she wrote "Healter Skelter" [*sic*].

It's apparent that the group's crimes, hallmarked by writing on the walls in blood, are all connected—not three episodes of coincidence. This was so apparent in 1969 that Sergeant Paul Whiteley, and other investigators from the Hinman investigation, sought out the LAPD detectives assigned to the Tate-LaBianca homicides and tried to tell them. As Stephen Kay, the Manson Family co-prosecutor recalled, "Two of the homicide investigators, Charlie Gunther and Paul Whiteley, went over and said, 'Look, we have this murder of Gary Hinman and there's writing in blood on the wall in Hinman's blood, and in the Tate house and LaBianca house there's writing on the walls all in blood.' So they said, 'Look, we think these are connected. Ours, your two, all connected.' The LAPD investigators sent them away, said, 'Nah, they're not connected.'"

The murders were clearly connected, *but what was Charlie Manson's true motive behind the LaBianca murders?*

The answer could be in Venice, California.

As part of disclosure in the original Manson Family trial, the prosecution notified the defence that they planned for Linda Kasabian to testify about where the group went *after* the LaBianca murders. According to Linda, she, Charlie, Clem, and Sadie left the LaBianca house and drove to Venice Beach. In a statement to the court Bugliosi said, "Manson, Susan (Sadie), and Clem are the only persons in the car after the LaBianca murder. The same night they go down to Venice and [Charles Manson] asked them to commit another murder." The prosecution insisted that Manson's alleged motive was once again to murder a random person, frame a black person, and thus fuel the race war. But in this instance, Linda Kasabian thwarted the murder. According to Linda, she causally told Charlie about a male friend she had in Venice, and in a spur of the moment decision, Manson told the group that they would go to Venice and murder this person. When they arrived in Venice, Linda led them to her friend's apartment building but deliberately knocked on the wrong door to prevent her friend's murder. Nobody answered and, apparently, they all went back to Spahn Ranch. This testimony was not allowed to be heard in front of the jury, because Manson, Sadie, Katie, and Leslie were all tried together. Since Sadie, Katie, and Leslie were not present for the Venice trip, the testimony was ruled to be not part of the crimes for which they were being tried.

According to Linda, the apartment building that she took Manson and the others to was on Ocean Front Walk. It was later reported that the apartment belonged to a Lebanese actor named Saladin Nader who had picked up Linda and Sandra Good while they were hitchhiking at some point in the month prior to the murders. Allegedly, Saladin took the girls back to his apartment and had sex with Linda while Sandra took a nap on his couch.

In hindsight, the Venice Beach story doesn't make a lot of sense. Linda could have just said she couldn't remember where the actor lived or taken Charlie to the wrong building altogether. But for some reason she allegedly thought the best way to prevent the murder was to knock on a door very close to her friend's apartment—even though she was the only one who knew where he lived. Also, Venice Beach is a forty-minute drive across west Los Angeles from the LaBianca house, so if Charlie was so hell-bent on killing another person, why did he give up so easily? Also, why would Charlie carefully distance himself in the eight preceding murders, but on a potential ninth murder be willing to go into an apartment building with the killers?

Curiously, Sadie testified that even though she was supposedly present, she didn't recall this incident at all. She claimed that she fell asleep in the car after they hid the wallet, and when she woke up, they were back at Spahn Ranch.

There is something that jumps out with respect to the location of that apartment. The address of Saladin Nader's apartment was a short walk from the Straight Satans' clubhouse. The same Straight Satans that Charlie had approached to protect the ranch in light of the Bernard Crowe shooting, and the same Straight Satans that Bobby was still indebted to.

In the fifties and sixties, Los Angeles motorcycle gangs would often claim hot dog stands as their fronts to meet up and do business. The Straight Satans had claimed a Venice Beach hot dog stand called The Saucy Dog, which was located on the corner of Pacific and 18th Avenue, about a block in from the beach. If you go there today, it's noticeable as it's on the last remaining brick street left in Venice Beach. Across the street from The Saucy Dog was a dive bar called The Silver Dollar, which is where the Straight Satans hung out. Their clubhouse was located on top of The Silver Dollar in a small apartment.

In the alternate theory, after Manson shot Bernard Crowe and believed that he had killed him, he feared retaliation and enlisted the Straight Satans for protection. Bobby Beausoleil compromised this protection by getting into a conflict with the Straight Satans over the one thousand dollars in supposedly bad mescaline, leading to the subsequent murder of Gary Hinman. If Manson took enough money from the LaBianca residence, he could have gone to Venice to settle the debt that Bobby Beausoleil still owed the Straight Satans from the Gary Hinman drug deal.

To corroborate this part of the theory, I asked Bobby what the Straight Satans' response was to the murder of Gary Hinman. Bobby confirmed that the Satans did indeed leave Spahn Ranch. "They went back to Venice," said Bobby. "Right after I got arrested, man. [The Straight Satans] they were scared, they took off."

This confirms the idea that the departure of the Straight Satans left the ranch open to an attack from the Black Panthers—at least in Charlie's mind. Manson going to Venice with the money he stole from the LaBiancas makes sense; paying the Straight Satans would have settled Bobby's debt, regained protection for the ranch, and enabled the group to help Bobby.

According to Linda Kasabian, the morning after their Venice Beach trip Charlie told her to go see Bobby Beausoleil in prison. In the alternate theory, it's clear that Charlie sent Linda to go tell Bobby to keep his mouth shut because they had taken care of everything. I asked Charlie if he recalled whether this was his intent. "Bobby was straight up," Charlie replied. "Bobby didn't lie, he didn't snitch, he rode a straight saddle, man. All the way down the line."

# The Informant

*"I'm an animal and I'll do anything it takes to survive, it's that simple. And I look out for this guy right here, number one. I've always been that way, and I explained that to all the people I was with."*
    *- Charles Manson, 1977*

There's a fascinating twist to the group's weekend of mayhem; unbeknownst to any one of them, they were all under police surveillance the entire time.

In the months leading up to the murders, LAPD officers and deputies from the LA County Sheriff's Department became a constant presence at the ranch. Bobby recalled that the Sheriff's Department would drive through two or three times a day. "Most of them probably just wanted to see some naked hippie chicks or something," Bobby recalled. "See if they could get lucky, you know."

According to police records, on July 15, 1969, an LAPD officer spotted a stolen vehicle near the main entrance to the ranch while on a routine patrol. This was three weeks before the Tate-LaBianca murders. Authorities began a focused investigation into the Manson commune for auto theft and discovered numerous reports of stolen vehicles in the area. A week later, sheriff's deputies went to Spahn Ranch and spoke with Manson personally. Manson denied any knowledge of the stolen vehicles and even bragged to police that the group living on the ranch was well-armed and would fend off intruders if needed. Investigators subsequently discovered that the group was selling stolen auto parts to a local dune buggy shop, only a few miles from the ranch, and initiated increased surveillance to catch them in the act.

The stolen auto parts investigation was lengthy and in-depth. Authorities flew helicopters over the ranch and interacted with members of the group numerous times throughout the weekend of the Tate-LaBianca murders. Despite the surveillance, authorities had no idea the group had gone out and killed seven people. Police even noted Gary Hinman's VW bus parked on the ranch and never put it together that Bobby—who was in custody—was a part of the group, so no one in the Manson commune was even questioned about the Hinman or Tate-LaBianca murders at the time.

By Monday, August 11, life at Spahn Ranch had more or less returned to normal. Down the road though, panic had overtaken Los Angeles as the victims' butchered bodies were discovered by friends, family, and police. The death of Sharon Tate dominated the headlines, and word of what had happened began to ripple through the commune at Spahn Ranch. The Tate-LaBianca murders became the focus of the LAPD, so the LA County Sheriff's Office took the lead on the auto theft and Hinman investigations—which were thought to be unrelated.

On Thursday, August 16, four days after the Tate-LaBianca murders, the Los Angeles Sheriff's Office executed a pre-dawn search warrant, storming the ranch at 6:00 a.m. Most of the group was fast asleep and awoke to the shouts of armed deputies pulling them out of their makeshift beds all around the property. Twenty-six adults and five children were rounded up and detained. Charlie was found hiding face down under the saloon by a sheriff's deputy. He was arrested and transported to the Malibu County Jail with the other adults, while the children were taken into protective custody.

It's been long speculated that the police raid was aided by Donald "Shorty" Shae, a cowboy who had lived at the ranch, off and on, for almost a decade. He would become the final victim of the Manson Family.

In 1969, Donald Shae was a thirty-five-year-old, out-of-work cowboy. Like most others at the ranch, Shae was a California transplant, originally from Massachusetts. When he was nineteen, he served in the Korean War but was discharged in 1956 and moved to California, finding a home at Spahn Ranch. He was originally hired by George Spahn to take care of the horses in exchange for room and board. Part of Shorty's job was transporting the horses to other area ranches to be used in movie sequences. While moving horses from Spahn Ranch to a neighbouring ranch, called Corriganville Ranch, Shorty was recruited to help with an ongoing live animal show for children. Shae helped corral the horses and performed small stunts in the show, falling in love with stunt work. He began dedicating himself to becoming a professional stuntman, training endlessly at Spahn Ranch for the next few years. In 1959, Shorty befriended several movie producers and for many years thereafter would call them frequently, trying to get his foot in the door as an actor and stuntman in western movies being filmed around LA.

Around the same time, Shorty met a thirteen-year-old girl named Sandra Harmon, who frequented Spahn Ranch to ride horses. When she turned eighteen, in 1961, they were immediately married—Shorty was twenty-seven at the time. Over the next four years they had three kids but were divorced by 1965. Sandra immediately remarried and actually asked Shorty not to see his children anymore so they could more easily accept their new father. Shorty tearfully obliged, never seeing his kids again.

Shorty spent the next several years making ends meet. He worked in salt mines, lived off and on at Spahn Ranch, and found small movie roles. He honed his craft as a stunt performer and became an expert at quick draw. In late 1968, Shorty met Manson for the first time while the group was living at an abandoned house not far from the ranch. By all accounts, Manson and Shorty disliked each other immediately, and Shorty's feelings only intensified when Manson and the group moved to Spahn Ranch and took over.

At one of Clem's final parole hearings he described Charlie's escalating dislike of Shorty prior to the raid. "It was like a growing hostility—Charlie didn't like him because he was always drinking and he thought [Shorty] was a slob."

In the spring of 1969, Shorty took a brief job as a club bouncer and met a cocktail waitress and topless dancer who went by the name Nikki. She was a beautiful African-American woman who was taken by Shorty's rugged good looks and charming stories about working in the film industry. At the time, interracial dating was still somewhat controversial; despite this, the couple was married on July 1, 1969 (coincidentally the same night as the Bernard Crowe shooting). The ceremony was brief with friends at a Las Vegas wedding chapel. Shorty was offered a job by a friend, and the couple planned to find an apartment and start a new life in Nevada. Once married, however, they faced some harsh realities. Shorty and Nikki encountered intense discrimination in the more conservative state and quickly left, returning to the more tolerant hippie culture of Topanga Canyon in Los Angeles. When Shorty and Nikki arrived in LA, they began living at the Wilcox Hotel just off Hollywood Boulevard. Shorty pawned some movie guns he owned to pay for the room.

At that time, Shorty had not been to Spahn Ranch since the early spring and was having trouble finding work. Nikki suggested she return to topless dancing while they figured things out, but Shorty vehemently opposed and vowed to take any job he could to prevent her from returning to the club. It was then that Shorty made the fateful decision to go back to Spahn Ranch, bringing Nikki with him. Shorty toured Nikki around the ranch and introduced her to his friends, as well as Charles Manson and George Spahn. With all the free labour from the Manson commune, George Spahn didn't currently need another ranch hand. But on the day of the Sheriff's Department raid, Shorty called Nikki and told her that George Spahn had asked him to stay at the ranch and work for a short period of time—until those who were arrested came back. The timing of the offer coincided with a difficult period in Shorty and Nikki's marriage. They were constantly fighting about money and Nikki wanting to go back to the club. Shorty vowed to work at the ranch for some quick cash and return in a week.

Two weeks later, Nikki was growing concerned as she had not heard from Shorty. She called the ranch and left a message with an unknown female member of the commune. The next day, a woman called her back and told her that Shorty had moved to San Francisco. Nikki searched for Shorty, fruitlessly, and filed a missing person's report on Dec 12, 1969, with the LA County Sheriff's Office. It was not followed up on for a year until members of the commune voluntarily told the Gary Hinman investigators that Manson and others had killed Shorty.

Allegedly, Manson believed Shorty was a snitch working with the police. It is clearly indicated on the search warrant that an informant from the ranch was providing information to the police, so it's at least plausible that Shorty was that informant. But I've yet to come across an explanation as to how or why Charlie allegedly came to believe this. Though Charlie told me about life on the ranch often, we never talked about Shorty. Bruce Davis, who had been with the group since 1968, corroborated the alleged motive for Shorty's murder at a 2014 parole hearing, saying, "I was there when Charlie said we're going to kill Shorty because he's a police informant." Bruce claimed that at the time he did not how Charlie came by this information.

It should be noted that at trial, the prosecution further claimed that Manson had Shorty killed because Manson was a racist and disapproved of Shorty's interracial marriage. Once again, how they surmised Manson's views on the marriage or why it mattered to Manson was never explained.

It's also not clear when exactly Shorty was killed. At his last parole hearing, Clem claimed that in the fall of 1969, Charlie woke him up, handed him a pipe wrench, and told him to get into a car with Tex and Shorty. The plan was to club Shorty over the back of the head once Tex gave the signal. Allegedly, Shorty was under the impression that he, Tex, and Clem were going into Los Angeles to exchange or sell some auto parts. Tex sat in the passenger seat, Shorty was driving, and Clem was in the back seat behind Shorty. Tex directed Shorty to an isolated area near Spahn Ranch claiming that he had stashed some parts. When they pulled off the road, Tex got out of the car and pretended to look around in the bushes. He then looked back at Clem and gave the signal.

Clem, having never clubbed someone over the head with a pipe wrench before, hesitated—half-uncertain and half-reluctant. Growing impatient, Tex turned back and came toward the car, drawing a large knife. Shorty snapped his head toward Tex, saw the knife, and reacted with confusion. At that point Clem hit Shorty in the back of the head, but the blow from the pipe wrench didn't have the intended effect. Shorty remained conscious and jumped across to the passenger seat to make a run for it.

Prior to this, Shorty had been holding the car in gear with his foot on the brake, so when he jumped over and out, the car lurched forward with Clem in the backseat. Clem dropped the wrench, reached into the front, and struggled to control the car. The car lurched forward and came to an abrupt stop in a ditch. Clem looked over and saw that Shorty hadn't gotten far. Tex had caught up with him and plunged the knife into Shorty's back.

As Shorty lay on the ground stabbed and bleeding, Manson and Bruce Davis allegedly pulled up. (Manson always denied that he was present for Shorty's murder.) According to trial testimony, the four stood over the dying cowboy. Tex handed his knife to Clem who violently thrust it twice into Shorty's chest. The small group took turns slashing at Shorty until he was dead, and someone dragged his corpse into the bushes. Bruce Davis later told people that before they returned to the ranch, they cut off Shorty's head.

The night Shorty was killed, Clem and others returned to dig a shallow grave. The location was such that mother nature covered the grave in mudslides and debris. Shorty's body would most likely have never been found except Clem drew a map for authorities almost a decade later in 1977. Based on Clem's map, the Los Angeles County Sheriff's Department searched and dug up the side of the Santa Susana Pass Road for six weeks. Shorty's skeleton was finally recovered, one hundred and fifty feet off the road, one mile west of Topanga Boulevard, buried in an embankment—his head still attached.

Bruce Davis had apparently embellished the details of Shorty's murder by saying that Shorty had been decapitated. It's unclear as to why. When Manson was later tried for Shorty's murder, he made an attempt to plead guilty in protest for not being able to act as his own lawyer. Manson said to the judge, "I enter a plea of guilty. I chopped his head off." Manson made this statement in 1971, which was six years before Shorty's remains were recovered. In this court exchange, Manson repeated the embellished version of Shorty's death, which he had presumably heard from Bruce. This could be evidence that Manson wasn't present for Shorty's murder or he would have known that Shorty wasn't decapitated.

Donald "Shorty" Shae's murder and the increasing scrutiny from the sheriff's office motivated the Manson commune to find somewhere else to live. They ultimately settled at another ranch near the Nevada border.

Barker Ranch was an old mining property in Death Valley that was established in 1940 and purchased by a couple named James and Arlene Barker in 1956. The ranch consisted of three wooden structures in the middle of nowhere. There were no proper roads leading to the ranch and no neighbours for miles. Barker Ranch was at least a five-hour drive from Los Angeles, making it very isolated. On most days the ranch sat empty, except when visited by the Barkers, who often took along their granddaughter Catherine. By 1969, Catherine was living with the Manson Family under the nickname Cappi.

Cappi recalled, "We went to the desert because of me. My favourite place besides the ocean. I was born on the ocean and I lived in the desert, and I love the desert, so I offered up the desert." According to Cappi, she was the one who insisted they leave Spahn Ranch. Word of the murders was filtering throughout the group, and many were talking about leaving. The group was becoming unsettled, and Charlie was uncertain about what to do next. People in the group were offering suggestions, and Cappi recalled, "I was jumping up and down saying we should go to Barker Ranch."

The group's stay at Barker Ranch was short-lived because they caught the attention of the local sheriff's office. The isolation of the ranch should have prevented this, but Cappi told me a spontaneous scavenging trip brought them the unwanted attention. According to Cappi, the group had settled into Barker Ranch in the wake of the murders, finding peace and tranquility. Cappi told the group about some hot springs in the area, which she used to visit as a child while on vacation with her family. Cappi and a few others piled into dune buggies and drove around the barren landscape searching for the hot springs, scouring the same place that has now become home to the Burning Man Festival. After several hours, they found the hot springs but were devastated to see that they were being filled in as part of a local construction project. Work had ceased for the day and the group explored the site, coming across a Caterpillar 988 Loader. Cappi was incensed that the establishment would dare violate the natural landscape etched into her childhood memory, and she made a plea to the group. "I suggested that we should burn it," Cappi recalled.

This task was easier said than done. The ninety-five-thousand-pound bulldozer was made of sheet metal, and the group had not come prepared to burn industrial-grade construction equipment. This didn't stop them from causing some destruction—melting the tires and rendering the loader severely damaged. "That was the trip wire right there," Cappi said. The vandalism was reported to the Inyo County Sheriff's Office, who in response turned their attention toward the group of hippies that Arlene Barker's granddaughter had brought to their family ranch.

Just like authorities had in Los Angeles, Inyo County officers raided the Death Valley ranch on October 12, 1969. Twenty-four members of the group were arrested. Once again, police had no idea they were the same people involved in any of the murders making national news. All the killers, and Manson, were taken into custody—except for Tex Watson.

After Tex led the murder parties on that fateful weekend, he went on to do some leisurely travelling. This contrasts starkly with the prosecution's claim that he was a mindless robot, completely subservient to Manson. Tex went home to McKinney, Texas, to visit his family, he took some time in Mexico, he spent time in Hawaii, and he returned to Los Angeles, all without mentioning a word to anybody about his experiences with Manson and the group.

After the arrest in Death Valley, Katie, who was an integral member of both the Tate and the LaBianca murder parties, was bailed out of prison by her father and went back to her childhood home in Mobile, Alabama. Likewise, Linda Kasabian was bailed out by her parents and left California for New Hampshire. Before anyone else could arrange for bail, Susan Atkins (Sadie) suddenly and voluntarily confessed to the murders.

To be clear, even though Manson was in custody, neither the LAPD or the Inyo County Sheriff's Office had any idea that Manson—or any other member of the group—had anything to do with the murders that were currently driving the largest investigation in the history of Los Angeles. LA County Sheriff's investigators believed that Gary Hinman's murder and Bobby Beausoleil were connected to the other murders, but they were dismissed by the LAPD. Although it's hard to appreciate in hindsight, at that point no one had heard of Charles Manson.

When Charlie was arrested with the group at Barker Ranch and booked into jail, his arrest form listed his name as "Charles Manson, aka Jesus Christ, God." Charlie always had a fascination with messianic themes and Christian mythology. According to Manson, "When you get spiritual, you get Jesus. When you get on Jesus, man, you're crucified. You're not going to believe anything less than death. The Christian's got to have a Jesus."

October 12, 1969 was a significant day to Manson because it was the last day on earth he spent as a free man. I asked him about this day, but Manson was caught up in rambling about Christian mythology, comparing his plight to that of Jesus Christ. "It's very simple, but the Christians don't want to make it simple, because they want to hide their fucking treachery," Manson said, referring to his own story and the biblical story of Jesus at the same time.

chapter fourteen
sadie

# Sadie

*"She said that she had [Sharon Tate's] blood in her hand and she looked at her hand and she took her hand and she put it up to her mouth and she said, 'To taste death and yet give life, wow, what a trip.'"*
  *- Virginia Graham, December 6, 1970*
   *Prosecution witness testifying to Sadie's confession of the Tate-LaBianca murders.*

Charlie and I spoke about many different things during the final year of his life. There were times when he seemed angry, times when he wanted to know things about me, and times when he just wanted to talk. On one occasion, he called me and before I could say hello, he began speaking intensely as if we had been in the middle of a conversation that had been going on for hours. I could tell by the tone of his voice that he did not want to be interrupted. I don't know what spurred him to impart this bit of wisdom to me, but I can say that he felt it was important:

> If you spend five years in solitary confinement watching spiders eat cockroaches, you'll find different levels of awareness, different levels of life that doesn't exist in humans. Everything in life has a capacity. A raven has capacity but not as much as a hawk. All things have a balance with survival. The greatest

creature on the planet is supposed to be, at least according the bible, the boss of all dogs. But, it's not that way. The germs far outweigh us. Bugs and birds live on levels that humans can't touch.

I watched a spider for a year, and then one day there was a bigger spider in the nest, and I could hear him talking. The big spider said, "I'm hungry man."
The little spider said, "Not me."
The big spider said, "I'll whoop your ass, and there's nothing you can do about it. You can run around but I'll catch you."

So they talk about it for a couple of days and then the bigger spider goes over, sticks his stinger in the little spider, sucks out the juice and kicks him out of the nest.

The human part of my mind makes me mad at the big spider. I wanted to step on him. That's how stupid humans are. That's what the big spider was supposed to do because he's a spider. How can I take my human capacity and blame a little creature like that? The guy can't eat anything unless he kills it. You know how powerful that is? If you had to get up and hunt and kill your food every day, you'd be a hell of a warrior, man.

I asked Stephen Kay, the former Manson Family prosecutor, "Do you remember the first time you ever heard of Charles Manson?"

"I think I first heard of Charles Manson maybe sometime in November 1969," Stephen began. "The prosecution had made a deal with Susan Atkins. She is the one who broke the case. I mean they didn't know that it was Charles Manson or Susan Atkins or anything until she blabbed to two of her cellmates. Fortunately, those cellmates, aside from both being high-priced hookers, were law-abiding citizens. And, when Susan Atkins told them about the murders, they phoned the police and told them about it. That's literally what broke the case."

Phil Kaufman remarked to me that when he learned Susan Atkins, a woman he'd recently had sex with, had confessed to the highest-profile murder in the history of Los Angeles, he was not surprised. "That was her, that was very much her. Charlie would have been better killing her and he probably would have gotten away with it a little bit longer," Phil said.

It's incredible to think that if Susan Atkins had not voluntarily confessed to the murders, the police might never have solved them. The LAPD was not closing in on Manson. As of October 1969, they were nowhere near an arrest. They had not located the gun, they had dismissed the idea of Gary Hinman's murder being related to their investigation, and none of the Manson Family were suspects. Tex, Katie, and Linda had all fled the state, and Sadie, Leslie, Bobby, and Charlie were all in jail facing charges unrelated to the Tate-LaBianca investigation.

The week before Sadie's confession, the LAPD held a press conference announcing that after months of intense investigation, all they had was a pair of glasses found in Sharon Tate's living room, which they could not identify. They had examined the glasses thoroughly and determined that the Tate-LaBianca killer was a man, twenty to forty years old, with a small head and one ear a quarter inch lower than the other. Other than that, the case was essentially cold. They had no clue that some of the murderers had posted bail, and others were still sitting in the LA County Jail. The LAPD also had no idea that they already had the murder weapon—the gun—sitting in a storage locker in an LAPD substation.

On the night of the Tate murders, Linda had thrown the gun out of the car window as they drove away from the scene. It rolled down an embankment and settled into some thick grass. Three weeks later, it was found by a sixth-grader named Steven Weiss, who carefully picked up the gun by the tip to ensure any fingerprints were undisturbed and brought it home. Steven and his father called the LAPD, telling them they thought they had found the murder weapon used in the Sharon Tate murders. When an officer responded, he dismissed their concerns as unfounded and, despite their objections, handled the gun with his bare hands, destroying any fingerprint evidence. The officer then booked the gun into evidence, and it was forgotten for four months.

At the same time, the Manson group was arrested at Barker Ranch, and those who could not make bail remained in jail awaiting trial. Sadie was housed in the same cell block as a call girl named Virginia Graham. While making our documentary, we were able to track down Virginia Graham living in Phoenix, Arizona. She was incredibly gracious with her time, and we were able to get her first-hand account.

When Virginia was thirty-seven, she'd gone from a promising career as a Hollywood model to imprisoned for cheque forgery. Allegedly, she'd suffered through domestic violence and tried to cash a bad cheque in a desperate bid to escape, ending up with a short stint in the Sybil Brand Institute, which was a Los Angeles County Jail for women.

According to Virginia, "Susan Atkins plopped herself down and she sat on the bunk and we started talking, and she started to tell me how 'stupid' and 'dumb' the police were. She said to me, 'You know those murders up in Benedict Canyon? You know who did it, don't you?' And I said, 'No.' And she said, as cold as can be, 'You're looking at her.'"

Interestingly, despite her candour with Virginia, Susan never mentioned two key words, "Helter Skelter."

"She didn't say 'Helter Skelter,'" Virginia said. "I heard about 'Helter Skelter' later on, but I don't recall her telling me anything about it."

Susan Atkins was denied compassionate release in 2008 for being associated with the Manson Family crimes, and she died from brain cancer in prison. In 1969, however, the DA was willing to overlook the brutality of her actions. When the grand jury was convened on December 5, 1969, to seek an indictment against Charles Manson, Tex, Sadie, Linda, and Katie, the prosecution's star witness was Sadie, who testified to the specifics of the murders that took place on August 8 and August 10, 1969. Atkins began her testimony solemnly saying, "My life doesn't mean that much to me, I just want to see [this] is taken care of."

During the course of the hearing—in which twenty-two witnesses were called—there was no mention of a race war. In fact, the prosecution didn't ask a single witness about a race war, and the term "Helter Skelter" was only discussed briefly—in so much as it was the title of a Beatles song that had appeared at one of the crime scenes.

Susan Atkins made no mention of a race war, and despite being an active participant in the Tate murders, she was able to make a deal with the prosecution to testify for a reduced sentence. As Stephen Kay explained to me, "The deal with Susan Atkins, was that she could plea to second-degree murder, which thank goodness that didn't happen because she stabbed Sharon Tate to death, and Tex was in on murder of Gary Hinman."

The moment that stuck out in Stephen's mind was how callous Susan was when confronting Sharon Tate after her three friends had been slaughtered in front of her. Stephen said, "Sharon was begging for her life. She was being held by Susan Atkins and Sharon said, 'Please don't kill me, please don't kill me. I just want to have my baby. Please let me have my baby.' And Susan Atkins looked her in the eye, and pardon my English, but she said, 'Look bitch, I don't care about you or your child. You're going to die, and you'd better be ready for it, and I don't feel a thing behind it.'"

Susan Atkins herself recalled this moment in a 1976 interview, saying, "I felt nothing, I felt absolutely nothing for her as she begged for the life of her baby."

I asked Stephen, "Do you think Susan Atkins was a true sociopath?"

He replied, "Well, she was definitely a sociopath, but I think of all of them—I would describe her as the craziest of all of them, and the most under Manson's influence. One time, Manson told her to go get him a coconut down in Brazil and she went out the front door like she was going to go down to Brazil to get him a coconut. She was pretty strange. I thought the strangest of the family members was Susan Atkins and Nancy Pitman. Nancy Pitman was scary. She would, like, stab you in the back without thinking twice about it."

With this in mind it's hard to fathom why the Los Angeles District Attorney's Office was on the cusp of allowing Susan to serve a reduced sentence in exchange for her testimony. Shortly after Susan "Sadie" Atkins broke the case, the LAPD Chief, Ed Davis, held a press conference on December 1, 1969, at which point he announced that they had solved the Tate-LaBianca murders. He named Charles D. Watson, Patricia "Kern-winkle" (he pronounced her name wrong), and Linda Louise Kasabian as the accused killers. When reporters asked how they had solved the case, Davis outright lied and said the "tenacious investigation carried on by the robbery homicide detectives—developed a suspicion and caused them to do a vigorous amount of work in this Spahn Ranch area, and the people connected with Spahn Ranch, which led us to where we are today."

Behind the scenes, two lead prosecutors named Aaron Stovitz and Vincent Bugliosi had been assigned to the case and negotiated the deal with Susan "Sadie" Atkins to testify.

Aaron Stovitz died in 2010 at the age of eighty-five after a lengthy battle with cancer. Stovitz was a no-nonsense lawyer who had come to California from New York after serving in the US Army Air

Force. Stovitz was removed from the case in September of 1970 after he joked with reporters about Susan Atkins allegedly faking an illness in court. It was also speculated that he had given an interview to *Rolling Stone* magazine in violation of a gag order in place at the time. Stovitz claimed that he thought he was speaking to the reporter for background research and was unaware his interview was going to be published. The removal of Stovitz paved the way for Stephen Kay to join the case, alongside lead prosecutor Vincent Bugliosi.

According to Stephen, Vince wasn't popular in the DA's office. He was overly ambitious, and his take-no-prisoners attitude had a tendency to put him on shaky ground. He was known in the DA's office as "The Bug," a nickname he despised as his name was in fact pronounced "Boo-lee-oh-see"—the "g" was silent. Like Stovitz, Bugliosi was not from California; he was native to a small town called Hibbing, Minnesota. When he took on the Manson case, Bugliosi was only five years out of law school, but his legendary work ethic and ambition had made him a candidate to lead the largest case in the history of Los Angeles.

When Stephen Kay began working alongside Bugliosi, Stovitz pulled him aside saying, "Don't worry Steve, this is just another big case in LA. Five years from now no one will even remember it." Stephen laughed, as Vince had the entirely opposite opinion. "Vince, he knew that this was his meal ticket," Stephen recalled.

When Stephen Kay walked into court, he noticed a man sitting behind the prosecutors' table scribbling notes. Stephen didn't recognize him as an LA reporter and was later shocked to learn the man was Curt Gentry, an author Vince had hired to write a book about the case before it was even tried. "He didn't tell me that he was writing a book during the trial," Stephen recalled. "He didn't tell anybody about it. He knew this was gonna make him rich and famous."

Knowing that Vince Bugliosi was writing his now-infamous book, *Helter Skelter*, prior to and during the trial is unsettling because it changes his motivation from seeking justice to establishing a sensational narrative to further his own fame. Though he couldn't know it at the time, *Helter Skelter* would go on to become the bestselling true crime book of all time, defining who Charles Manson was to the general public. How can a prosecutor be seeking truth or considering justice if his underlying motive is celebrity and personal fortune? As a district attorney, the lawyer's clients are the people in the district he represents. Bugliosi was tasked with representing the people who make up the state of California. His personal interest in furthering the successs of his book is a clear conflict of interest and brings into question the true reason he adamantly promoted his Helter Skelter theory.

I asked Stephen Kay, "Do you remember what ran through your mind once the team got behind the Helter Skelter theory?"

"Well, I think I found out about that when they were going to the grand jury," Stephen told me. "Aaron Stovitz. He told me about it, and to say it was an unusual motive is an understatement."

"But at the time you must have thought, 'How are we going to sell that to a jury? It's so weird,'" I said.

"Well, it is weird," Stephen replied. "But fortunately, there was a lot of evidence."

This is, in summary, the Helter Skelter theory that was presented to the jury in the Charles Manson trials:

After being released from prison in 1967, Manson formed a religious cult of obedient followers who wanted to drop out of society. They looked at him like a god and followed his every instruction without question. He controlled them with ideological indoctrination, drugs, and sex, then taught them how to commit murder. The connection between Manson's cult and the Bernard Crowe shooting is unknown as the motive was not explored by the prosecution.

While forming his cult, Manson also wanted to be a rockstar and was obsessed with The Beatles. He met The Beach Boys through Dennis Wilson and wanted Dennis's friend Terry Melcher to further his non-existent career. When Melcher refused, Manson came to resent Terry Melcher, considering Melcher's house a representation of "the establishment."

At the same time, Manson believed that The Beatles were predicting an apocalyptic race war through hidden messages embedded in their songs from *The White Album*, specifically the song "Helter Skelter." After hearing *The White Album*, Manson further brainwashed his cult to believe in the coming race war and ordered them to kill Gary Hinman. Manson realized he would need a significant amount of money to prepare for the race war, and his followers believed that Hinman had money in his home—what the money was to be used for specifically was never explained by the prosecution.

Meanwhile, Manson became impatient and decided he would start the race war himself. It's unclear why Manson thought he needed to do this himself, since all of his actions up to this point were supposedly justified by his belief in the future prophesied by The Beatles. For some unexplained reason Manson had lost faith in the impending conflict and decided that he needed to take an active role to kick it off. To start the the race war, Manson decided to murder white people and frame black people. To do this, according to the prosecution, he indirectly ordered his followers to kill whoever lived at Terry Melcher's house. The next night, Manson chose a house at random and indirectly ordered its occupants to be killed as well.

Manson's plan to frame black people for these actions involved having his followers leave indirect references to The Beatles' *White Album* at the crime scenes. Manson believed that both the police and black people would understand these references, and this would lead to the race war. As the prosecution explained, Manson believed that a black person would see words like "Pig" and "Helter Skelter" and explain to other black people that these were references to The Beatles' *White Album*. Those people would in turn understand that *The White Album* was obviously predicting a race war, and they would interpret the crime scenes to mean that the race war had started, and they should all join in.

Once the race war began, Manson and the family would hide in a secret cave in the desert. After the war, the prosecution explained, Manson would emerge and become the leader of the victorious black army. Manson was a racist who believed black people to be inferior; yet he wanted to be in charge of all of them in a post-apocalyptic scenario where white people had been decimated. At that point, he would rebuild the society that he and his followers were trying to drop out of in the first place.

People like Bobby Beausoleil who have spent the majority of their lives in prison because of the Helter Skelter theories shudder when they hear the words. "It's such an insidious book," Bobby told me. "It's a curse having to live with it." We spoke about it further at which point Bobby laughed and replied sarcastically, "Yeah, I've been listening to Beatles records, I've been getting these messages and I need to go out and kill some piggies so that we can start a race war. I mean *Jesus-fuck*, I just can't even believe that was ever bought."

In listening to the interviews from the original investigation by the Los Angeles District Attorney's Office, it's compelling to hear prosecutors ask people about Helter Skelter. In one such interview with Phil Kaufman, who was interviewed by Aaron Stovitz on January 27, 1970, Stovitz asks Phil about music recordings Manson had made, "Anything on the recordings that you know of whereby he speaks of his philosophy of Helter Skelter, the ruination and damnation of this world?"

"No," Phil replies definitively. I asked Phil directly if he remembered being interviewed and if he felt they were trying to get him to say he knew about "Helter Skelter."

"I was really not a friendly witness," Phil recalled. "I was on parole for one thing. I really didn't, you know, want to get connected with these people. And this DA comes out to my house and tries to get stuff out of me that wasn't there."

In a conversation I had with Charlie, he summarized the infamous theory that led to his conviction in a way only he could. "They know how to milk the cow, man. And they do it so well the cow don't even know it.

chapter fifteen
the conspiracy

# The Conspiracy

*"Life is the struggle and the experience of existence. Some people don't like the struggle, but I do."*
*- Charles Manson, 1977*

On April 1, 1967, a Contra Costa Sheriff's deputy responded to a burglary complaint in North Richmond, California. When he came upon the scene, he ran into a twenty-two-year-old black man named Denzil Dowell who was unarmed, carrying a wrench and a hammer. It's unclear what was said between them but within minutes, Denzil was dead—shot six times in the chest with a shotgun. Two weeks later, a coroner's inquest ruled that the incident was a justifiable homicide. The event sparked outrage in the black community at a time when civil unrest over race relations was reaching a fever pitch. The following week, on April 25, 1967, the Black Panther Political Party (Oakland Emeryville Branch) published their first pamphlet—the headline read "Why Was Denzil Killed?"

Seven days later, on May 2, 1967, the governor of California, and future president of the United States, Ronald Regan, was on his way to the west lawn of the state capitol when a large group of Black Panthers stormed the building. The group of about thirty men—armed with pistols and rifles—marched straight through security onto the assembly chamber floor while the assembly was in session. The protestors held their weapons close, citing their right to bear arms under the second amendment, and demanded action for the police murder of Denzil Dowell.

The incident occurred a decade before the NRA was transformed into a fervent defender of the second amendment, so the Panthers' interpretation was a novel form of expression and political protest. Security guards forcefully wrestled their guns away, amidst the Black Panthers' screams that their constitutional rights were being violated. After the incident, the Black Panthers took to patrolling the streets armed with shotguns to monitor police activity in response to numerous incidents of systemic racism across California. The Black Panthers' interpretation of the second amendment was considered so radical that California Republicans passed a bill to strip Californians of their right to openly carry firearms. White lawmakers were so terrified of an armed black militia that they were willing to impose strict gun control across the board.

It's not an overstatement to say that people across the country heard of these incidents, saw the rifle-carrying Black Panthers, and legitimately feared that a black versus white race war was on the horizon. I searched available archived newspapers from 1966 and 1967 in California alone and found more than thirty thousand meta tags in reference to a potential race war. White versus black relations were written about daily in the editorial sections of California newspapers. This was unequivocally part of the public consciousness when Manson was set free for the final time in the port of Los Angeles. It's this context that makes the racial components of the Helter Skelter theory somewhat understandable.

A key component of the theory had been Manson's views on race, and this was something he and I spoke about. Having a swastika carved in his forehead made Manson something of a racist icon. Many people who supported Manson during his years in prison have told me that his swastika was actually meant to be representative of Tibetan Shamans or Eastern spirituality. When he first appeared with the swastika in 1971 and was asked about it, Manson gave a long rant to reporters saying in part, "The mark on my head simulates the dead head black stamp of rejection, anti-church, falling cross, devil sign, death, terror, fear. It is also the mark of the beast." At no point did he mention his understanding of the swastika's Eastern philosophical context. From a practical standpoint, Manson was a lean five foot two and convicted of being a racist cult leader; having a swastika on his forehead enabled him to curry favour with Aryan nation members whose protection he undoubtedly needed in prison.

In our calls, Manson was outspoken in his racism. He saw black people as inferior and was outraged at the election of President Obama. "They let a negro in the president's office," Charlie said, beginning a racial rant out of nowhere. "Negros are not humans, they were running around wild in the motherfuckin' jungle, man, with no shoes on. We domesticated them. We brought them over here and they play acted like they were people. Come on man, go to Africa and look around."

In addition to his personal racism, there's something inherently racist about the idea of Charles Manson. It's not a coincidence that there were no black people in the Manson Family. It's also not a coincidence that all the people who befriended Manson in prison throughout his entire life are white. Manson's brand of anti-establishment philosophy is something that seems to resonate predominantly with white men. The idea that Manson was misrepresented by the culture at large seems to connect with that small group of men who also see themselves as marginalized.

*\*\**

In speaking with Charlie—and developing an alternate theory around the murders—this question constantly plagued me: *What was the point of making up Helter Skelter?* Was it just about demonizing the sixties counterculture? Was it so Bugliosi could become famous or to drive book sales? It certainly accomplished these things, but are any of these truly the reason?

At first, I speculated that it had to do with Sharon Tate.

When Tate was murdered, it sent Los Angeles into a panic. A gorgeous Hollywood sex symbol had been butchered amongst her affluent friends. There's no question there was tremendous pressure on the LAPD and the District Attorney's office to solve the case. When they uncovered Manson and his hippie commune, I speculated that the prosecution thought a bizarre crime required a bizarre explanation. They were under intense media scrutiny, and the public wanted satisfying answers. A group of dirty hippies, engaged in a complex web of sordid

193

transactions, who randomly killed a movie star would have been an unsatisfying explanation for the general public—and hard to understand for the jury. In addition, understanding Manson's role in all of it was not an easy task. He had certainly broken the law in many instances but his culpability—at least in the Tate murders—was very circumstantial.

When I met Gary Fleischman—one of the Manson Family attorneys—I asked him what the defence collectively thought of the prosecution's case against Manson. "I thought it was a horrible case against him," Gary said. "He was forty miles away when the murders took place. So, he was an *armchair murderer*."

The prosecution's main problem, putting aside all the spectacle, was that they had to prove Manson had directly ordered the murders, or had committed an overt act as part of the conspiracy to commit them. After months of investigation they couldn't prove either. During the grand jury sessions, Bugliosi asked Susan Atkins plainly, "On the date August 8, 1969, did Charlie Manson instruct you and other members of the Family to do anything?"

"I never recall getting any actual instructions from Charlie," Susan replied.

What the prosecution needed was to find something in the law that would allow them to circumvent the evidence they didn't have. The best evidence the prosecution could come up with—showing Manson's direct involvement—was that he drove to the LaBianca house on the night of the murders and left the car for a couple of minutes. Because Tex was not brought in as a witness and Susan Atkins was asleep in the car at the time, there was no one who could give testimony placing Manson inside the house. The prosecution could therefore not legally establish Manson's actions. There was hearsay evidence that Manson may have known about the murders after the fact, but no one would testify that they heard Manson say the group should murder people—so at best Manson could only be implicated as an accomplice after the fact.

This may have been enough to convince a jury that Manson was guilty of conspiracy to commit murder, but the prosecution didn't like the uncertainty. The prosecution wanted Manson to go down for first-degree murder—an almost impossible task given that Manson wasn't present when the murders took place. How do you convict someone of murder when that person was undeniably miles away at the actual time the murders happened? How do you prove your case when there is no direct evidence that a person enabled the actions of the killers? The answer is legal gymnastics. The prosecution in the case against Charles Manson, the most evil man in the world, had to bend the law to convict him.

During the grand jury sessions, the prosecution talked about a concept called "vicarious liability," which is the idea that a given person can be held responsible for the actions of another. It's a scenario with the same ramifications of a conspiracy charge—without all the pesky legal requirements. This concept is almost never applied to criminal cases; instead, it's often relevant in civil law when someone is injured or killed as the result of negligence.

For example, if a person goes to a bar, gets drunk, and drives home and kills someone, the victim's family can not only file a civil suit against the drunk driver, they can also file suit against the bartender or even the bar owner, claiming their actions or negligence contributed to the fatal accident. In a case like this, the court can recognize that multiple people are to blame for the actions of one person, even though there was no malicious plot to harm anyone. The bartender and even the bar owner can be found vicariously liable for the actions of the driver. There was no conspiracy to murder the victim but they're all responsible for the death, so they all have to pay. In the case of the State of California v. Manson et al., the Los Angeles District Attorney took this concept into uncharted territory.

The prosecution contended that by indoctrinating his "followers" with his Helter Skelter philosophy, Manson became vicariously liable for the murders. After Manson and the others were indicted, Bugliosi told members of the press, "[Manson] can be watching television or bowling when the crime is committed, but he is still equally guilty. I don't think Adolf Hitler murdered anyone in particular himself."[12]

The Helter Skelter theory was not only sensational, it established the elements of murder and conspiracy to commit murder under California law. According to all witness testimony, Manson never gave any orders, never handed anyone a weapon, and never wrote anything down. This was always a problem for the prosecution. To be found guilty of conspiracy to commit murder under California law, the defendant

---

[12] United Press International. (1970, May 19). Manson expected to be sole defense witness. *The Desert Sun*, pp. 3.

must agree to commit a crime and also commit an overt act in furtherance of that agreement.

In speaking to Manson, he was well aware of this. "I didn't break the law because I've been in prison all my life and I know the law," Manson said. "I know what conspiracy is. I'm not going to conspire to do something. That's kind of stupid isn't it? I'm not a stupid dude. I'm dumb but I'm not stupid."

When Manson told me this, I realized that I finally understood the implications of everything he had been saying. He never denied involvement in the events of the summer of 1969. Manson had no problem telling me that he shot Bernard Crowe, that he'd been involved with drugs, that he'd hired the Straight Satans, and that getting Bobby out of prison was the motive for actions taken later. But when it came to the murders, he steadfastly maintained that he'd purposefully kept himself at a distance. That was the point of Helter Skelter—it's what the prosecution needed to sell the idea that Manson was guilty of conspiracy and murder under the requirements of the law.

The prosecution had to describe a scenario where Manson ordered the murders without actually saying the words. Bugliosi's argument was that by preaching Helter Skelter, which included the implication that his co-conspirators should murder people, Manson was guilty of conspiracy to commit murder. By virtue of being part of that conspiracy, he was vicariously liable for the murders—thus making him also guilty of first-degree murder. It's a circular argument: Manson is guilty of murder because he's guilty of conspiracy, and he's guilty of conspiracy because he's guilty of murder. This subverts the entire reasoning behind the law regarding conspiracy to commit murder. Once someone is found to be part of the conspiracy and not the primary actor, the focus turns to the person who actually committed the murder. In the case of Charles Manson, the fact that he wasn't the primary actor was used to justify the idea that he somehow might as well have been. The entire reason for a conspiracy to commit murder law is that people who orchestrate murders can't also be found guilty of first-degree murder. In Manson's case, the prosecution literally argued the opposite.

I felt like this was a breakthrough in understanding Manson's claims of injustice. When I told him, he seemed excited. According to Charlie, I had finally figured it out. "There you go, there you go," Charlie said. "It's not true on the level that it was presented to you."

I put this to co-prosecutor Stephen Kay who confirmed it was indeed true that they had to come up with a way around the fact that Manson never spoke the words. "I mean they all knew about Helter Skelter, but we didn't have any evidence that on that specific night Manson said, 'Go out and start Helter Skelter.' He just said, 'Go with Tex, and do what Tex tells you to do.'"

This logic outraged Charlie, who surprisingly had a strong grasp on the argument against him. "All that broad said is I think he said go in there and kill those people, well she can think a pink elephant that's hearsay. They had no evidence against me, none. The press convicted me."

The prosecution used the race war as the basis of their legal argument. They claimed that Charlie convinced people in the abstract that other people needed to die to fulfill his prophecy. When people died, he was therefore just as guilty as the murderers. If we consider the drunk driver analogy, Charlie isn't the driver or the bartender. He's the owner of the bar who had policies that inadvertently encouraged people to drink. By preaching Helter Skelter, he theoretically created a situation in which he knew people would be murdered—therefore he's vicariously responsible.

This brings about a massive question and one that we based our documentary on. If Helter Skelter isn't true—and if the alternate theory is correct—might the prosecution have ignored the true nature of events to gain a conviction?

Whatever Manson's crimes are, do the legal ends justify the means?

With the Helter Skelter theory ready to present to the jury, the prosecution had one big problem. They might have satisfied the legal hurdles to convict Manson, but they still needed someone to corroborate it. They needed one member of the Family to testify that Manson had told them about Helter Skelter—and that this philosophy implied that they should kill people. The prosecution didn't have that person, but what they did have was Susan Atkins, who was still coming down from several years of LSD trips. She was unreliable, prone to digressing into bizarre ramblings, and didn't seem to know anything about Helter Skelter.

This was something that Manson's defence team was keenly aware of but didn't seem to capitalize on. At the time, Manson, Sadie, Katie, Linda, and Leslie were all tried together but each was assigned an individual attorney. Gary Fleischman, who was Linda's attorney, told me, "I think if [Manson] had a competent lawyer, he would have either walked on the trial or walked on appeal because there just wasn't sufficient testimony to convict him of anything."

The prosecution knew that their witness testimony was thin and so had no choice but to try and work with Susan Atkins. At the same time, arrest warrants were issued for Charlie, who was still in custody, as well as Tex, Katie, and Linda who had all left Los Angeles.

Tex was picked up near his home in McKinney, Texas. By all accounts he had settled into a normal life with a new girlfriend and had tried to put behind him the fact that he'd led the slaughter of eight people. When he was arrested by local authorities, his father was quoted as saying, "I don't think he done it." According to Tex Watson's father, they were under the impression he had been going to school in California and had seen him a couple of times over the years, during which nothing seemed out of the ordinary. When Tex returned to live with his family prior to his arrest, he had been helping his father at the grocery store where he worked. Tex was taken to the county jail and his family immediately hired a lawyer, who vowed to fight Tex's extradition back to California.

The police found Katie who had also returned to a normal life in her childhood home of Mobile, Alabama. She was pulled over riding in a car with a young teenage boy, arrested without incident, and immediately returned to California.

On December 2, 1969, four months after the death of Sharon Tate, the final murderer—Linda Kasabian—was captured. After the murders, Linda had called her mother and asked if she could come home. Her mother was delighted to have Linda back in New Hampshire and welcomed her with open arms. Linda spent Thanksgiving 1969 with her family and didn't mention a word about Charles Manson, "the Family," or the fact that she had been involved in the multiple murders that were making national news. After Thanksgiving, Linda's mother picked up a newspaper and read on the front page that Linda was wanted in California for the murder of Sharon Tate and six others. Linda's mother confronted Linda who broke down, admitting that she was involved. Linda's mother drove to ask the town's police chief for advice, and he called the State Police. That afternoon Linda was en route to Logan Airport to be flown in custody to California when she broke down. She begged State Police to allow her to see her daughter before she went. The

State Police obliged and arranged to meet Linda's mother with Linda's daughter, Tanya, in a church parking lot fourteen miles east of Milford. There, Linda was allowed to give her daughter a proper goodbye. It strikes me that no such compassion was given to Sharon Tate the night she pleaded for her life and the life of her baby as Linda stood guard— allowing the others to carry out their horrific acts of violence.

When Linda landed in California, she was taken immediately to the jail where her lawyer, Gary Fleischman, was waiting to speak with her. Gary was in a unique position—he received Linda's entire unfiltered account of whatever she saw and did while with Manson and the group. "But I have to admit when I first talked to her it was pretty frightening," Gary said. "I was only in my thirties, and it was scary hearing the story. I heard her version of it the first night they brought her back and I talked to her. The only conversation I can tell you is I said, 'keep your mouth shut and keep it shut in that jail. Don't talk to anybody about this and we'll see what we can do for you.'"

What no one realized at the time was that Gary had a plan, and that plan would change everything.

Late one evening Charlie called me, quickly asking me some random questions like if I'd talked to this person or that person. As the time limit on our call approached, he changed course to talk about the documentary—specifically Linda Kasabian. "When everybody is persecuting one person they all find it easy because that person doesn't have any backup to help with what his problem is," Charlie said. "So they don't consider that what they're doing is contrary to what they said and what their commitments were. So, I'll get back to you to try and explain but be careful with these phone calls and don't use them to cause any more persecution to my friends, my family. Peace, I gotta go, my phone time's up."

chapter sixteen
darling

# Darling

*"[Charlie said] that everything was alright, there was no wrong."*
*- Linda Kasabian, July 28, 1970, testifying for the*
*prosecution.*

It's not an overstatement to say that Charles Manson was
convicted of being a racist hippie cult leader based on the testimony of
one witness—Linda Kasabian. It's amazing to read the court transcripts
and realize that the prosecution's entire case came down to one person.
Linda, who was nicknamed "Darling," was one of the four people who
carried out the Tate murders. She was also with Manson and the others
on the night of the LaBianca murders. Prior to that, she had only been
with the group for about thirty days and had spent very little time with
Manson himself.

Manson and I spoke about Linda on several occasions, and he
was well aware of the tactic used by the District Attorney in his case.
"What they did was they got a woman who didn't know me. The women
that knew me stood up," he said, meaning that the other women held their
ground by not turning on him. "They're still standing," Charlie insisted.
"When it comes down to it those women will always stand up because
they are me." Charlie took a long pause before adding, "I can't get in

your mind." Charlie always took exception to the idea that he was capable of any sort of mind control.

Before Linda had even contemplated testifying, she was extradited to California and found herself in the LA County Jail sitting across a small wooden table from her attorney Gary Fleischman. When I met Gary, I wanted to find out as much as I could about Linda's motivations. "In Linda's trial testimony, she always maintained that she didn't really know what was going on—making it seem like she was in the wrong place at the wrong time," I said to Gary. "Did Linda minimize her role in the murders?"

Gary paused, contemplating what he was allowed to say—his attorney-client privilege was still in effect. "She was betwixt and between," Gary said. "She had to go along with the murders because they had her baby—they had Tanya back at the ranch. So, she was in a mess and she didn't have a lot of options. After she was caught, her only option was to do business with the DA, and at first she wouldn't do it because she considered that snitching." Gary said that he had to convince Linda that working with prosecutors was their only play—or the gas chamber awaited. As her defence attorney, it was his job to do whatever it took to keep her alive and, if possible, out of prison, although the latter seemed unlikely. "I talked to her about it. I said, 'Linda, you either snitch or you're gonna to go to trial and then God help us.'"

At the time of Linda's arrest, Gary's negotiating power was limited because Susan Atkins, a.k.a. Sadie, had already turned state's witness. Gary knew something had to change. As long as the prosecution had Sadie in their back pocket there was no need to make a deal with Linda—she would stand trial alongside Leslie Van Houten, Patricia Krenwinkel, and Manson. Gary told Linda that they could turn the tide in their favour by sabotaging Sadie's testimony and forcing the DA to the bargaining table. "I had Linda pass kites to [Sadie] in jail," Gary told me.

"Kite" is prison slang for a contraband letter. Inmates will write letters, often in code, and fold them up into little squares shaped like a child's kite. The prisoners attach string or dental floss to the bottom of a kite and pull the string to slide the kite across the floor from cell to cell in order to avoid detection.

Gary instructed Linda to write letters full of Manson's rambling philosophy, which he thought would resonate with Sadie. "It was Charlie talk," Gary told me. "It was things like, 'The DA is your lawyer, Charlie is the DA, they are all one.' It was just nonsense, and Atkins was a little nut, so it had some sort of meaning to her." Linda managed to get the kites to Sadie undetected, and Sadie became engrossed in the writings. Soon after, Sadie informed her lawyer that she was no longer willing to testify. As Gary recalled, "They were left with Linda, period."

Going into the Christmas break of 1969, unbeknownst to the media, the DA's case against the Manson Family had completely fallen apart. Sadie recanted all of the testimony that had garnered the prosecution their grand jury indictments, and with the actual trial approaching, the prosecution had little physical evidence and no corroborating witnesses. Sadie's prison confession was hearsay and not one of the murderers was willing to tell the jury what had actually happened or—most importantly—why the murders were carried out. Without the latter, Manson would walk—he was nowhere near the murders and no one was willing to say he had ordered them.

Gary recalled that when they reconvened in early 1970, he knew the prosecution was backed into a corner. They immediately met with Gary and offered a plea deal, proposing that Linda would plead to second-degree murder in exchange for testifying. "I said no," Gary told me definitively.

The DA came back offering Linda the opportunity to plead to involuntary manslaughter. They proposed that Linda tell the jury she willingly got into the car on August 8 but didn't know where the murder party was going when they left the ranch. She would concede that her behaviour was reckless enough to be considered unlawful, but she would not have to admit to being part of the actual killings. Her crime would be that she should have helped Sharon Tate and the others or told someone immediately after the fact to save the LaBiancas. Once again, Gary outright refused their offer. "Look, she was technically guilty of first-degree murder before *and* after the fact," Gary recalled to me. They'd come this far, he reasoned, why settle for manslaughter? The DA couldn't risk letting Manson go free.

At that point negotiations stalled, but Gary knew complete immunity was still a possibility. The DA was desperate and somehow had to reconcile with the optics of letting one of the killers go free in order to make a deal. Before Linda, Sadie had been willing to plead to second-degree murder for her testimony; she would have received a reduced sentence, but prison time nonetheless. Gary wasn't willing to make that deal; he wanted Linda to be released on time served.

In order to get the deal done, the DA would need assurances as to what Linda was actually going to say once she got on the stand. Gary knew that Linda didn't know anything about Helter Skelter, but, with the opening day of trial fast approaching, he reached out to a friend in the Robbery Homicide Division of the LAPD. Gary asked his friend to go to the DA and tell him that he had heard that Linda knew enough to put Charlie in the gas chamber. A few days passed with no word. Then Gary finally received the phone call he'd been waiting for. "They came to me and said we'll give her complete immunity, and finally asked, 'what's she gonna say?' I told them Linda was going to testify that before they left the ranch Manson *told* them to kill all those people."

On August 8, four people went into Sharon Tate's house and slaughtered her friends, before butchering her and her unborn baby. On that night, she surely endured inconceivable terror, and the DA made their case by letting one of her killers go free. Charlie's plan to make others complicit failed in a way he never imagined—someone agreed to snitch despite having blood on their hands. Manson had counted on the killers being unable to testify against him because they couldn't tell the prosecutors what they themselves had done. Charlie didn't foresee that prosecutors would be so desperate to convict him they would overlook whatever horrific crimes the snitch had committed. "Nobody ratted on me, except Linda but she didn't rat because she didn't know anything," Charlie told me, still dumbfounded about this turn of events after fifty years. "If you read the transcripts, you'll find nobody said that I did anything."

After agreeing to terms with the DA, Gary recalled that things moved very quickly. "We typed up an immunity agreement, which said, "Linda Kasabian will receive immunity if she testifies to the truth in the so-called Manson murders. The truth is as follows..." I pressed Gary, asking, "Who determined what the truth was?"

Gary conceded that he was the one who wrote "the truth" on the agreement. "I knew exactly what was necessary to convict him," Gary told me. "Whether that was true or not, it wasn't my business to decide. That was Vince Bugliosi's business. I took the agreement to Linda and said, 'Linda if you testify to this, you're going to walk out of that courtroom.'"

On July 27, 1970, over a torrent of objections from all the attorneys for the defendants, Linda Kasabian was sworn in to testify in front of the jury. Ironically, the first statement from Linda was, "I strongly believe in the truth, and I feel the truth should be spoken."

Linda remained on the stand for eighteen days, testifying to every aspect of the Manson Family. Linda was questioned at length about the dynamics of the group and talked in depth about Charlie's tactics of manipulation and beliefs about Helter Skelter, which she'd miraculously developed insight into even though she had spent about a month with Manson in total. She'd also had none of this knowledge prior to trial. Ironically, in the years after the murders, Linda spent more time testifying about the group than she'd actually spent with the group. In the brief time Linda had spent with the group, she testified that she'd had sex with most of the men at the commune, including Tex, Bruce, Clem, Bobby, and Charlie, among others. Bobby and Charlie adamantly denied this, saying they couldn't even remember what Linda looked like.

Linda first came to Spahn Ranch on July 4, which was the same time that Bobby began staying at Spahn Ranch with his pregnant girlfriend Kitty. Two or three days later, Bobby was involved in the Straight Satans-Gary Hinman ordeal, so if Bobby and Linda did have any sort of relationship it had to have been within the few days after she arrived. According to Bobby, Linda's story was complete bullshit. "I saw her at the ranch before this shit happened, she had just shown up and it had something to do with her kid. I had no relationship with her, didn't know her at all. Whatever she was saying is all her bullshit," Bobby told me.

Despite having spent very little time with Charlie personally in her short time on the ranch, according to Linda's testimony she had fallen in love with Charlie and come to believe Manson was "the Messiah come again, the second coming of Christ."

"What was your impression of Linda?" I asked Cappi.

"Oh!" Cappi said, letting out a long, frustrated sigh just hearing Linda's name.

"My impression. I let her live." Cappi paused. A polite way of saying, Linda is only alive because I didn't kill her. Cappi's resentment toward Linda Kasabian was self-evident, and she wasn't shy about saying it. I didn't know what to say in response, so I laughed nervously. "I'm just being honest," Cappi said sternly. "She wasn't with us very long and she wasn't a terribly sincere sort of person. She wasn't *real*."

Cappi recalled being in the courtroom for Linda's testimony, saying she did everything she could not to burst out laughing. "You should have seen my face when I was sitting in the courtroom and Linda came up with the demure look. This whole gold cross that she was fingering and got up on the stand and said, 'I'm just an angel sent here from Heaven to tell the world that Charlie's the devil, not Jesus Christ.'" According to Cappi, nothing could be further from the truth. She recalled Linda vividly as a latecomer trying to save her own ass, enraging everyone who was truly a part of the group.

Midway through Linda's testimony, a reporter yelled a question at Charlie during a break. "Charlie, what were you thinking of when saw Linda Kasabian yesterday?"

Charlie turned casually from his seat at the defendants' table and smiled. "I was thinking how pretty she looked."

"Are you upset with Linda?" another reporter yelled.

"No, not at all," said Charlie.

"Even though she will testify for the prosecution?"

"That's up to her, that ain't got nothing to do with me," Charlie replied.

When I spoke to Charlie, he said he vividly recalled Linda's testimony but said he didn't think much of it at first. "She never really said that I did anything."

In a way Charlie was right. I told him, "Linda said a lot of things like, 'I think Charlie said…'"

"Right," Charlie did a paraphrase of Linda's testimony. "He may have said this or, 'I can't remember.' No one ever really snitched on me." According to Charlie, he thought Linda's testimony was all heresay and was certain the jury would see that there was little substance to it.

In another bizarre twist, Linda was not formally granted immunity by the court until after her testimony. Although Gary had an immunity agreement sitting in his pocket, which detailed what Linda would say, nothing was presented to the court until two weeks *after* she testified. Manson's lawyer, Iriving Kanarek, presented a motion for the defence arguing that by holding back Linda's agreement, the prosecution assured she would tailor her testimony to fit their case—or risk losing her deal. This is exactly what the prosecution was doing. They claimed, however, that they had held back the agreement out of concern for Linda's safety. This rationale was accepted by Judge Charles Herman Older who later signed the immunity agreement and granted Linda her freedom.

"Was Linda involved in the murders?" I asked Cappi.

"I know how involved she was, and I won't say, but she was definitely involved, yes," Cappi said definitively.

After several days of testimony, Vincent Bugliosi asked Linda Kasabian on the stand, "During the day of August 8th, 1969, do you recall Mr. Manson saying anything about Helter Skelter?"

"Yes, I do," Linda responded. Linda told the jury that Manson "used to say that Blackie was much more aware than Whitey, and super together. Whitey was just more un-together."

Bugliosi pressed Linda, "What did [Manson] say about bringing the white man together to be more like Blackie?"

"He said he had a way to do it, and his way was the only way to bring the white man together," Linda explained.

According to Linda's testimony, on the night of August 8, all the members of the group got together for a large meal in the saloon at Spahn Ranch. Afterwards, Charlie approached Linda on the porch and told her to get two sets of clothing and her driver's licence. After Linda found her driver's licence in George Spahn's house, she retrieved a knife from the saloon, then reported back to Manson who told her, "Go with Tex and do what he tells you to do."

Linda testified that she got into the car and Charlie stuck his head in the window saying, "Leave a sign, you girls know what I mean, something witchy."

Bugliosi argued that these eleven words were an "operative fact," meaning that those words said by Manson in that context at that time became the specific moment he entered into a conspiracy to commit murder. I asked Charlie if he recalled this moment, and he said it was all "crap"—he never said anything like that. "She never lied about me. The truth is they never told the truth about me. No one ever told on me, that was bullshit."

A curious piece of evidence that could implicate Linda as an active participant in the murders is the metal gate at the entrance to 10050 Cielo Drive. According to Linda's testimony, when the murders began, she ran down the hill and waited by the car. In Susan Atkins' grand jury testimony she confirmed this saying, "When we got to the car, we saw Linda Kasabian in the car. She started the car and Tex ran up to her and said, 'What do you think you're doing?'"

Linda may have gone down ahead of the others, but that doesn't mean she wasn't present for the murders. Remember that when Tex and the girls first arrived at the house, they couldn't get through the entrance gate—they had to climb over the adjacent barbed wire fence using the coiled rope Tex brought. When Linda went down the hill, that rope was tied around Sharon Tate and Jay Sebring's necks, where it remained until the coroner removed it the next day. To get through the gate—the only remaining exit point—and to the car, Linda would have had to open the gate using the electronic button on the inside. When the first LAPD officers arrived on the scene the next morning, an officer named Jerry DeRosa opened the gate and inadvertently destroyed a bloody fingerprint left by one of the murderers on the electronic button. The LAPD was subsequently unable to lift the print because the officer had smudged it. If Linda wasn't present when the murders took place—leaving the house to go back to the car before anyone else—she was the first to open the gate, thus leaving the bloody fingerprint. If she wasn't there for the murders, how did she get blood on her finger?

As Linda's testimony came to a close, Manson became increasingly disillusioned with the entire trial—a feeling he carried with him up until his death. "There's no rights in the court of law, the courts are filled with bureaucratical horseshit. You've got a lot of people locked up because of rumours," Charlie said, referring to himself.

"That's why you're locked up?" I asked.

"I know it. I've been screaming all my life for my wife. And, there ain't no such thing. It's how are you going to be represented on the battlefield when you can't be represented in the courtroom," Charlie said, in a way only he could.

Linda testified that immediately after the Tate-LaBianca murders she escaped Manson's group. According to her trial testimony, Linda recalled packing a sleeping bag and diapers for her one-year-old daughter. She said she hid the supplies in a gully, under the guise of going to deliver a message to Bobby in jail. Linda took one of the communal cars, drove away, and never looked back. According to Linda, she tracked down her ex-husband and returned home to New Hampshire, where she confided in friends what she knew about the Sharon Tate murders—telling them she was afraid for her life.

There are many problems with this account. First, it's unclear why Linda would have been instructed to go speak with Bobby in prison. Bobby told me, "She hadn't been there long enough to be close to anybody or to know much about anything. I never even had a conversation with her, so she didn't know me at all. If she came to the jail to come and talk to me, I don't know anything about it. I don't believe it's true."

Second, even though Linda said she carefully planned to escape with her daughter, she inexplicably left her behind. Linda didn't take her one-year-old child with her when she left Spahn Ranch. Linda also didn't make any attempt to get her daughter away from the people she was allegedly so terrified of. In fact, Linda's daughter was still with the commune when they were arrested in the Inyo County raid about two months later. The child was placed in foster care, and Linda flew back to Los Angeles from New Hampshire to retrieve her. At that time Linda had ample contact with authorities but didn't mention anything about her knowledge of the Tate-LaBianca murders.

Linda's story was further brought into question in 1970, when an anonymous young man came forward with a detailed written account of meeting Linda on August 14, 1969. According to the article, which was first published in the Harvard University newspaper, *The Harvard Crimson,* the author was a Harvard student who met Linda while hitchhiking. Contrary to Linda's account of immediately escaping from Charlie and the commune after the murders, Linda is quoted at length speaking about Manson positively, even offering to take the author and his friends to Spahn Ranch.

When Linda's mother talked to the press—in great detail—about Linda's return to New Hampshire, she claimed that Linda didn't mention anything to her family or friends about Manson or the murders. All of this adds up to a cloud of suspicion that hangs over Linda Kasabian's account of the Tate-LaBianca murders.

For Charlie's part, Linda's testimony only confirmed what he already thought. "There's no law. Law's a game. It's who you're afraid of."

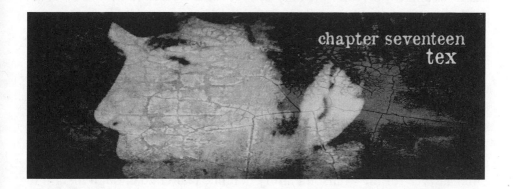

# Tex

*"I was doing what Charles Manson told me to do."*
  *- Tex Watson, September 2, 1971,*
    *testifying on his own behalf.*

A month after Linda Kasabian and the prosecution entered into a formal immunity agreement, Tex was finally extradited to California. After Tex's arrest, California Governor Ronald Reagan personally asked Texas Governor Preston Smith to return Tex. Though Governor Smith publicly said he was more than willing to ship Watson back to LA, Tex lucked into a good lawyer who made a compelling argument to prevent it. Watson's lawyer was a born and raised Texan named Bill Boyd, a former deputy district attorney and family friend of Watson. Boyd argued that the massive publicity surrounding the murders was prejudicial and would prevent Tex from receiving a fair trial in Los Angeles—he should therefore be held and tried in Texas.

Interestingly, Charles Manson's defence team had presented the same argument to the trial judge in California. The motion was written by Gary Fleischman, the only Manson Family lawyer with any criminal law experience, on behalf of his client Linda Kasabian. As Gary remembered, it was those common-sense arguments that brought scorn from the LA District Attorney. "They wanted to get rid of me. I went to

Stanford and I was really the only lawyer for the defence who knew what the hell was going on," said Gary. "We filed a very detailed motion to get the case out of LA County. It had a hundred newspaper clippings in it, and I claimed that the bad publicity was instigated by the prosecutors. That's enough to get the case dismissed, at least on appeal. The Manson case should never have been tried in Los Angeles county, but when me and Linda made a deal with the DA's office, I withdrew the motion." If Gary's motion on behalf of Linda had been successful, all the defendants would have benefited, but since Gary had made a deal with the prosecution, he withdrew the motion to let the trial proceed. Since no other lawyer for the Manson Family defence team had enough insight to file a similar motion, the trial moved forward. Meanwhile, the publicity argument was compelling enough to delay Tex's extradition for the better part of a year. Tex's lawyer appealed through the lower courts, the Texas Supreme court, even the US Supreme Court. All the while, Tex was held comfortably in the town jail by the local sheriff.

Tex grew up in McKinney, Texas and the sheriff knew the Watson family well because they owned and operated the local general store. While fighting extradition, Tex was able to avoid the scrutiny of the media circus and public attention in a retrofitted holding cell a few miles from his parents' house. Tex was allowed extensive visits with family and friends and access to hot beverages as needed. His parents even cooked for him and brought his meals to the jail to make things more comfortable. In the fall of 1970, Tex lost his final appeal and was ordered back to California.

On September 18, 1970, a clean-cut Tex Watson arrived back in California in the custody of the LAPD. Tex was dressed in a double-breasted blue blazer, red tie, and polished black loafers. He greeted everyone by putting on a thick Texas drawl and liberally applying pleasantries like "hello sir," "Yes, sir," and "No, sir." A stark contrast to the drug-dealing homicidal hippie he'd been for the previous few years.

Because of Tex's prolonged extradition, it was too late to include him in the Manson Family trial alongside his four codefendants; however, nothing was preventing him from being called as a witness for the prosecution. Despite this, Bugliosi made the stunning announcement that Watson would not be called, leaving the jury to rely solely on Linda's testimony.

*\*\**

Halfway through the trial, Squeaky stood outside the courtroom amidst a throng of reporters. The young woman stood her ground with dozens of microphones being shoved in her face. Sandra Good politely fought for room to breath, hugging Squeaky's right shoulder. Squeaky's vibrant red hair was parted in the middle, and she was well-dressed in an uncharacteristic black pantsuit. Squeaky stared at the yelling reporters with quiet patience and answered their questions with simple but cynical answers.

"Did Manson tell you to come to court?" yelled a reporter.

"You have the loveliest green eyes," another commented.

"When you saw Mr. Manson this morning how did he look to you?" another anonymous voice called from the crowd.

Squeaky laughed, "He looks however you think he looks."

After laughing off another barrage of questions, Squeaky revealed her true reason for appearing in front of the media. In her hands, Squeaky held a letter written by Charlie. With the press listening intently, Squeaky read the letter addressed to the judge on behalf of Charlie. "I'm writing to you because I don't think I'm getting a fair trial. I have this belief for a number of reasons some of which I will state to you. First of all, I am an individual standing alone defending myself. Contrast this with the facilities you have available to you. Hundreds of attorneys working for you, hundreds of investigators. Thousands of Los Angeles police department officers, many of whom are working on this case."

What Manson was attempting to express was that he was only one man, trusting no one, and he had to defend his complicated actions up against an entire system. This moment stood out to Manson. He explained it to me saying, "As the convicts say, if you do all the talking you got to be all the right. If I can call you fifteen minutes a day, and you can call somebody five hours a day, who is going to be right?" Charlie paused, "You understand that?"

Having spent the better part of a year talking to Manson, I did understand. The prison phone calls were limited to fifteen minutes, after which they would abruptly cut out. Charlie saw this as a metaphor for his trial, and his life in general. Whether in or out of prison, he was always constrained by some similar limitation. As a child, he was constrained by poverty and a reluctant mother. As a young man, he was constrained by societal laws and his inability to cope with any form of authority. As an adult, he was a literal prisoner serving a life sentence.

Manson experienced life looking through a keyhole, imprisoned by a society he could manipulate but never really understand.

After years of thought, Cappi came to a poignant conclusion about what had really happened to Manson. She shared his belief that he was a victim of circumstance. "The reason this whole thing happened the way it did was because they were trying to put a cap on the sixties, and they succeeded," said Cappi. "They killed the sixties. People were questioning the government, demanding answers. They had to put a cap on that, and Charlie was the cap. No more communes. No more LSD."

It's not hard to see why members of the Manson commune would feel persecuted—at least to some degree. In the midst of the trial President Nixon weighed in using unscripted remarks at a press event and calling Manson unequivocally "guilty." Having the president of the United States declare a defendant guilty was controversial at the time— and possibly so prejudicial it should be grounds for a mistrial. Manson Family defence attorneys—aside from Gary—did file motions asking for a mistrial. "We know this is unprecedented in the history of jurisprudence," said Paul Fitzgerald, attorney for Susan Atkins. "If the President of the United States is going to say this then the ball game is over."[13]

Nixon responded to the controversy issuing a statement reading in part, "To set the record straight, I do not know and did not intend to speculate as to whether the Tate defendants are guilty, in fact or not. All of the facts in this case have not been presented. The defendants should be innocent at this stage of their trial."

Trial Judge Charles Older declined the defence motion for a mistrial, reasoning that the jury was sequestered and therefore not exposed to the publicity surrounding Nixon's comments. The day after his ruling the *Los Angeles Times* ran the headline, "Manson Guilty, Nixon Declares," in giant bold letters across the front page. Judge Older had ordered security to ensure that the jurors would not see the paper; however, Daye Shinn, Susan Atkins co-counsel, somehow managed to bring a copy through security and left it sitting on the defence table. As court was about to begin, Manson grabbed the paper, held it above his

---

[13] Associated Press. (1970, August 4). Defense attorneys ask mistrial in Tate case. *The Odessa American*, pp. 6-B.

head, and showed it to the jury. Jury members gasped, lawyers began screaming, and a bailiff jumped on Manson trying to hide the headline.

The incident gave the defence new grounds to ask for a mistrial, but after questioning the jury—many of whom admitted they'd seen the headline prior to Manson's outburst—Judge Older once again concluded that there was "no exposure" and ordered the trial to continue.

chapter eighteen
the devil incarnate

# The Devil Incarnate

*"In a communist or racist or dictatorship country, when they want to get somebody, they stage events for the public. They stage events so that the public will become roused against a certain person. And then they come in and destroy the person that they have made the public mad at. In connection to Mr. Manson, it is being done as of this date."*
*      - Irving Kanarek, Manson's defence attorney, October 19, 1971*

I often wondered why Vincent Bugliosi decided that he had to portray Manson with such grand theatrics. At trial, he described Susan "Sadie" Atkins as Manson's "bloodthirsty robot" who "worshiped" him and Tex Watson as "Charles Manson's head zombie on the night of the LaBianca murders."

The prosecution had established their strategy of *vicarious responsibility*, contending that Helter Skelter made Manson legally responsible for the murders. Why also portray him as the devil incarnate? Manson could have been found guilty regardless of any sort of maniacal intent. In California, the legal elements of a conspiracy only require that an individual act in accordance with the group. There is nothing that states the group has to be completely obedient to any one person. In this case, the DA needed to prove that Charles Manson knew about the plan and/or did something to help push it forward. They went well beyond that, constantly portraying Manson as a "maharaja" or a "Svengali" or, most significantly, a "god."

"Remember," Bugliosi told the jury as part of his closing arguments, "Manson is supposed to be [Tex Watson's] God, or at least Godlike to him, his father figure, the superior being." In the courtroom, it didn't matter if Tex or anyone else in the Family saw Manson as a god. Even *if* this caricature was true, it was completely superfluous. The only thing the argument achieved was to feed the growing legend of Charles Manson as evil genius, so why include it?

I think the answer is twofold. First, as already discussed, Bugliosi had the obvious incentive to create a sensational narrative to boost book sales and further his own fame. Second, and perhaps more importantly, it satisfied a basic need for the jury. The twelve men and women—who ultimately found Manson guilty—needed to understand why anyone would listen to a crazed ex-convict obsessed with sex and death, which was what the prosecution alleged. How could good-natured, pretty young women be seduced by a dirty hippie cult leader? As Phil Kaufman, the ex-convict who lived with the group prior to the murders, told me, "I can't imagine what it takes, to listen to somebody who tells you to go out and kill people? What could be the reason? I could never conceive of what would allow [the killers] to be influenced like that. And, they didn't just kill people, they butchered people! And, to make it worse, these were the very people that I'd been sleeping with."

Bugliosi knew that Helter Skelter was a bizarre and outrageous idea—one that could leave the jury struggling to understand how it could inspire anyone to commit multiple murders. Why wouldn't members of The Family get together and say, "What if Charlie is wrong? Maybe we shouldn't murder people in their homes? Maybe this isn't the best course of action?" How could anyone be so naive as to believe that a race war was on the horizon and Manson's nonsensical murder plot would benefit them? The jury would have inevitably asked these questions, which would have at least opened the door to reasonable doubt. However, because the prosecution was intent on proving in court that The Family literally saw Manson as a god, they ensured that door stayed shut.

If a god asks you to do something, and you truly believe that being is a god, the specifics and the horrors of the orders become

218

irrelevant. You have no choice but to obey without question because you've given up any semblance of control.

This is why Bugliosi had to make Manson a god. If Manson had been a peripheral collaborator, he would have met the legal burden to be held accountable as a co-conspirator; but the jury would still have been left struggling to understand why anyone would have listened to him in the first place. Bugliosi had to set Manson apart, pushing the jury to believe that these murders were not just committed *by* him or *with* him but *for* him. That wouldn't change Manson's culpability, but it would enable the jury to understand him, and therefore allow them to convict.

Unfortunately for Manson, his behaviour—and that of his friends—only fed into this narrative. Squeaky, Gypsy, Brenda, Cappi, Sandy, and others held vigil outside the courthouse, sitting on the corner of Temple and Broadway speaking to anyone who would approach them. They mimicked Charlie's beatnik style of speech, rambling about love and half-hearted philosophy, allowing everyone to believe that Manson had brainwashed them.

Midway through the trial, Manson managed to carve an X in his forehead with a prison-issue razor blade, shocking everyone when he was brought in for court. Manson told reporters he was being "X'ed" out of the trial, therefore he had chosen to be X'ed out of the world. Soon thereafter, Manson's codefendants, Sadie, Katie, and Leslie, were brought into court all having done the same, with fresh cut X's in their foreheads.

In a phone call with Michael Channels, which he provided us with for our documentary, Manson explained the X's saying, "They don't realize that the X on them heads means the head is gone, man. You know, they still think that person's there because they got a head, you dig? But I took the head. I got it on my belt." Whenever the X's were brought up, Manson was downright proud—and he truly meant that he had taken the "heads." The X's were the physical manifestation of the commune's true motivation—one many members have passionately expressed over the years, yet something most people have failed to recognize. They wanted *out*; not just out of LA, out of society. Under Manson's guidance, they thought they could find a better way to live— away from authority, money, politics, hang-ups—away from everything. They shed their personas and tried to "drop out," but the realities of the world kept pulling them back in. They needed things like food and shelter, and the bigger the group got, the more they needed—so they made a commitment to blow up the system and try to ruin the society they couldn't escape from. Facing the death penalty, Charlie was determined to show that he and his Family would find a way to "drop out," if not physically, then mentally. For Charlie, the X's showed that no matter what cage they put him in, he was still in control. "They'll never break me," he often told me, "because there's no such thing." Charlie thought it didn't matter what they did to him, because in his mind he was always in control—reality was a ruse. In his head he could come and go as he pleased, and to Charlie the X's were his proof.

Within hours of Charlie being escorted into the courtroom with a freshly carved X in his forehead, Squeaky, Cappi, Brenda, Sandy, and two others were back on the corner, all with their own freshly carved X's. This time they had also packed provisions like food, water, and sleeping bags and vowed to stay on the corner until Manson was released. They were all arrested for loitering and endangering public safety. As the trial wore on, getting arrested on the corner became a routine. After setting up for the day, the group would be picked up, brought into a local LAPD substation, booked, charged, and released for time served, after which they'd return to the corner and start the process all over again. Ironically, it was this seeming blind allegiance to Charlie outside of the courtroom that corroborated the prosecution's allegations inside it. Walking past the young women holding vigil, their foreheads still raw from mutilating themselves to mimic Charlie, how could the jury not think that Charles Manson was a dark messiah?

At trial, Manson was represented by an outlandish attorney named Irving Kanarek. It remains unclear as to why Manson picked Kanarek to defend him. It's apparent from reading the trial transcripts that Kanarek was out of his depth. To be fair, not very many defence lawyers would have been prepared to represent Charles Manson, but Kanarek had never been involved in anything close to a serious criminal trial. Kanarek was a loud, dishevelled man, who looked and acted more like a man pretending to be a lawyer than someone actually capable of practising law. He was boisterous, often shouting and screaming in the courtroom, relentlessly objecting to things that would make a first-year law clerk blush. He constantly drew the ire of Judge Charles Older, and the jury complained Kanarek's seemingly endless rants were putting them to sleep.

When speaking to Stephen Kay, I asked him about his memories of Kanarek, and he laughed out loud describing him as truly awful. Kay recalled petitioning the judge for a motion to order Kanarek to take a bath. "He really smelled," Kay recalled, saying that the intensity of Kanarek's odour was an actual problem for the trial proceedings.

During the trial there were rumours that Manson and Kanarek came to blows behind closed doors as the trial progressed. There were also rumours that the girls were paying Kanarek with sex. All of this remains uncorroborated.

Twenty years after the trial, Kanarek had a very public nervous breakdown after divorcing his wife. He burst into the office of the Torrence District Attorney screaming and was subdued and subsequently committed to a mental health ward. Kanarek was accused of several counts of malpractice and his licence to practise law was stripped. He began living in hotels and gave rambling interviews to local newspapers claiming his disbarment was a conspiracy against him. Shortly before the year 2000, Kanarek dropped off the grid, hidden from the world by his remaining family, living in obscurity.

While making the documentary, we discovered that Irving Kanarek was still alive at ninety-two years old and living in hiding in California. We were able to track him down and made contact through his family. To our surprise he agreed to meet us for an interview but asked that we not disclose his location. We agreed and rented a house near Los Angeles. We arrived a couple of hours early to set-up and waited patiently. Kanarek arrived right on time, driven to the location by a family member, but instead of coming inside, Kanarek's driver came in alone while Irving waited in the car.

"He won't come in the house," the driver said. It was relayed to us that on the way over Kanarek had not only decided he didn't want to do the interview but had also inexplicably decided he didn't like me in particular—even though we had never met or even spoken on the phone. Irving's driver suggested I go outside and talk to him personally to see if I could change his mind. I walked out to see Irving Kanarek sitting in the passenger seat of the car, his seatbelt still on, staring straight ahead. His window was rolled down, so I went over and greeted him. "Hello Mr. Kanarek," I said. "It's a pleasure to meet you. I've read a lot about you." Irving Kanarek didn't move a muscle. He kept staring straight ahead, not acknowledging my presence in any way, shape, or form.

I thought there was a chance he didn't hear me. "Mr. Kanarek?" I said. "Mr. Kanarek?"

221

Irving breathed heavily, apparently content to pretend that I didn't exist. I stood staring into the passenger side widow for ten minutes, occasionally trying to make small talk, unwittingly entering into a battle of wills with Charles Manson's former attorney—which I was losing.

I opened the back door and sat in the back seat. I figured that he had to listen to me if I was in the car with him. I told Irving about the film, how I had been speaking to Manson, and what I had learned about the trial. I talked for thirty minutes, pausing every so often to say, "Mr. Kanarek? Mr. Kanarek? Can you hear me?"

Nothing.

It was hot so I went back into the house determined to keep trying. I retrieved the driver and a couple bottles of water. We went back outside. "Would you like some water, Mr. Kanarek?"

Nothing.

I put the water bottle in his hands.

Nothing.

After thirty more minutes of talking, at which point Irving Kanarek had not moved for an hour, I gave up. The driver apologized profusely then made the not so subtle suggestion that we should bribe him to get Irving to talk. At that point we concluded our business with Irving Kanarek and watched him drive away.

I later told Manson I had tracked down his old friend, thinking he would be impressed. He laughed and said he didn't give a fuck.

# Locked Up

*"There were a number of kids who were cut off without any money,
begging on the streets, who wanted to go someplace. All they wanted
to do was get away from one kind of life that was beating them
around and get into another one. Now, that is our crime and you all
know it."*
> *- Lynette "Squeaky" Fromme, 1971,*
> *lecturing the court at Manson's sentencing hearing.*

On March 29, 1971, in the Superior Court of Los Angeles,
Charles Manson, Patricia Krenwinkel, and Susan Atkins were sentenced
to death. The penalty of death was affixed to each count of murder and
one count of conspiracy to commit murder, meaning they were each
given eight death sentences. Leslie Van Houten was convicted of two
counts of first-degree murder for her part in the murders of Leno and
Rosemary LaBianca and one count of conspiracy to commit murder,
giving her only three death sentences.

"I'm legally a mass murderer," Charlie told me.

After Manson, Van Houten, Krenwinkel, and Atkins were
convicted and sentenced, Tex Watson finally had his day in court. His
trial began on August 2, 1971, with Tex pleading not guilty by reason of
insanity. His defence contended that Watson was a victim of

circumstance who had become "mentally deranged" from extreme amounts of LSD and other hallucinogenic drugs. Using the prosecution's own words from the first Manson Family trial, Tex's defence concurred that Tex was a mindless "robot" slavishly obedient to Manson; thus, Tex must be found legally insane as he could not appreciate the wrongfulness of his own actions. This left the prosecution in a position where they had to argue against their own arguments from the first trial. Vincent Bugliosi and Stephen Kay had to contradict what they had told Manson's jury by telling Watson's jury that Tex was completely in control of his own actions, operating as an independent co-conspirator alongside Manson and the others.

Their arguments from Tex's trial are a stunning display of contradiction. At Manson's trial, on December 23, 1970, Bugliosi passionately told the jury, "There is no way in the world that Charles "Tex" Watson could have been the decision maker. He was simply doing what he had always done, following Charlie's instructions, because true robots, true zombies, don't talk back." One year later, Bugliosi told Tex Watson's jury the opposite, describing Tex as "thinking clearly," on the nights of the Tate-LaBianca murders and saying, "Watson knew exactly what he was doing. He took every step to ensure he would not get caught and he couldn't have deliberated and permitted these murders any more than he did."

Even though both arguments can't be true—either Manson was in complete control or he wasn't—the prosecution prevailed on both sides of the argument. After a three-month trial, on October 25, 1971, Tex was convicted on seven counts of murder and one additional count of conspiracy to commit murder. After a post-conviction hearing determined that Tex was competent for sentencing, he received a death sentence and was scheduled for execution in the gas chamber of San Quentin State Prison along with Manson, Krenwinkel, Atkins, and Van Houten.

Over the years, Tex has maintained his re-characterization as a Manson "zombie." At a 2016 parole hearing he told the board, "I continued to slowly give myself over to the delusional beliefs of Manson and everybody there. You know it kind of happens like this, I think. You know when you don't have significant goals in your life and you don't have any direction in your life, you begin to pick up the goals of people around you, you know. And then if you have all this ideology going on, Manson's delusional beliefs and that are constantly being talked about and you're feeling like—I was feeling like I wasn't enough, that I wasn't really—you got to realize there was a lot of group pressure and peer pressure going on at the same time."

Charles Manson and the others would surely have been executed if not for a botched heist that occurred three years before they even met each other. On April 8, 1965, a scrawny twenty-two-year-old black man named Robert Page Anderson—completely unassociated with the Manson affair—walked into a pawn shop in a working-class area of San Diego. Anderson attempted to negotiate the sale of a diamond ring he intended to pawn to shop owner Louis Richards, a cantankerous sixty-one-year-old white man. Their exchange turned heated, and Anderson interpreted the shop owner's reluctance to give him a fair price as racially motivated. Anderson pretended to let the slight go and began to shop for other items, including a .30 calibre rifle and ammunition, which were both in a nearby display. When the shop owner saw Anderson load the gun, he ran for the door, but Anderson swivelled and, in a split second, aimed and fired.

The blast caught Louis Richards square in the back and burst through his chest, shattering the glass front door. Richards slumped to the ground and died instantly. Anderson inspected the shop owner's body and was overcome with shock at the sight of it. Within seconds, Anderson could hear the police sirens screaming and building with intensity as they rushed toward the pawn shop. Anderson ran back toward the gun cases and started smashing the glass, preparing as many guns as he could get his hands on as the San Diego Police Department arrived on scene.

When the first responders got out of their squad cars, they had no idea that Anderson was still inside and armed to the teeth. The corpse remained face down in the doorway, clearly visible, so officers drew their firearms and began announcing that they were coming inside. They were met with eighty rounds that shattered the shop's main windows. The cops dove for cover, narrowly escaping the hail of bullets, and within minutes more than sixty officers had surrounded the shop and opened fire, unleashing over eight hundred rounds of ammunition. Concussion grenades broke the remaining plate glass windows, filling the shop with smoke. Crowds gathered nearby, screaming and cheering the police on. The armed standoff continued for hours resolving in a dramatic one-on-one confrontation between Anderson and a police sergeant, which left Anderson shot in both arms with a twelve-gauge shotgun. Anderson was pulled out of the wreckage of the pawn shop, pouring blood and cursing the police who had ended the siege. Incredibly only one officer was wounded, and he fully recovered.

Anderson was tried and given a death sentence in 1966; however, the sentence was overturned on appeal in 1968 because one of the jurors in the original trial—who was philosophically opposed to the death penalty—had been removed by the trial judge. This was deemed unconstitutional, and Anderson was given a re-sentencing hearing. He was sentenced to die a second time. The case, however, was caught up in the growing debate around the death penalty.

Many republicans like California Governor Ronald Reagan favoured the death penalty as a tough-on-crime approach—especially in response to growing anti-establishment culture and high-profile California crimes, like the murder of Sharon Tate. Far-left liberals opposed the death penalty on moral grounds, especially in response to the gruesome imagery being broadcast from Vietnam. More moderate liberals opposed the death penalty because it created endless legal proceedings, and they saw it as a highly ineffective use of time and money while ultimately leading to little resolve for victims' families.

By chance, Anderson's case was taken up by a young lawyer named Jerome B. Falk, who was eager to gain appellate experience and secured funding from the Legal Defense Fund. Falk pushed Anderson's appeal to the California State Supreme Court, arguing that the death penalty violated the Constitution's prohibition on "cruel and unusual" punishment. On February 8, 1972, the Court issued a 6-1 opinion saying in part that the death penalty "degrades and dehumanizes all who participate in the process." California became the first state ever to legally oppose the death penalty, and Anderson was re-sentenced and paroled ten years later.

This sweeping decision meant that all the men and women on California's death row were being held on sentences that were deemed unconstitutional. Charles Manson, Tex, Katie, Sadie, and Leslie were all re-sentenced to life in prison, which, in California, automatically carries with it the possibility of parole. The republican legislature reintroduced the death penalty in California within a year, and it was reestablished in 1974, but for Manson the politics were inconsequential. He had beaten the system again. He was sentenced to death eight times and survived. In an interview that we unearthed for the documentary, Manson was interviewed in his cell by California reporter Stan Atkinson. Atkinson asked, "Do you believe there should be a death penalty?"

"A death penalty?" Manson asked, pondering the question.

"Yes, for someone who commits a murder or something like that," Atkinson said.

Charlie responded quickly, "Aren't we all born to die? We're born with a death penalty."

"But, in the gas chamber?" Atkinson attempted to reason.

"I see what you're searching for," Manson replied, calmly stroking his beard.

Atkinson attempted to ask the question again, "Should there be a supreme penalty for committing a crime?"

"What do you think?" Charlie said.

"I'm the one who's asking you," Atkinson replied.

"I don't have the authority to say anything like that," Manson said confidently.

"You have the authority to believe," Atkinson challenged.

"I believe what I'm told to believe. Don't you?" Manson said, winning the exchange.

\*\*\*

Bobby Beausoleil's case stands out from the other convictions because he was actually tried twice, once before the Helter Skelter theory was established and then again after.

The first trial took place on November 12, 1969. At that time Manson and Susan "Sadie" Atkins were in jail for auto theft but their full involvement in the Tate-LaBianca murders had not been revealed. Bobby had been in jail since before the murders, so he also didn't know that his friends were the "ritualistic" murderers sought by police.

The trial lasted two weeks, and prosecutors claimed that Bobby had killed Gary because of a dispute over money. Their star witness was one of the Straight Satans who described the gang's arrangement to protect the ranch and described hearing about the murder second-hand from Bobby—an unlikely scenario because Bobby fled the ranch in fear of the Satans immediately after Gary's death. The witness testified that "a guy named Charlie," had cut Gary's ear with a sword, and that Bobby had staged the crime scene to frame the Black Panthers. There was no mention of "Helter Skelter" or The Beatles or a cult or any of the other

227

common Manson mythology. As Bobby recalled, "The first trial was just a quiet little trial in Santa Monica, the jury was hung 8 to 4. I didn't even testify because the case was really very weak."

The following April, five months later, in the midst of the Manson Family trial, prosecutors announced they would not only retry the case against Bobby, but they would also seek the death penalty. Bobby Beausoleil was rebranded as a "member of the Manson Family," and he elected to act as his own attorney, even calling himself as a witness to claim that it was Manson himself who stabbed Gary Hinman to death. This testimony was in 1970 when Bobby was twenty-one—nearly fifty years before I met him. In those five decades he'd truly accepted responsibility for his actions and refused to tell anything but the truth about them. Looking back, Bobby recalled that what sealed his fate was the Helter Skelter narrative that had been embraced by the prosecution. "They brought up this race war thing and all of that. It was horrible, man—they did a lot of insidious things," Bobby told me.

On June 15, 1970, Bobby was convicted in a dramatic court hearing in which he screamed at the judge, "He who judges his brother shall be judged. He who leadeth into captivity, shall be led into captivity." [14] Bobby was sentenced to death, and his sentence was commuted along with the others in 1972.

While Bobby was on death row, Bruce Davis was arrested in spectacular fashion during the original Manson Family trial. Bruce had been wanted in connection with the murder of Gary Hinman for nine months. While the Manson trial was on a recess, a barefoot Bruce Davis, complete with an "X" carved in his forehead, wandered up to the courthouse, greeting the gaggle of Manson Family women at their daily vigil on the corner. Davis was arm in arm with Brenda and announced to reporters that they had wed in Las Vegas. He then surrendered to police. Davis announced to reporters, "They want to kill bodies. They're putting murder charges on everybody." He was taken into custody and charged with murder.

A year later, on May 22, 1971, Susan Atkins—then sitting on death row—pled guilty to the first-degree murder of Gary Hinman in

---

[14] Beausoleil loses in bid for new trial; Given sentence. (1970, June 16). *The Van Nuys News*, pp. 14.

exchange for an additional life sentence. Manson and Bruce Davis were also charged, tried, convicted, and sentenced to death.

Mary Brunner was also charged in connection to Hinman's murder but agreed to testify for the prosecution in exchange for immunity. Even though she avoided prison for the Hinman murder, she ended up serving time for a Manson Family crime that took place after the trial.

On August 21, 1971, shortly before 9:00 p.m., Mary Brunner and four others stormed a gun shop called Western Surplus in Hawthorne, California, armed with a sawed-off shotgun. They burst through the front door screaming for everyone to take cover or be killed. The store's occupants—two customers and three clerks—cowered in terror and were forced to lie face down on the floor. The robbers announced they were taking guns and hostages. Using the butt of the shotgun, one of the robbers smashed a display case, and the group began scooping up any firearm they could get their hands on. Within seconds, Mary and the others were heavily armed and ready for a fight. The group kicked open the back door to the shop, where Gypsy was waiting in a 1966 white Ford van, ready to load the hostages and guns. At trial, Gypsy later testified that she didn't know about the robbery when she pulled the van around back and waited for her friends.

Unbeknownst to the robbers, one of the store clerks had triggered a silent alarm, and the call was picked up by two officers just blocks away. When they arrived at the front of the store, they could see activity inside and called the watch commander who drove around back. That officer saw the white van parked near the rear door and a man coming out toward it. Without hesitation, the man spun and fired at the cop car. A deafening gunshot blasted through the passenger side of the front window, sending glass shards flying. The blast tore through the passenger seat and the watch commander threw his hands up to shield himself from the blast. Miraculously, the officer was unharmed, but the echoing gunshot signalled that a shootout was imminent.

Before any officer could return fire, the shooter got off a second shotgun blast, destroying the lights on the top of the police car. The watch commander dove out of the car, scrambling to hide behind a small retaining wall, and drew his service weapon, a .38 calibre revolver. Peeking over the wall, the officer could see the white van pulling away, so he stood up and unloaded his weapon, filling the driver's side of the van with bullet holes. By that time, the other two officers had come around the building in response to the gunshots and also began shooting at the van. The occupants of the van returned fire, and the alley filled with gunpowder smoke.

In a surreal moment that could only happen on the streets of America, the watch commander ran out of ammunition, and a neighbour who was watching the shootout ran out of his house to give the police officer more .38 calibre rounds—allowing the gun battle to continue uninterrupted.

After several minutes the gunfire ceased, and no more activity appeared evident from inside the van. One of the officers carefully approached the driver's side door and opened it. Gypsy, covered in broken glass, fell out of the vehicle onto the pavement, blood gushing from three gunshot wounds. She wept and told the officers, "I'm sorry," as they radioed for an ambulance and additional backup.

Inside the store, Mary and the others were not finished. They opened fire on the officers, who took cover. Additional units responded until more than thirty police officers were surrounding the store exchanging shots, wary that they would hit the hostages still inside. An LAPD helicopter swooped overhead searching the area. The man who had originally shot out the watch commander's window with a shotgun had taken refuge under a parked car and escaped in the initial gun battle. He was later identified as Chuck Lovett, a member of the commune who'd joined later, after becoming enamoured with Manson during the trial.

After about thirty minutes the gunshots coming from inside the store subsided. No one was hit with a bullet, but the robbers were heavily injured by breaking glass and buckshot, leaving them all bleeding and ready to surrender. All were taken into custody and charged with armed robbery. Along with Mary Brunner, Gypsy, and Chuck Lovett were Kenneth Como, a man who was in love with and later married Gypsy, Dennis Rice, a bearded young father who had read about Charlie in the newspaper and went to Spahn Ranch to join them, and Lawrence Bailey, a.k.a. Little Larry, a teenage occasional member of the commune who lived at Spahn Ranch prior to the murders but was not part of them.

Dennis Rice and Chuck Lovett were tried separately, served time in prison, and were released on parole. But Mary, Gypsy, Little Larry, and Kenneth Como opted to be tried together, all requesting to act as their own attorneys, and all pleading insanity.

Though the exact motive for the robbery has never fully been explained, it's been alleged that the group planned to load up on weapons and take the hostages to an airport where they would board a commercial airliner and demand the release of Manson and the others. Once reunited they would have the plane fly them to another country. Their plan worked in a small sense, as they were all reunited when the defence called Manson to testify at trial. A barefoot Manson was led into the courtroom in chains, where he was sworn in as a witness and questioned at length. Manson took the opportunity to say the Manson Family didn't exist. "These people are just part of a group that the newspapers made up…and there was no motivating force other than a lot of people having fun."[15]

Mary, Gypsy, and Little Larry were all sentenced to life in prison with varying terms for paroles. All three were paroled and distanced themselves from Manson.

Many of those convicted for the Tate-LaBianca murders remain in jail. Leslie Van Houten has been granted parole on numerous occasions but because of her association with Charles Manson her parole has been continually overturned. "It's all political perspectives, they're all using everybody," Manson told me. "They won't let Bruce out of jail," Charlie said, referring to Bruce Davis. Bruce is also serving a life sentence and has been paroled multiple times, yet he's kept in prison at the behest of the governor of California, Jerry Brown. "Bruce has been paroled four times, and Governor Brown wants to keep him. Everybody's using us," Charlie said.

Leslie Van Houten, who joined Katie and Tex in butchering the LaBiancas, took a different path after she received a death sentence alongside Manson, Katie, and Sadie. Leslie was the first to renounce Manson and—for a short period of time—was released from prison altogether.

Immediately after her initial sentence, Leslie's new defence team appealed her conviction on the grounds of ineffective assistance of counsel. The sixth amendment of the US Constitution guarantees individuals the right to a competent defence. Leslie had a strong claim as her defence attorney went missing halfway through the original Manson

---

[15] Farr, W. (1973, February 27) No 'Family' exists media created it. *The Los Angeles Times*, p. 5.

Family trial. When the court broke for Thanksgiving, Stephen Kay recalled Manson being upset with Leslie Van Houten's attorney, Ronald Hughes. Hughes was an imposing 250-pound man, bald with a giant combed beard. "I remember we broke for the weekend," Kay recalled. "It was a Friday afternoon. Manson pointed directly at Ronald Hughes and said 'Attorney, I don't ever want to see you in this courtroom again."

That night, Ronald Hughes took advantage of the trial break and went camping with a couple he knew. The trio ventured to Sespe Hot Springs, part of the massive Los Padres National Forest, an hour north of Los Angeles. Hughes and the couple camped Friday night, but on Saturday morning the couple decided to leave because of increasing rain. Hughes told his friends that he wanted to stay by himself, despite their concerns that the storm would worsen. The rain was worse than either Ronald or his friends expected—intense flash floods were reported, making many areas inaccessible. The couple ended up stuck in the mud trying to drive back to the city, so they abandoned their vehicle and managed to hitchhike back to Los Angeles safely. Once home, they had no way to check on Hughes and assumed he had continued camping despite the weather.

On Monday morning when court resumed, Hughes was a no-show. Realizing that no one had heard from him since the camping trip, the court immediately reported him missing, and authorities launched an air and ground search of Los Padres National Forest. At first, sheriff's investigators theorized that Hughes may have become stranded due to flooding and sought refuge in one of the many remote cabins in the area. As the days turned into weeks, it was clear that Hughes was most likely dead.

In mid-December, Judge Charles Older decreed that the trial would move on without Hughes, and Leslie Van Houten was assigned a new attorney. Leslie literally screamed at the judge, demanding a mistrial, saying, "Every time you dismiss us, it's obvious that you deny we even exist."

In retrospect, Leslie was absolutely right. Legally she should have been granted a mistrial due to ineffective assistance of counsel. How could anyone receive a competent defence under the sixth amendment when their lawyer vanishes halfway through the largest trial in LA history? Leslie screamed at the judge, "We can't put on a defence!" Judge Older responded by ordering that she be forcibly seated and when a bailiff attempted to make Leslie comply, she slapped him across the face. This drew further scorn from the judge who ordered that Leslie be removed from the courtroom for the day. As deputies dragged her out of the room, Leslie continued flailing and kicking and screamed at the judge, "During the weeks' postponement, my attorney somehow disappeared. I ask you what you did with him!"

In March of the following year, two trout fishermen found a body near Sespe Creek and called the Sheriff's Department. Deputies recovered the corpse of a large man so badly decomposed that the coroner was unable to determine his identity or cause of death. Fellow lawyer Paul Fitzgerald, who represented Susan Atkins, viewed the body and declared it was Ronald Hughes. The Sheriff's Department theorized that a torrential rainstorm had caused a flash flood in the area where Hughes was camping and that he'd drowned. To this day, fellow defence attorney Gary Fleischman disagrees. "I'll bet your bottom dollar that he said something that got under Charlie's skin and Manson had him killed," Gary said. "I mean, they said he went up to Sespe Hot Springs and all of a sudden he dies. I don't believe it was an accident."

The disappearance of Ronald Hughes gave Leslie Van Houten grounds for appeal in 1976, and she prevailed. Her convictions of two counts of murder for the LaBianca murders and one count of conspiracy to commit murder with Charles Manson were all vacated, and she was ordered to be retried or released. She was immediately retried, and her defence presented the same strategy that Tex Watson's defence had unsuccessfully attempted five years earlier. Leslie pleaded not guilty, the result of "diminished capacity due to mental illness induced by Charles Manson and prolonged use of hallucinogenic drugs that Manson supplied."[16]

The prosecution countered, claiming that Leslie was of sound mind and was an active collaborator in the murder plot and subsequent home invasion of the LaBiancas. Leslie's defence team took the defence one step further, actively admitting that Leslie participated in murdering the LaBiancas. This forced the prosecution to concede that Leslie did not participate in the Tate murders. This strategy was beneficial to the defence since admitting to killing the LaBiancas didn't take away from their argument that Leslie was essentially "insane" while doing so. It did

---

[16] Pfeiffer, R. (2019, June 29). Petition for writ of habeas corpus; Memorandum of points and authorities. p. 11.

hurt the prosecution who was still trying to tie Leslie to a conspiracy to murder Sharon Tate and the others.

This second trial occurred five years after the initial trial, and in the interim the legend of Charles Manson and the Manson Family had been established. The feature documentary *Manson* (1972) had been nominated for an Academy Award, promoting the story that Manson was an evil Svengali who had corrupted innocent young women to become killers. In the film, Susan "Sadie" Atkins is described as a "new mother," Leslie Van Houten is introduced as a "girl scout—an all-A student homecoming queen," and Patricia Krenwinkel is "a Bible student Sunday school teacher who planned to become a nun."

Vincent Bugliosi's book *Helter Skelter* was in wide release at this time and a TV movie by the same name, starring Steve Railsback as a wild-eyed, hysterical, buckskin-clad Manson, was a major event. Images of doe-eyed girls helpless to the maniacal charisma of Charles Manson permeated the media, so Leslie's defence that Manson had caused her insanity resonated with the jury.

After thirty days of deliberation, the jury announced it was helplessly deadlocked and a mistrial was declared. The prosecution planned to go to a third trial but wanted additional time to prepare. With no conviction, and an undetermined date for another trial, Leslie Van Houten was released from prison.

At the third trial, the prosecutors changed their strategy, completely ignoring Leslie's state of mind. Instead, they charged her with murder under California's felony murder law. California has a unique rule as part of the state definition of a first-degree homicide. If a murder is committed as part of certain felonies, like arson, rape, kidnapping, burglary, etc., then all those involved in the felony are guilty of first-degree murder, regardless of who actually committed the murder. For example, if two people rob a convenience store and the first robber leaves but the second robber stays and shoots the clerk, then both are guilty of first-degree murder. If a murder is committed as part of a felony it doesn't matter who pulls the trigger—everyone tied to the commission of the felony is guilty of murder.

When Tex, Leslie, and Katie went into the LaBianca home and tied them up, they committed kidnapping—a potentially applicable felony. But Leslie had also taken a box of collectible coins when they left the LaBianca house, which translated into robbery—another applicable felony. Under California's felony murder rule, Leslie was charged with first-degree murder related to the commission of robbery. She was therefore guilty of murder regardless of whether or not she actually intended or even actively participated in the LaBianca murders. On July 5, 1978, Leslie was convicted of first-degree murder and sentenced to serve seven years to life with the possibility of parole. Her time served made her eligible for parole on the day she was sentenced.

Leslie was subsequently denied parole nineteen times, until she met a lawyer named Rich Pfeiffer, who I interviewed for my documentary. On April 14, 2016, Rich argued on Leslie's behalf and a parole board deemed her suitable for release. Before Leslie could actually be let out of prison, her parole was blocked by Governor Jerry Brown. Leslie was found suitable for release again six months later, and once again Governor Brown blocked her release.

According to Governor Brown's decisions, Leslie has minimized her role in the murders by shifting blame to Charles Manson, thus failing to take full responsibility for her crimes. According to Rich, "the government's not playing fairly." Rich, and many others, clearly see the governor's continual actions to keep Leslie in prison as politically motivated, with no basis in law. "This is a Catch-22," Rich wrote. "If Ms. Van Houten fails to recognize the true facts [as to] how Manson controlled the cult, she has no insight and remains a risk of danger [to society] because someone else might control her upon release. If she does testify to that control, she shifts some blame to Manson and does not take full responsibility and is denied parole for that reason. The Governor cannot have it both ways."[17]

***

Donald "Shorty" Shae was ambushed by Steve "Clem" Grogan and Tex Watson on a dirt road near Spahn Ranch. Bruce Davis and Charles Manson arrived a short time later and participated in the beating and stabbing of Shorty. His body was hidden in an unmarked grave near Spahn Ranch.

Manson, Bruce Davis, Tex Watson, and Steve "Clem" Grogan were charged with Shorty's murder as well as an additional charge of

---

[17] Pfeiffer, R. (2019, June 29). Petition for writ of habeas corpus; Memorandum of points and authorities. p. 8.

conspiracy to commit murder. Clem renounced Manson and lobbied to be tried separately. At his first individual trial the prosecution insisted on questioning other members of the Manson Family about their involvement with Manson. Clem's lawyers argued that this was prejudicial and were granted a mistrial. In a second trial, Clem was found guilty of murder but not conspiracy and sentenced to death on December 23, 1971.

Clem became the first—and as of 2018, the only—member of the Manson Family to receive a death sentence and get out of prison. After Clem's death sentence was overturned along with all the others, he was re-sentenced in 1972 to life with the possibility of parole. In 1985, he worked with authorities to recover Shorty's remains and was paroled, living in obscurity ever since.

In a bizarre decision by the Los Angeles District Attorney's Office, the murder charges against Tex Watson for Shorty's murder were dropped, even though all involved contended that he was the person who physically killed Shorty. In a written statement provided to me by the Los Angeles County District Attorney's office, they offered the following explanation: "The DA decided not to charge Charles Watson because he already was convicted of murder and faced the death penalty." This seems logical until you realize that immediately after dropping the charges agains Tex, the same DA's office refiled consolidated charges against Charles Manson for the Shae and Hinman murders and went to trial.

Manson was tried for both murders in a brief trial in October 1971. His lawyer, Irving Kanarek, continually lobbied the judge to postpone the trial because Manson had become so famous for the Tate-LaBianca murders that his reputation would be prejudicial to the jury. In open court, Kanarek argued that Charles Manson's fundamental rights had been denied. "Where else in history do you have a jury, where the jury knows that the [defendant] has got eight death [sentences] against him?" Kanarek asked.

The judge responded, "The court believes the defendant's position is not well taken, legally or otherwise." Manson was found guilty on both counts and given two additional life sentences.

Considering the heinousness of their actions, it surprised me to research the actual specifics of the trials and realize how many hurdles the various prosecutors had to clear to convict the Manson Family. Bobby Beausoleil's first trial ended in a hung jury, and the prosecution completely changed strategies for his second trial, which resulted in a conviction. Leslie Van Houten's conviction was vacated, and her prosecutors also completely changed strategies to gain a conviction after her second trial resulted in a hung jury. Tex Watson and Leslie Van Houten went into separate trials with the same defence—one resulted in a conviction, the other did not. The prosecution was forced to argue against their own arguments on multiple occasions and was granted victories regardless of which side they took. Leslie Van Houten was the only person convicted under the California felony murder rule although it would have applied to many others who didn't go to prison. Linda Kasabian was given complete immunity despite clearly being guilty of murder under the felony murder rule. When you stand back and look at the legal twists and turns that ultimately landed Charles Manson, Bobby Beausoleil, Bruce Davis, Tex Watson, Susan Atkins, Patricia Krenwinkel, and Leslie Van Houten in prison for life, the only consistency is the prosecution's drive to ensure they all went to prison.

At Manson's original trial it's crystal clear that the prosecution claimed that all the members of the Family were under Manson's spell. As Bugliosi reiterated in his closing arguments, they were "slavishly obedient to one man, their master, their leader, their god, Charles Manson." But if the Family was brainwashed, how are they also culpable for the crimes? If Manson psychologically tortured them, rewrote their very personalities in his own image, forced them to take mind-altering drugs, used his mystical charisma to turn them into "robots," and sent them out on a "mission of murder," as Bugliosi described, then aren't they victims of Manson as well? Shouldn't they be in hospitals instead of prisons? Don't they deserve our compassion for what they endured?

At the time of the Manson Family trials, California followed the M'Naghten rule, a precedent from 1843 English law that states: "To establish a defence on the ground of insanity, it must be clearly proved that, at the time of the committing of the act, the party accused was labouring under such a defect of reason, from disease of the mind, as not to know the nature and quality of the act he was doing; or, if he did know it, that he did not know he was doing what was wrong."[18]

This seems to fit Bugliosi's description of the Manson Family perfectly. According to Bugliosi, Manson was a dark messiah who

---

[18] R v M'Naghten, 8 E.R. 718; (1843) 10 Cl. & F. 200

corrupted lost souls. "[Manson had] absolute and complete control over his Family." Bugliosi argued to the jury that the "Family" were "robots," a term he used over and over again throughout the trial. "Charlie was not going to go to sleep that night," Bugliosi said, referring to August 8, 1969, the night of the Tate murders, "[Charlie] sent his robots off on a mission." After the Tate murders, Bugliosi told the jury, "it wasn't enough that [Charles Manson's] robots had just viciously cut down and slaughtered five human beings at the Tate residence, their blood probably still trickling out of their dead bodies when Tex reported to Manson; that wasn't enough for Charlie. Charlie wanted assurances from all of them that they had no remorse." How can mindless "robots," who Manson supposedly controlled to the point that they had no understanding that what they had done was wrong, be held accountable under California law?

It seems like the M'Naghten rule was made for people who were brainwashed by psychopathic cult leaders. It's such a perfect fit that almost all the members of the Manson Family subsequently adopted the argument, only to be told by various prosecutors that they were minimizing their actions—by agreeing with the original prosecutors. It's a nonsensical argument yet one accepted by numerous courts across decades, and it was the governor of California's official reasoning for denying parole

chapter twenty
death of the boogeyman

# Death of the Boogeyman

*"Burn in Hell"*
*- Front page of the New York Daily News on November 20,*
*2017, in response to Manson's death.*

According to Manson's death certificate he died on November 19, 2017 at 8:13 p.m. local time. His death was listed as "heart and respiratory failure" brought on by end stage colon cancer. I had not spoken to Charlie for several weeks, and I had suspected he was nearing the end. It was widely reported that he'd been in and out of the hospital for months. At times when he would call, he would take a break to talk to a nurse, and I could hear the hospital setting in the background. Several months before, he had called and his speech was noticeably slurred, as if he'd had a stroke. He was difficult to hear and not making a lot sense— even less sense than usual. I thought that would be the last time I spoke with him, but a few weeks later he called and seemed sharp, his voice clear and coherent.

When Manson died, our documentary was practically finished. By that time, we had connected with legendary musician and filmmaker Rob Zombie, who had come on-board to narrate the film. I was a massive fan of Zombie's films like *House of 1000 Corpses*, *The Devil's Rejects*, and *31*. In one of the opening scenes of *House of 1000 Corpses*, one of the main villains named Baby Firefly, played by Sheri Moon Zombie, recites a curious piece of dialogue about killing. People well-versed in the Manson mythology will recognize the quote as originally said by Manson Family member Sandra Good in the 1973 documentary *Manson*. It's one of many Charles Manson references in Rob Zombie films. In the sequel to *House of 1000 Corpses*, another villain stands after a gory murder and says to the corpse, "I am the devil and I'm here to do the devil's work."

At that time, we had decided to call the documentary *Manson: The Voice of Madness*—a play on the idea that Manson's voice would be heard, and the story would be insane. We had already submitted to several film festivals and had a planned premiere in early 2018, but when Manson died everything changed. The ongoing interviews I had conducted with him became the final interviews anyone would ever conduct with him. We completed everything within the span of a few days, and Rob Zombie graciously worked an incredibly long day to finish the narration. We completed the edit over the weekend and, working with our broadcaster REELZ Channel, changed the name of the documentary to *Charles Manson: The Final Words*.

The documentary premiered at the Atlanta DocuFest and won the Audience Award for Documentary Feature, before winning the award for Best Dramatic Documentary at the Red Rock Film Festival. The film was covered in numerous publications including *Rolling Stone*, *InTouch,* and *Newsweek*, and listed as recommended viewing by both *The New York Times* and *The Washington Post*. I was invited to appear on the *Today Show* to promote the film alongside Dianne Lake, a former member of the Manson Family who was promoting a book. I had tracked down Dianne Lake during the course of filming, and she'd hung up on me when I introduced myself.

Dianne met Charlie in the fall of 1967, when she was thirteen years old. Her father had become captivated by the writings of Allen Ginsberg and Jack Kerouac and sold all of their family's worldly possessions before moving them into a commune. Dianne was free-spirited, and her parents gave her written emancipation, encouraging her to go out on her own. She met Charlie shortly thereafter and fell in with the group. She was given the nickname "Snake," after doing a jovial snake impression for the girls—they looked after her like older sisters.

When I met Dianne on the *Today Show*, she had recently published a memoir called *Member of the Family*. I later got to know her better when we collaborated on two subsequent projects. Dianne's book endorses the prosecution's Helter Skelter theory, and during the Tate-

LaBianca murder trial she gave testimony saying she heard Manson talk more generally about starting a racially motivated revolution—not specifically related to the Tate-LaBianca murders. I have always found Dianne to be a credible source when it comes to life inside the Family, but when it comes to the underlying motives for the actual murders, I don't believe she has great insight.

There's no doubt Manson talked about a revolution; the growing civil unrest of the time was a common topic of conversation. But Dianne wasn't part of Manson's inner circle—at least when it came to the underlying reasons for the murders. She didn't find out the group was even involved in the murders until months later, when they moved to Death Valley. Dianne was fourteen for the majority of her time with the Family, and there's no question that makes her a victim in many ways. No one that age should be left to their own devices to navigate the world; however, I also think that her perception of the murders is clouded by the fact that she was incredibly immature at the time. All her insights were shared years later—when the Helter Skelter narrative had become widely accepted and disseminated.

After the *Today Show,* I was presenting the film at a screening in Utah when I noticed Gray Wolf walking into the auditorium with a big smile on his face. I was shocked to see him but gladly sat with him during the showing. Afterwards, Nate Harper, the director of photography, and I took Gray Wolf out to Applebee's (a different location from the one where I first got the phone call from Manson). Gray Wolf ordered a vegan meal, while Nate and I knocked back some beers and party platters. We talked about the film and our memories of Charlie. Gray Wolf gave the film a reluctantly positive review, despite not caring for the "bloody" parts, all while expressing his sorrow over the death of his friend. For his part, Gray Wolf didn't believe Charlie had died in the conventional sense, describing Manson as if he had undergone a transformation—becoming ever-present and powerful.

When Manson died, several people tried to claim his remains, and Michael Channels was among them. I wasn't surprised by this turn of events—while Manson was alive, Michael had told me he fully intended to seek control of Manson's body and estate once Manson died. Michael claimed to have a will written by Charlie, giving Michael everything. Michael and I discussed making a documentary about the whole process if Michael was successful. We stayed in touch sporadically during the various legal hearings until Michael ultimately lost his bid in court. The judge ruled that the will presented by Michael and his attorneys was not a valid legal document, and those contesting Channels suggested it was forged.

Ultimately, Manson's body was awarded to his grandson, a man named Jason Freeman, who was the son of Manson's first child Charles Manson Jr. (later known as Jay White). Jason's father had committed suicide when Jason was a teenager, and Jason and his family had gotten to know Manson in letters and phone calls in the years leading up to Manson's death. While I was speaking to Michael Channels, Jason was working with another documentary crew to film his pursuit of Manson's remains and Manson's subsequent funeral. The project was picked up by the REELZ Channel—the same network that had funded my first documentary—and I was hired to direct based on my previous Manson experience. Crafting the documentary, I spent the summer of 2018 with Jason, his family, and those who attended Manson's funeral. The final product was called *Charles Manson: The Funeral,* which premiered on the REELZChannel on April 13, 2019.

Manson wasn't the only person who died after we completed filming *Charles Manson: The Final Words.* Barbara Hoyt died from kidney failure on December 3, 2017. While meeting her it was apparent that she wasn't in good health—she had trouble moving around and used a motorized scooter. I found her to be a lovely woman, and her time with the Manson Family carried an immense emotional burden for her. We didn't stay in touch after the interview, and I read about her death online in a Facebook post by Sharon Tate's sister Debra. Barbara and Debra became friends in later years, working together to oppose the parole of those still incarcerated for the Tate-LaBianca murders.

Catherine Gillies, a.k.a. Cappi, died on June 29, 2018. I had continued to speak with her after the documentary came out, and I last called her a few months before she died. She said she'd enjoyed the documentary and thanked me for trying to get the truth out, even nearly fifty years later. Cappi expressed to me that she truly loved Charlie and all the others she had met in the summer of 1969. The murders truly broke her heart—her family was taken away from her. Up until her death she looked back on those times with great affection.

After the trial, Gary Fleischman left Los Angeles and changed his name. He laughed when I asked him the reason, saying he was worried that Squeaky was going to kill him. In a more serious tone, he recalled a memorable moment from the courtroom. "Charlie went like this to me," using one finger Gary motioned across his throat, "meaning 'I'm going to cut your throat' and I said to him 'Charlie, when you get out of jail I'm going to have an old man turkey neck so bring a sharp knife to cut it.'" As Gary recalled, Charlie couldn't maintain his menacing behaviour and broke out laughing.

Stephen Kay recalled a more ominous encounter. "One night during the first trial on my way to the parking lot where I had parked, Squeaky and Sandra Good snuck up behind me and said they were going to do to my house what was done at the Tate house." Kay said that he took the threat very seriously and had kept a watchful eye ever since, though no serious threat ever manifested. I later asked Sandra and Squeaky about this event, and they both denied it ever happened.

Vincent Bugliosi died in 2015. His book *Helter Skelter* became gospel in terms of information on Charles Manson with over seven million copies sold.

\*\*\*

The fundamental question I considered throughout my time with Charles Manson was not whether or not he was *innocent*. Charles Manson was many things, and innocent was not among them. Manson was a career criminal who revelled in his life in the underworld, but he wasn't a serial killer, thirsty for blood. When interviewed about the documentary, I was often asked if I thought Manson was "evil." The simple answer is no. He was more misunderstood than he was evil, which is not to say that he was virtuous, but rather that he liked to play the part of "evil."

Manson was born and bred to care about himself above everyone else. In the summer of 1969, he was at best indifferent if innocent people were killed to further his own aims. He didn't relish in the suffering of others, but he also had a very black-and-white view of the world: *you get caught off base and you get tagged out*. Evil is the villainous archetype that was assigned to Manson, and that's at the heart of what I came to wonder about him. The Russian philosopher Fyodor Dostoyevsky is often quoted as saying, "A society should be judged not by how it treats its outstanding citizens but by how it treats its criminals." Was Manson treated fairly, regardless of who he was?

The fundamental question I considered was: *should those in power be allowed to construct their own truth in the pursuit of justice?*

As Gray Wolf said to me, "I don't care who it is, if somebody doesn't get a fair trial then we're all in trouble."

Charlie had long made his peace with the fact that he was imprisoned for a crime he didn't really commit; or rather, imprisoned for a crime he *did* commit but not in the way he was prosecuted and convicted for it. This is what he meant when he said he was innocent, and like almost everything Manson said, he was right—in a manner of speaking.

Charlie had a philosophy he called "My-Me" that he spoke about to many people, including me. As Charlie explained it, "There is no other people, only *my* and *me*." Manson believed that a personal sense of self was all that existed. "I am you," he would often say. The outside world was irrelevant. I thought this was poignant in considering Manson's untold story.

In reality, Manson was little more than a clever convict, adept at the ways of the world after living through a hard upbringing. He was well-suited for his time and place, and through a series of events—many of which he had little to do with—he was recast as a caricature of evil. The devil incarnate; a dark messiah. As his legend grew, Manson became a cultural icon who appealed to white, disaffected men—the swastika on his forehead a not so subtle nod. The killer hippie; the ultimate anti-establishment outlaw bringing to life a male fantasy of creating a sex cult of pretty young women who will act slavishly obedient. Little of this was true, but it didn't matter to Manson. He was willing to adopt any persona to become greater than the man he actually was. To Manson all that mattered was how he saw himself, and if society wanted to portray him as a hippie cult leader, that was their trip, not his.

All this begs the question, did Manson get a fair shake? Surely his own actions largely determined his fate. Can we judge a society based on how the worst of us are treated? I put this question to Gary Fleischman who said, "Do I think Manson suffered an injustice?" He laughed, "Not really, not in my heart of hearts." After a moment, Gary looked at me seriously and thoughtfully and said, "Look, as a matter of litigation, yes. He did suffer an injustice. Did he morally suffer an injustice? I don't think so." Gary's point was clear. Manson was railroaded in a sense, but—based on what Manson had actually done—the ends justify the means. This still leaves me asking: *If the prosecution had pursued the alternate theory with its brutal but less sensational elements, would anyone even know who Charles Manson is? And, would he have died in prison?*

I believe that if Manson had been convicted of the crimes he actually committed, we wouldn't know who he was. He would have died an old parolee, living in obscurity like many others who were convicted of murder in the 1960s and subsequently released.

Charlie often spoke about death. On one occasion Charlie said, "How many times have we all died. What is died? No one really dies and no one's really born. We made up all those things. It's eternal." Charlie had a fundamental belief that life was a fleeting circumstance—a never-ending game that he'd somehow won because he could see it for what it really was.

Charlie said, "The sun makes all the light in the world and the universe; look at the stars at night, man, how many thousands of millions of light years has that sun been lighting all those stars? How can you slow yourself down to one lifetime?"

epilogue
paroled

# Epilogue - Paroled

In late 2018, Bobby called me and told me his next parole hearing was coming up. I wasn't optimistic—Bobby had been denied parole eighteen times in his forty-nine years in prison. "This one feels different," Bobby said, sounding full of hope. To aid his bid for release, Bobby asked me if I'd write him a letter of support to the parole board, which I gladly did:

To Whom It May Concern,

My name is James Buddy Day, and I am a documentary TV and film producer, director, and writer. Over the past few years, I have gotten to know Bobby Beausoleil and would like to offer my support for his release.

All homicides are tragic, and I can only imagine the pain that Gary Hinman's death has brought upon his family. I understand this must be considered; however, I do believe that Bobby understands the gravity of his actions from 1969 and is reformed.

According to statistics published by the California CDC, the average time served for first-degree murder (crimes committed pre-November 1978) was 408.8 months. Bobby was arrested on August 6, 1969 and has been in custody for over 591 months. This means that his sentence has thus far been fifteen years longer than the average person convicted of the same crime. This additional time is due to the fact that Bobby has been labelled as a member of the Manson Family.

Unfortunately, when tragedy becomes the focus of national attention the truth often becomes distorted and more people suffer as a result.
I have undertaken a significant amount of journalistic work on the subject of Charles Manson, and I can say with certainty that Bobby's characterization has been unfair. During his incarceration, Bobby has been forthright and honest about his transgressions. He has demonstrated accountability and remorse in spite of continual personal scrutiny and consistently strived to demonstrate that he is fit for release.

Despite his lengthy incarceration, Bobby has become an accomplished musician and has attempted to better himself through art, education, and spiritual growth. I have had the opportunity to work with him on a feature documentary, which was featured in *Rolling Stone, The New York Times, The Washington Post*, and the *Today Show*, among numerous other media outlets.

If paroled, I believe Bobby will be a respectful member of the community. I would welcome the opportunity to work with him further and aid in helping him find employment in the entertainment industry. I would be eager to work with Bobby, and not just as a subject but as a musical collaborator, advisor, or other production specialty. I ask you to please consider my support in considering his parole.

Sincerely yours,

James Buddy Day

I sent the letter to Bobby's attorney Jason Campbell, and Bobby and I continued to keep in touch. As the date of his parole hearing approached, I was surprised at Bobby's increasing level of optimism. He truly felt something had changed—that people had begun to see him as something other than the Manson Family cast member he'd be erroneously portrayed as.

There is no question that Bobby killed his friend Gary Hinman, and in my mind, there is no question that Bobby did so for bad reasons unassociated with Helter Skelter. I've spoken with Bobby at length about the day he murdered Gary, and Bobby is full of sorrow, emotional burden, and guilt. The sad truth is that Bobby made an egregious mistake, and only the Hinman family can decide if he should be forgiven. But as a society we've decided that people who commit murder—in the same way Bobby did—have the opportunity to be released from prison if they are no longer a risk to the public. Bobby is a high-profile, low-risk individual. He has many friends and family members in the community, he understands that what he did was wrong, and he carries immense remorse. There is absolutely no legal reason to keep him in prison, other than his unfortunate association with Charles Manson.

I wrote to Bobby on January 2, the day before his parole hearing, and wished him luck. I told him I was "anxiously optimistic," although I truly didn't believe he would be successful. The biggest problem he would face is that he'd been adamant about the truth of his crimes. He's refused to lie and "admit" that he was a "Manson Family" villain from the pages of *Helter Skelter*. The problem is that the *Helter Skelter* narrative *is* the official record, and under California law it is considered fact to the parole board members who weigh Bobby's potential release. I frankly did not have faith that anyone reviewing Bobby's case would take the time to properly research the intricacies of the Manson Family saga, before hearing what Bobby had to say in his defence.

I was wrong.

Late in the evening on January 3, 2019, my phone buzzed on my bedside table. It was a text from Gray Wolf telling me that Bobby had been recommended for parole. I texted back my amazement and began reading about the decision online. I hurriedly emailed Bobby some hearty congratulations.

Immediately after Bobby's parole decision, Debra Tate, Sharon Tate's sister, began publicly opposing his release. In the decades after her sister's murder, Debra Tate became an advocate to keep all members of the Manson Family in prison for life. After Bobby won his parole, Debra was quoted as saying, "This man does not belong outside the walls of prison."[19] It's unclear to me how she believed she knew this as Debra had no contact whatsoever with Bobby. Debra Tate also posted a petition on her website (noparoleformansonfamily.org) to block Bobby's release.

As terrible as Bobby's crime was, his actions had nothing to do with the death of Sharon Tate. Bobby was in an LA County Jail on August 8, 1969 and had absolutely no involvement with the planning or execution of the home invasion that killed Debra's sister—he didn't even know it was happening. Bobby has not paid a debt to society for the Tate-LaBianca murders because he had nothing to do with the Tate-LaBianca murders. I can completely understand Debra's vehement opposition to Tex Watson or Patricia Krenwinkel being released—they stared her sister in the eye as she begged for her life. But I can't help but feel that her continued opposition to Bobby's release is misplaced.

Working in Bobby's favour was the 2018 gubernatorial election. Governor Jerry Brown, who had blocked the parole of Bruce Davis and Leslie Van Houten on numerous occasions, was no longer in office. Governor Brown had been long opposed to the release of members of the Manson Family, which may have been related to Lynette "Squeaky" Fromme's attempt to assassinate President Gerald Ford. Governor Brown served as governor on two separate occasions (1973–1975 and again 2011–2019). It was during Governor Brown's first term that Squeaky put a gun to the head of President Ford, who was walking across a street toward a meeting with Governor Brown. Fromme was still paroled in 2009. She, along with Clem, Mary, Brenda, Gypsy, and Sandra Good are the only members of the Manson Family who have been granted parole and have not had it overturned by the governor. Sandra Good and Brenda served time in prison for offences unrelated to the Tate-LaBianca murders.

The decision to stand aside and allow Bobby's release to proceed fell on incoming Democratic Governor Gavin Newsom. In California, once an inmate is found suitable for parole the decision is automatically sent for a 120-day review by the California Board of Parole. If they affirm the decision, then the governor has thirty days to respond. The governor has three options. First, the governor can support the decision,

---

[19] Thompson, Don. (2019, January 4th). Charles Manson follower, murderer recommended for parole. *The Mercury News*, Retrieved, January 2019, https://www.mercurynews.com/2019/01/04/first-time-parole-recommendation-for-charles-manson-follower/

in which case the inmate is released. Second, the governor can reverse the decision, in which case the inmate stays in prison and gets another parole hearing within one year. Third, the governor can do absolutely nothing, in which case the inmate is released after the thirty-day response period.

Adding to the politics of Bobby's potential release is the parole of Leslie Van Houten. Since our documentary's release, Leslie's attorney Rich Pfeiffer has remained tirelessly fighting on her behalf. "I'm going to get her out," Rich told me. "The government's not playing fairly." Leslie had been denied parole nineteen times before Rich won her first parole hearing in 2016. This parole decision was overturned by Governor Jerry Brown. The same thing happened again the following year, and less than a month after Bobby was found suitable for parole, Leslie was also found suitable for parole (for a third time).

What that meant was newly elected Governor Gavin Newsom would have to decide the fates of both Bobby and Leslie at virtually the same time. If he denied their parole, he also faced the prospect of having to keep denying their parole every year for his entire term.

Apparently, this was the road that Governor Newsom was willing to go down.

I heard from Bobby on April 30, 2019. He was devastated to learn that Governor Newsom had overturned his parole decision. In a written opinion, Governor Newsom justified overturning Bobby's parole saying, "Mr. Beausoleil helped perpetrate the first of the Manson Family's atrocious high-profile murders in an attempt to start a civilization-ending race war. Mr. Beausoleil and other Manson family members kept Mr. Hinman hostage and tortured him over several days in an attempt to finance their apocalyptic scheme. When Mr. Hinman refused to cooperate, Mr. Manson sliced Mr. Hinman's throat and severed his ear, before Mr. Beausoleil stabbed him to death."

It's stunning to me that a life-changing decision made by the California governor could be written so ignorantly. Even setting aside the incorrect "race war" motive, Newsom's description of the crime is just factually wrong—not the least of which includes describing Gary Hinman as having his throat slit, which he plainly didn't. Even though Governor Newsom doesn't seem to be aware of the actual circumstances of Bobby's crimes, the details of how the crime was committed are actually irrelevant in terms of his parole. Bobby's sentence is life *with the possibility of parole*. Bobby can't do anything about the circumstances of his crime. If those circumstances are a determining factor in whether or not he should be released, then the governor is in effect changing his sentence to life with *no* possibility for parole—since the crime itself will never change.

The governor is essentially saying that no matter how much Bobby fulfills the suitability requirements for parole, he will always be a member of the Manson Family and thus can never be released—regardless of the law. Governor Newsom doubled down on his decision two months later on June 3, 2019, by ruling against Leslie Van Houten's parole, once again citing the Family's ambitions to start a race war. Leslie Van Houten is a master's degree-educated, self-help counselling, sixty-nine-year-old woman, who was eligible for parole on the day she was sentenced, forty-one years ago. Her master's degree thesis was on sustained rehabilitation. But according to Governor Newsom, she is an "unreasonable risk to society." In both Bobby and Leslie's cases, they obviously pose no risk and are being held in prison because of who they supposedly are or were and not because of what they've done. Nobody is entitled to parole, but if the government determines that it's in the best interest of the community to keep Bobby and Leslie in prison, the decision needs to be based on valid reasons. Bobby and Leslie should not continue to be punished because of the mythology they've become associated with.

People often ask me, "Why are you so fascinated with the Manson murders?" To me, the Manson story has become American folklore—in the same vein as Lizzy Borden or Bonnie and Clyde. A "true" crime story full of Jungian archetypes: heroes, outlaws, lovers, and sages. In the over fifty years since 1969, the details have become fuzzy, clouded by time and oral history. It's truly unfortunate that the myth of the Manson saga has replaced the reality in most people's minds.

That's why unravelling the truth resonates with me, because it matters, and it just disappears as time goes on.

## The Manson Family

**Susan Atkins, a.k.a. Sadie Mae Glutz**. As a teenager, Susan was abandoned by her alcoholic father after her mother died from cancer. Atkins became a heavy user of LSD and was working as a topless dancer in San Francisco when she met Manson. Atkins was present for the murder of Gary Hinman and was one of the four who participated in the Tate murders. In prison, Atkins married twice. She died from brain cancer in 2008.

**Bobby Beausoleil, a.k.a. Cupid**, met Manson while both were active in the Topanga Canyon music scene in 1968. Several of the Manson Family women met Manson through Bobby, including Katherine "Kitty" Lutesinger, Catherine "Gypsy" Share, and Leslie Van Houten. Bobby was the first person in the Manson commune convicted of murder, after he stabbed Gary Hinman to death on July 27, 1969. In 2019, Bobby was found suitable for parole, a decision that was blocked by the Governor of California, Gavin Newsom.

**Ella Jo Bailey** met Manson and several of the Manson Family women in San Francisco, at approximately the same time as Susan Atkins. Bailey and Patricia Krenwinkel, were later picked up hitchhiking by Dennis Wilson, facilitating his introduction to Manson. Bailey's statements to investigators and subsequent testimony were the basis for the allegation that Charles Manson sought money from Gary Hinman to further the "Helter Skelter" race war. Bailey left the commune the day after the Hinman murder. She died in 2015.

**Mary Brunner, a.k.a. Mother Mary**, is often referred to as the first member of the Manson Family. Mary met Manson while she was working at UC Berkeley in San Francisco. Mary gave birth to Manson's child named Son-stone (raised by Mary's parents as Michael Brunner). Mary was present for the Gary Hinman murder but not prosecuted as part of an immunity deal for her testimony—which she later renounced. Mary was convicted for her role in the 1971 Hawthorne shootout with police and served six and a half years in prison. After her release she lived in anonymity in the Midwest with her family.

**Bruce Davis** first met Manson and several of the Manson women in Oregon in 1967, and he became an active member of the commune. Bruce drove Beausoleil, Atkins, Brunner, and Manson to Gary Hinman's apartment on the day of the Hinman murder, and he also participated in the Donald "Shorty" Shea murder— he was later convicted of both. Bruce went into hiding during the Tate-LaBianca murder trial but voluntarily turned himself in to police in front of reporters at the courthouse. As of 2018, Bruce had been found eligible for parole five times but remained in prison because of continual opposition from the former Governor of California, Jerry Brown.

**Lynette Fromme, a.k.a. Squeaky**, met Manson in Venice Beach, California, after escalating tensions with her authoritarian father resulted in her leaving home. After Manson's arrest, Lynette assumed a leadership role in the commune. In 1975, Lynette was convicted of attempting to assassinate President Gerald Ford and served thirty-four years in prison. She was paroled in 2009 and published a memoir, *Reflexion*, in 2018.

**Sandra Good, a.k.a. Blue**, met Manson and the women while on vacation in 1968. Within a few days she quit her job, electing to stay with the commune. She never returned home. Good grew up in an affluent family but suffered from numerous respiratory conditions requiring multiple surgeries as a child. Good has described her home life as extremely abusive, claiming her mother wanted her to die. Good was later convicted of conspiracy to send death threats through the mail related to Lynette Fromme's attempt to assassinate President Gerald Ford. Sandra Good was paroled in 1985 over her own objections—she wished to stay in prison to show solidarity with Manson and the others.

**Catherine Gillies, a.k.a. Capistrano or Cappi,** met Manson and the women sometime in 1968 and became a beloved member of the commune. Gillies' family owned the Death Valley properties that became home to the group after the murders. They were ultimately arrested there in October 1969. Gillies died in 2018.

**Steve Grogan, a.k.a. Clem,** was a runaway who met Manson and the others at Spahn Ranch in 1968. Grogan was in the car on the night of the LaBianca murders and participated in the Donald "Shorty" Shae murder. Grogan was never prosecuted for the LaBianca murders due to a lack of evidence, but he was convicted of the Shae murder after two trials. Grogan was paroled in 1985, in part because he aided authorities in recovering Donald Shae's remains.

**Barbara Hoyt** was a California native from a middle-class family who met Manson and the women after running away from home. Hoyt later testified at the Tate-LaBianca and Shae trials. Several of the women conspired to prevent her from testifying by providing her airfare to Hawaii and poisoning her with an LSD-laced hamburger. Barbara later went back to school, becoming a nurse. She died in 2017 from kidney failure.

**Linda Kasabian, a.k.a. Darling**, met Manson and the others three weeks before the murders, after a falling out with her husband. Linda participated in the Tate-LaBianca murders but was not prosecuted due to an immunity deal with the Los Angeles County District Attorney's Office. After the trial, she went into hiding but did a series of interviews in 2009 associated with a documentary. As of 2019, she is the only person still living who participated in the Tate-LaBianca murders and is not in prison.

**Patricia Krenwinkel, a.k.a. Katie,** came from a dysfunctional family largely due to conflicts involving her older half-sister, Charlene. After her parents divorced, Krenwinkel lived with Charlene who became addicted to heroin. Desperate to leave, Krenwinkel met Manson, Mary Brunner, and Lynette Fromme in 1967 and began to travel with them. Krenwinkel participated in the Tate-LaBianca murders, notably stabbing Abigail Folger and Rosemary LaBianca and writing on the LaBianca walls in blood. As of 2019, she remains incarcerated in the California Institute for Women.

**Dianne Lake, a.k.a. Snake,** met Manson and the group in the fall of 1967, when she was fourteen years old. At the time, her parents had given her written emancipation, encouraging her to go out on her own. Dianne was given the nickname "Snake" after doing a snake impression for the girls. Lake was one of the youngest in the group, along with Cappi. Dianne was arrested with the others in the Death Valley raid, and she was later admitted for an extended period of time to a state psychiatric hospital. Her mental health was a source of contention during the trial, but she was ultimately found competent to testify on behalf of the prosecution.

**Nancy Pitman, a.k.a. Brenda,** grew up in an affluent home but left due to tensions within her family. Pitman was introduced to Manson through a mutual friend sometime in 1968 and became a vocal supporter of Manson and the others during the Manson Family trials. She testified for the defence on several occasions. Pitman was later incarcerated for numerous offences including attempting to smuggle LSD to Manson in prison and being an accomplice to a double homicide that took place in 1972.

**Catherine Share, a.k.a. Gypsy,** was born in France where her father was killed, and her mother committed suicide after being raped and forced into prostitution during World War II. Share was adopted by American parents, but her adoptive mother also committed suicide after becoming ill with cancer. Share became estranged from her adoptive father and began dating Bobby Beausoleil, who introduced her to Charles Manson. Catherine was later convicted for her role in the 1971 Hawthorne shootout with police and served five years in prison. She later went into hiding to raise her son.

**Leslie Van Houten, a.k.a. Lulu.** After her father had an affair, Leslie's parents divorced, leading her into depression and drugs. Leslie became pregnant and her mother arranged an illegal abortion. Leslie subsequently became involved in the hippie subculture of the San Francisco Haight-Ashbury district, where she met Bobby Beausoleil and Catherine Share, leading to her introduction to Manson. Leslie participated in the LaBianca murders and was convicted alongside Susan Atkins, Patricia Krenwinkel, and Manson. Her initial conviction was overturned in 1976, and she received a lesser sentence after two additional trials. As of 2019, Leslie had been found suitable for parole twice, but both times were blocked by the Governor of California.

**Charles Watson, a.k.a. Tex or Tex Watson,** moved to California from Texas, working in sales and dealing drugs in the late sixties. He met Manson through Dennis Wilson and became a fixture of the commune. Tex led the Tate, LaBianca, and Shae murder parties and carried out the majority of the violence. Tex was tried separately because of a lengthy legal fight involving his extradition to California from Texas. Watson converted to Christianity in prison, became a minister, wrote numerous books, and fathered four children. (The California Department of Corrections later banned conjugal visits in 1996 for inmates serving specific sentences—this included Watson's.) He remains incarcerated at Richard J. Donovan Correctional Facility in California.

**Gray Wolf** met Squeaky and Blue while hitchhiking during the Tate-LaBianca trial. Gray Wolf briefly attended the trial and first met Manson in the courthouse visiting room, an experience Gray Wolf described as life-changing. Gray Wolf maintained loyalty to Manson and their shared environmental philosophy called ATWA (Air, Trees, Water, Animals), living near the prison where Manson was last incarcerated.

## The Victims

### July 1, 1969

**Bernard Crowe, a.k.a. Lotsapoppa,** was an African-American drug dealer who became involved with Tex Watson, and, later, Charles Manson. Crowe was shot in the stomach by Manson during a dispute. Manson initially believed that he had killed Crowe, and only learned that Crowe had survived when Crowe was called as a witness during the Tate-LaBianca murder trial.

### July 27, 1969

**Gary Hinman** was a UCLA graduate student and friend to many members of the Manson commune, including Mary Brunner and Bobby Beausoleil, who had both stayed at Hinman's apartment at various times. Gary was stabbed to death by Bobby Beausoleil in the presence of Susan Atkins and Mary Brunner. Bobby Beausoleil wrote "Political Piggy" on a wall near Hinman's body, using Hinman's blood.

## August 8, 1969 – The Tate Murders

**Abigail Folger** was the heiress to the Folger's Coffee fortune and a volunteer social worker for the Los Angeles County Welfare Department. She met her boyfriend Wojciech Frykowski in New York, moving to California in the summer of 1968. She was stabbed to death by Patricia Krenwinkel and Tex Watson.

**Wojciech Frykowski** was a Polish friend of film director Roman Polanski, and boyfriend of Abigail Folger. In the summer of 1969, Polanski asked Frykowski and Folger to stay with Polanski's wife Sharon Tate at their home on 10050 Cielo Drive, while Polanski was filming a movie in Europe. Frykowski was stabbed to death by Tex Watson.

**Steven Parent** was an acquaintance of William (Bill) Garretson's, the live-in caretaker at 10050 Cielo Drive. On the night of August 8, 1969, Steven visited Garretson and was leaving the property when he came upon Tex Watson, Susan Atkins, Patricia Krenwinkel, and Linda Kasabian. Steven was shot and stabbed by Watson—and possibly Kasabian.

**Jay Sebring** was an entrepreneur and celebrity hairstylist who was close friends with Sharon Tate. On the night of August 8, 1969, Sebring spent the evening with Tate, Folger, and Frykowski, drinking and eating dinner at the El Coyote Café in Beverly Hills, before returning to 10050 Cielo Drive. Sebring was shot and hung by Tex Watson.

**Sharon Tate** was a celebrity, actress, and model, married to film director Roman Polanski. Tate was eight and a half months pregnant at the time of her death, and the last to be killed on the night of August 8, 1969. Tate was hung and stabbed to death.

## August 10, 1969 – The LaBianca Murders

**Leno LaBianca** was the owner of a chain of grocery stores called Gateway Markets, founded by his father Antonio LaBianca. Leno met and married Rosemary Struthers in 1959, the second marriage for both. Leno was allegedly tied up by Manson—who left the scene prior to the murders—and stabbed to death by Tex Watson.

**Rosemary (Struthers) LaBianca** met Leno LaBianca while she was working as a waitress at the Los Feliz Inn. In 1968, the couple moved into Leno's childhood home at 3301 Waverly Drive. Rosemary was stabbed to death by Tex Watson, Patricia Krenwinkel, and Leslie Van Houten.

## August 28, 1969 (estimated) – The Shorty Shae Murder

**Donald Shae, a.k.a. Shorty**, was a ranch hand and stuntman working at Spahn Ranch. It is suspected that Shae was working with the Los Angeles County Sheriff's Office to provide information about Manson and his group. Shae and Manson had increasing animosity leading up to Shae's death. Shae was allegedly stabbed to death by Tex Watson, Charles Manson, Bruce Davis, and Steve Grogan. Tex Watson was not tried for this murder.

## The Prosecutors

**Vincent Bugliosi** was the lead prosecutor in the Tate-LaBianca murder trial and co-author of the bestselling true crime book *Helter Skelter: The True Story of the Manson Murders*. He died of cancer in 2015.

**Stephen Kay** was co-counsel in the Tate-LaBianca murder trial, taking over for Aaron Stovitz. Kay continued as a prosecutor in all the subsequent Manson Family trials and represented Los Angeles County in the first sixty parole hearings, until his retirement in 2005.

**Aaron Stovitz** was the original prosecutor in the Tate-LaBianca murder trial. He was removed from the case in September of 1970, after he joked with reporters about Susan Atkins' allegedly faking an illness in court. It was also speculated that Stovitz had willingly given an interview to *Rolling Stone* magazine in violation of a gag order. He died in 2010 after a lengthy battle with cancer.

## Others

**The Black Panthers, a.k.a. The Black Panther Party,** were a political organization founded in Oakland, California in 1966. The group came to prominence in Los Angeles in 1968 for protesting police brutality and racism against the African-American community. Though Manson had no known significant contact with the Black Panthers, he believed Bernard Crowe to be a member.

**Phil Kaufman** met Manson while both were incarcerated at Terminal Island Prison in the port of Los Angeles. Kaufman became friends with Manson and lived with the group for a short period in 1968. Kaufman became a successful road manager and record producer and released Manson's album *Lie: The Love and Terror Cult*.

**Terry Melcher** was a record producer and son of actress Doris Day. Melcher met Manson through their mutual friend Dennis Wilson. Melcher was living at 10050 Cielo Drive at the time he met Manson and the group. Melcher was an acquaintance of Manson's but became more friendly with Tex Watson, taking him to parties around Los Angeles—including 10050 Cielo Drive. He died in 2004.

**George Spahn** was the owner of Spahn Ranch, where the Manson commune was based at the time of the Tate-LaBianca murders. Spahn was a former dairy farmer who moved to California during the Great Depression, eventually buying Spahn Ranch in 1948. Spahn gradually allowed the group to stay at his ranch beginning sometime in 1967, becoming increasingly dependent on the care provided by the women. At the time Spahn met Manson, Spahn was eighty-one years old and blind. Spahn died in 1974.

**The Straight Satans** were a motorcycle gang based in Venice Beach, California. Many members began staying at Spahn Ranch after the Bernard Crowe shooting to protect the Manson commune from a perceived threat from the Black Panthers. According to Straight Satans' president Al Springer, The Satans were given free room, board, and access to the women in exchange for protection. The Satans disbanded sometime in the seventies.

**Harold True** was a UCLA graduate student who met Manson through his roommate Phil Kaufman. True and Kaufman lived next door to the LaBianca residence at 3301 Waverly Drive, and True told authorities he had given the Manson Family a map to the LaBiancas' residence so they could attend a party there.

**Dennis Wilson** was a co-founder of The Beach Boys, along with his brothers, Brian and Carl, their cousin Mike Love, and their friend AJ Jardine. Dennis met Manson after picking up Patricia Krenwinkel and Ella Jo Bailey, who were hitchhiking in Los Angeles. While the Manson group was living with Wilson, they were introduced to Tex Watson and Terry Melcher.

## Select Bibliography

Amarillo Globe-Times, Staff. "Hippie cult named in Tate murders." *The Amarillo Globe-Times,* December 2, 1969.

Anonymous Author. "Linda Kasabian, was she Yana the witch?" *Independent Press-Telegram*, March 8, 1980.

Associated Press. "Nixon backs off from trial comment." *The Odessa American,* August 4, 1970.

Associated Press. "Miss Tate hanged, stabbed." *The Petaluma Argus-Courier,* August 22, 1970.

Associated Press. "6 Manson followers held in freedom camping vow." *Democrat and Chronicle,* September 17, 1970.

Associated Press. "Cellmates say Tate suspect confessed." *Detroit Free Press,* October 10, 1970.

Associated Press. "Two more twists in Tate case." *Des Moines Tribune,* December 3, 1970.

Associated Press. "Mistrial refused over lost Tate lawyer." *Detroit Free Press,* December 22, 1970.

Associated Press. "Manson's mom tells her story." *Santa Cruz Sentinel,* January 26, 1971.

Associated Press. "Manson follower tells of wandering family." *The Naples Daily News,* February 3, 1971.

Associated Press. "Manson wears swastika to murder trial." *The Daily Mail,* March 16, 1971.

Associated Press. "Watson convicted of Tate murders; faces sanity trial." *New York Times*, October 12, 1971.
Associated Press. "Victim's son gets Manson royalties." *New York Times*, December 6, 1993.

Atkins-Whitehouse, Susan. *The Myth of Helter Skelter*. California: Menelorelin Dorenay's Publishing, 2012.

Bacon, James. "Hollywood Hotline, Wednesday, June 14, 1972." *Ithaca Journal*, June 14, 1972.

Browning, Norma Lee. "Sharon Tate casting aside sex goddess image." *Fort Lauderdale News*, August 18, 1968.

Byrd, Joyce. "Mother tells how Linda Kasabian has changed." *San Antonio Express*, August 30, 1970.

Bugliosi, Vincent and Curt Gentry. *Helter Skelter: the true story of the Manson murders*. New York: W. W. Norton and Company, 1974.

Champlin, Charles. "Vampire Killers' plays it ghoul." *Los Angeles Times*, September 13, 1968.

Cohen, Jerry. "Savage mystic cult blamed for 5 Tate murders, 6 others." *Los Angeles Times*, December 2, 1969.

Crabstreet, Dallas. "Girl with accent answers - after Gary Hinman killed." *The Bismarck Tribune*, January 19, 1970.

Deustch, Linda. "Court grants Linda Kasabian immunity." *The San Bernardino County Sun*, August 11, 1970.

Deustch, Linda. "Says Manson used to carry gun." *Springfield Leader and Press*, September 11, 1970.

Deustch, Linda. "Tate case judge substitute for missing lawyer." *The San Bernardino County Sun*, December 4, 1970.

Deustch, Linda. "Manson punches attorney, ejected." *The San Bernardino County Sun*, January 29, 1971.
Deustch, Linda. "Follower draws a vivid picture of Manson family's formation." *The San Bernardino County Sun*, February 1971.

Everett, Arthur. "Linda says she loved Manson as 'The messiah come again." *The San Bernardino County Sun*, August 1, 1970.

Everett, Arthur. "Manson shows Nixon's story to Tate jury." *Statesman Journal*, August 5, 1970.

Farr, William. "No 'family' exists media created it, Manson testifies." *Los Angeles Times*, February 27, 1973.

Jones, Jack, and Michael J. Goodman. "Beach Boys drummer Dennis Wilson, 39, dies while diving at marina." *Los Angles Times,* December 29, 1983.

LaBianca first homicide investigation progress report. Los Angeles Police Department, Robbery Homicide Division, August 1969.

Los Angeles County Sheriff's Department. Statement of Mary Brunner. Case No. 039-02378-1076-016, Dec. 4, 1969.

Los Angeles County Sheriff's Department. Numerous documents related to August 1969 raid of Spahn Ranch.

*Manson*. Theatrical documentary. Directed by Robert Hendrickson and Laurence Merrick. Los Angeles: American International Pictures, 1973.

Mettetal, Sandi. "Enter evidence linking Manson to Tate murder gun." *Valley News*, Sept. 11, 1970.

Mettetal, Sandi. "Girl from 'Family' testifies about life with Manson." *Valley News*, February 4, 1971.

Morain, Dan. "Both side point to death penalty decision of 1972." *Los Angeles Times,* February 18, 1986.

National Park Service. "Cultural landscapes inventory, Thompson/Barker Ranch." Death Valley National Park. 2005.

Newell, R. "Dream comes true for lad; He's going to Boys Town." *The Indianapolis News*, March 7, 1949.

Neiswender, Mary. "Mom claims cult girl lied." *Independent Press-Telegram*, June 10, 1970.

Neiswender, Mary. "Manson trial recesses in storm of tempers." *Independent Press-Telegram*, September 12, 1970.

Neiswender, Mary. "Tex Watson trial!" *Independent Press-Telegram*, February 5, 1971.

Peterson, Bettelou. "Jay Sebring, man with a successful idea." *Detroit Free Press*, August 14, 1969.

Pfeiffer, R. "Petition for writ of habeas corpus; Memorandum of points and authorities." June 29, 2019.

Ruth, Daniel. "Vincent Bugliosi has murder on his mind." *The Tampa Tribune*, October 1979, p. 51.

Serrano, Richard A. "I wish I never got off that bus." *Los Angeles Times*, April 3, 1990.

Skelton, Richard. "A seminal event remembered." *Los Angeles Times*, May 3, 2007.

Smith, Dave. "Mother tells life on Manson as a boy." *Los Angeles Times*, January 26, 1971.

Stack, James. "The unhappy odyssey of Linda Kasabian." *The Boston Globe*, March 14, 1976.

State of California Community Release Board. "In the matter of the life term parole consideration of Charles Watson." No. A-253156, Oct. 27, 1978. Additional parole hearings from The State of California Board of Parole Hearings including: Charles Manson, Susan Atkins, Patricia

Krenwinkel, Leslie Van Houten, Charles Watson, Steve Grogan, Bruce Davis, Bobby Beausoleil, and Lynette Fromme. Various years.

Stimson, George. *Goodbye Helter Skelter*. Cobb, California: The Peasenhall Press, 2014.

Tate first homicide investigation progress report. Los Angeles Police Department, Robbery Homicide Division, August 1969.

Thomas, Bob. Doris Day's son and the horrors of the Mansons. *Courier-Post*, May 16, 1982.

Thursby, Kieth. "Prosector was removed from Charles Manson case." *Los Angeles Times*, Jan 26, 2010.

U.S. Department of Commerce. *Social and Health Indicators System*, July 17, 1973.

United Press International. "Hold Nude Hippies for Bus Theft." *Independent*, April 23, 1968.

United Press International. "Sharon Tate killer left glasses at scene, police say." *The Atlanta Constitution*, October 24, 1969.

United Press International. "Eyeglasses clue in coast murders." *The Sentinel*, October 28, 1969.

United Press International. Prosecution plans to base trial on vicarious conspiracy. *The Desert Sun*, May 19, 1970.

United Press International. "Defendant's sister found dead." *The Daily Intelligencer*, June 22, 1970.

United Press International. "Body believed that of Ronald Hughes." *Redlands Daily Facts*, March 31, 1971.

Wilson, Earl. "Sharon Tate - a secret sex missile?" *The Cincinnati Enquirer*, May 22, 1966.

Trial transcripts retrieved from the Los Angeles County District
Attorney's Office, including:
People v. Manson, Atkins, Krenwinkel and Van Houten (Tate-
LaBianca Murders)
People v. Charles (Tex) Watson (Tate-LaBianca Murders)
People v. Leslie Van Houten (LaBianca Murders) (First and Second
Trial)
People v. Steve Grogan (Shae Murder)
People v. Manson, Davis, Atkins (Hinman Murder)
People v. Manson, Davis, Watson (Shae Murder) (First Trial)
People v. Manson, (Shae and Hinman Murders)

Investigation audio retrieved from the Los Angeles County District
Attorney's Office including: Charles Manson, Leslie Van Houten.
Danny DeCarlo, Ella Jo Bailey, Greg Jacobson, Dianne Lake, Rudy
Weber, Al Spencer, Harold True, Barbara Hoyt.

## Author Bio

James Buddy Day is an award-winning true crime producer, showrunner, writer, and director for numerous television and feature documentaries. Buddy's work has been showcased in numerous film festivals and featured in national publications such as the *Today Show*, *Rolling Stone*, *TMZ*, *The Daily Mail*, *Billboard*, *The New York Times*, and *The Washington Post*.

## Selected Filmography

*Charles Manson: The Final Words*
 (REELZ/Pyramid Productions)

*Charles Manson: The Funeral*
(REELZ/MyEntertainment/Pyramid Productions)

*Manson: The Women*
(Oxygen Channel/Glass Entertainment Group/Pyramid Productions)

*Sex, Lies & Murder*
(REELZ/Pyramid Productions)

*The Shocking Truth*
(REELZ/Pyramid Productions)

*Casey Anthony: Her Friends Speak*
(REELZ/Pyramid Productions/Kinetic Content),

*The Disappearance of Susan Cox Powell*
(Oxygen Channel/Texas Crew Productions/Everywhere Studios)

*The Slender Man Stabbing: The Untold Story*
(REELZ/Red Arrow/Dorsey Pictures).

www.pyramidproductions.tv

## Photo Credits

Epilogue – The Devil's Business

Los Angeles Police Department evidence photo of 10050 Cielo Drive, site of the Tate Murders, August 9, 1969. Courtesy of Los Angeles Deputy District Attorney Stephen Kay (retired).


Chapter One – Charlie

Mugshot of Charles Milles Manson, taken after raid of Spahn Ranch on August 16, 1969. Courtesy of cielodrive.com.


Chapter Two – Helter Skelter

Front entrance of Los Angeles Hall of Justice, location of the Tate-LaBianca murder trial. Photo by author.


Chapter Three – Survival

Michael Channels during filming of *Charles Manson: The Final Words*, 2016. Courtesy of Pyramid Productions Inc./Nathanial Harper.


Gray Wolf during filming of *Charles Manson: The Final Words*, 2016. Courtesy of Pyramid Productions Inc./Nathanial Harper.


Chapter Four – Bobby

Mugshot of Bobby Beausoleil, August 6, 1969. Courtesy of cielodrive.com.


Chapter Five – Manson Born

West Virginia State Penitentiary, Moundsville, West Virginia, 2018. Photo by author.


Chapter Six – The Family

Spahn Ranch, 1970. LAPD investigation photo courtesy of Los

Angeles Deputy District Attorney Stephen Kay (retired).

Chapter Seven – The Summer of 1968

Phil Kaufman during filming of *Charles Manson: The Final Words*, 2016. Courtesy of Pyramid Productions Inc./Nathanial Harper.

Chapter Eight – The Alternate Theory

Mugshot of Tex Watson, 1970. Courtesy of Los Angeles Deputy District Attorney Stephen Kay (retired).

Chapter Nine – Gary Hinman

Mugshot of Mary Brunner, 1969. Courtesy of cielodrive.com.

Chapter Ten – August 8, 1969

Front door of 10050 Cielo Drive, 1969. LAPD investigation photo courtesy of Los Angeles Deputy District Attorney Stephen Kay (retired).

Chapter Eleven – Sharon Tate

Street sign in front of Sharon Tate's former residence. Photo by author, 2019.

Chapter Twelve – Death to Pigs

Interior of the LaBianca living room, August 11, 1969. LAPD investigation photo courtesy of Los Angeles Deputy District Attorney Stephen Kay (retired).

Chapter Thirteen – The Informant

Mugshot of Bruce Davis, 1969. Courtesy of cielodrive.com.

Chapter Fourteen – Sadie

Mugshot of Susan "Sade" Atkins, 1969. Courtesy of cielodrive.com.

Chapter Fifteen – The Conspiracy

Corner of Temple and Broadway, where the Manson Family held vigil during the Tate-LaBianca trial. Photo by author, 2019.

Chapter Sixteen – Darling

Mugshot of Linda Kasabian, prosecution's main witness, 1970. LAPD photo courtesy of Los Angeles Deputy District Attorney Stephen Kay (retired).

Chapter Seventeen – Tex

Mugshot of Charles "Tex" Watson, 1970. LAPD file photo courtesy of Los Angeles Deputy District Attorney Stephen Kay (retired).

Chapter Eighteen– The Devil Incarnate

Mugshot of Charles Manson, October 12, 1969, Inyo County Sheriff's Office. Courtesy of Los Angeles Deputy District Attorney Stephen Kay (retired).

Chapter Nineteen – Locked Up

Stock photo of prison cell, 2017. Courtesy of Pyramid Productions Inc./Nathanial Harper.

Chapter Twenty – Death of the Boogeyman

Mugshot of Charles Milles Manson, taken after raid of Spahn Ranch on August 16, 1969. Courtesy of cielodrive.com

Epilogue

Photo by author, 2017.

## Acknowledgements

Throughout my career I've been blessed with the opportunity to work with very talented people. Every project I've undertaken has been a testament to the vital collaboration needed to succeed in entertainment. This book would not have been possible without the many people at Pyramid Productions who contributed to *Charles Manson: The Final Words*, including Nate Harper, Julie Sinclair, Dave Alderson, Jon Nadeau and Geordie Day. Also, thanks to Rob Zombie and Cuilla Management.

Pyramid Productions is a family company founded by my parents Kirstie McLellan-Day and Larry Day both of whom I owe a debt of gratitude for supporting all my endeavours. Our company is nothing without our broadcast partners, and we are incredibly proud of our numerous collaborations with REELZChannel, perhaps the greatest independent broadcaster in America. Special thanks to Rob Swartz, the most creative production partner I've ever encountered.

The Manson case is incredibly large and in-depth. I would like to acknowledge some of the many people who have spent hours with me providing insight, namely George Stimson, Gray Wolf, Sandra Good, Lynette Fromme, Catherine Share, Bobby Beausoleil, and Rich Pfeiffer. I was honoured to get to know both Catherine Gillies and Barbara Hoyt prior to their passing. Also, thank you to cielodrive.com, Dean Baxendale at Optimum Publishing, and Anne Joldersma.

Though not included in this work, I would like to thank the fantastic partners at Oxygen Channel, MyEntertainment, Glass Productions, and my agents at ICM Partners, Andy Stabile, Tyler Kroos, and Shade Grant for allowing me to continue to explore the Manson mythology beyond *Charles Manson: The Final Words*.

An extra-special-mega-thank-you to Kristin, Téa, Jaxon, and Griffin.

Finally, thanks to Charlie. I'll never know why he decided to allow me to tell his story but I'm glad that he did.

- James Buddy Day